SPEEDPRO SERIES

HOW TO BUILD & MODIFY SPORTSCAR & KIT CAR SUSPENSION & BRAKES

FOR ROAD & TRACK

ENLARGED & UPDATED 2ND EDITION

DES HAMMILL

VELOCE PUBLISHING
THE PUBLISHER OF FINE AUTOMOTIVE BOOKS

Also from Veloce Publishing:

SpeedPro Series
4-Cylinder Engine - How to Blueprint & Build a Short Block for High Performance by Des Hammill
Alfa Romeo Twin Cam Engines - How to Power Tune by Jim Kartalamakis
BMC 998cc A-Series Engine - How to Power Tune by Des Hammill
BMC/Rover 1275cc A-Series Engines - How to Power Tune by Des Hammill
Camshafts - How to Choose & Time them for Maximum Power by Des Hammill
Cylinder Heads - How to Build, Modify & Power Tune Second Edition by Peter Burgess
Distributor-type Ignition Systems - How to Build & Power Tune by Des Hammill
Fast Road Car - How to Plan and Build by Daniel Stapleton
Ford SOHC 'Pinto' & Sierra Cosworth DOHC Engines - How to Power Tune Updated & Revised Edition by Des Hammill
Ford V8 - How to Power Tune Small Block Engines by Des Hammill
Harley-Davidson Evolution Engines - How to Build & Power Tune by Des Hammill
Holley Carburetors - How to Build & Power Tune by Des Hammill
Jaguar XK Engines - How to Power Tune by Des Hammill
MG Midget & Austin-Healey Sprite - How to Power Tune Updated Edition by Daniel Stapleton
MGB 4-Cylinder Engine - How to Power Tune by Peter Burgess
MGB - How to Give your MGB V8 Power Updated & Revised Edition by Roger Williams
MGB, MGC & MGB V8 - How to Improve by Roger Williams
Mini Engines - How to Power Tune on a Small Budget by Des Hammill
Motorsport - Getting Started in by Sam Collins
Rover V8 Engines - How to Power Tune by Des Hammill
Sportscar/Kitcar Suspension & Brakes - How to Build & Modify by Des Hammill
SU Carburettors - How to Build & Modify for High Performance by Des Hammill
Tiger Avon Sportscar - How to Build Your Own by Jim Dudley
TR2, 3 & TR4 - How to Improve by Roger Williams
TR5, 250 & TR6 - How to Improve by Roger Williams
V8 Engine - How to Build a Short Block for High Performance by Des Hammill
Volkswagen Beetle Suspension, Brakes & Chassis - How to Modify for High Performance by James Hale
Volkswagen Bus Suspension, Brakes & Chassis - How to Modify for High Performance by James Hale
Weber DCOE, & Dellorto DHLA Carburetors - How to Build & Power Tune Third Edition by Des Hammill

Colour Family Album Series
Alfa Romeo by Andrea & David Sparrow
Bubblecars & Microcars by Andrea & David Sparrow
Bubblecars & Microcars, More by Andrea & David Sparrow
Citroen 2CV by Andrea & David Sparrow
Citroen DS by Andrea & David Sparrow
Custom VWs by Andrea & David Sparrow
Fiat & Abarth 500 & 600 by Andrea & David Sparrow
Lambretta by Andrea & David Sparrow
Mini & Mini Cooper by Andrea & David Sparrow
Motor Scooters by Andrea & David Sparrow
Porsche by Andrea & David Sparrow
Triumph Sportscars by Andrea & David Sparrow
Vespa by Andrea & David Sparrow
VW Beetle by Andrea & David Sparrow
VW Bus, Camper, Van & Pick-up by Andrea & David Sparrow
VW Custom Beetle by Andrea & David Sparrow

General
AC Two-litre Saloons & Buckand Sportscars by Leo Archibald
Alfa Romeo Berlinas (Saloons/Sedans) by John Tipler
Alfa Romeo Giulia Coupe GT & GTA by John Tipler
Anatomy of the Works Minis by Brian Moylan
Automotive A-Z, Lane's Dictionary of Automotive Terms by Keith Lane
Automotive Mascots by David Kay & Lynda Springate
Bentley Continental, Corniche and Azure, by Martin Bennett
BMW 5-Series by Marc Cranswick
BMW Z-Cars by James Taylor
British Cars, The Complete Catalogue of, 1895-1975 by Culshaw & Horrobin
British Police Cars by Nick Walker
Caravans, The Illustrated History 1919-1959 by Andrew Jenkinson
Caravans, The Illustrated History from 1960 by Andrew Jenkinson
Bugatti Type 40 by Barrie Price
Bugatti 46/50 Updated Edition by Barrie Price
Bugatti 57 2nd Edition - by Barrie Price
Caravanning & Trailer Tenting, the Essential Handbook by Len Archer
Chrysler 300 - America's Most Powerful Car by Robert Ackerson
Cobra - The Real Thing! by Trevor Legate
Cortina - Ford's Bestseller by Graham Robson
Coventry Climax Racing Engines by Des Hammill
Daimler SP250 'Dart' by Brian Long
Datsun/Nissan 280ZX & 300ZX by Brian Long
Datsun Z - From Fairlady to 280Z by Brian Long
Dune Buggy Handbook by James Hale
Dune Buggies by James Hale
Fiat & Abarth 124 Spider & Coupe by John Tipler
Fiat & Abarth 500 & 600 Second edition by Malcolm Bobbitt
Ford F100/F150 Pick-up by Robert Ackerson
Ford GT40 by Trevor Legate
Ford Model Y by Sam Roberts
Harley-Davidson, Growing up by Jean Davidson
Jaguar XJ-S, by Brian Long
Karmann-Ghia Coupe & Convertible by Malcolm Bobbitt
Land Rover, The Half-Ton Military by Mark Cook
Lea-Francis Story, The by Barrie Price
Lexus Story, The by Brian Long
Lola - The Illustrated History (1957-1977) by John Starkey
Lola - All The Sports Racing & Single-Seater Racing Cars 1978-1997 by John Starkey
Lola T70 - The Racing History & Individual Chassis Record 3rd Edition by John Starkey
Lotus 49 by Michael Oliver
Mazda MX-5/Miata 1.6 Enthusiast's Workshop Manual by Rod Grainger & Pete Shoemark
Mazda MX-5/Miata 1.8 Enthusiast's Workshop Manual by Rod Grainger & Pete Shoemark
Mazda MX-5 (& Eunos Roadster) - The World's Favourite Sportscar by Brian Long
MGA by John Price Williams
MGB & MGB GT - Expert Guide (Auto-Doc Series) by Roger Williams
Mini Cooper - The Real Thing! by John Tipler
Mitsubishi Lancer Evo by Brian Long
Motor Racing at Goodwood in the Sixties by Tony Gardiner
Motorhomes, The Illustrated History by Andrew Jenkinson
MR2 - Toyota's Mid-engined Sports Car by Brian Long
Pontiac Firebird by Marc Cranswick
Porsche 356 by Brian Long
Porsche 911R, RS & RSR, 4th Ed. by John Starkey
Porsche 911 - The Definitive History 1963-1971 by Brian Long
Porsche 911 - The Definitive History 1971-1977 by Brian Long
Porsche 911 - The Definitive History 1977-1987 by Brian Long
Porsche 911 - The Definitive History 1987-1997 by Brian Long
Porsche 914 & 914-6 by Brian Long
Porsche 924 by Brian Long
Porsche 944 by Brian Long
Rolls-Royce Silver Shadow/Bentley T Series Corniche & Camargue Updated Edition by Malcolm Bobbitt
Rolls-Royce Silver Spirit, Silver Spur & Bentley Mulsanne by Malcolm Bobbitt
Rolls-Royce Silver Wraith, Dawn & Cloud/Bentley MkVI, R & S Series by Martyn Nutland
RX-7 - Mazda's Rotary Engine Sportscar by Brian Long
Singer Story: Cars, Commercial Vehicles, Bicycles & Motorcycles by Kevin Atkinson
Subaru Impreza by Brian Long
Taxi! The Story of the 'London' Taxicab by Malcolm Bobbitt
Three Wheelers by Malcolm Bobbitt
Triumph Motorcycles & the Meriden Factory by Hughie Hancox
Triumph Tiger Cub Bible by Mike Estall
Triumph Trophy Bible by Harry Woolridge
Triumph TR2/3/3A, How to Restore, by Roger Williams
Triumph TR4/4A, How to Restore, by Roger Williams
Triumph TR5/250 & 6, How to Restore, by Roger Williams
Triumph TR6 by William Kimberley
Turner's Triumphs, Edward Turner & his Triumph Motorcycles by Jeff Clew
Velocette Motorcycles - MSS to Thruxton by Rod Burris
Volkswagens of the World by Simon Glen
VW Beetle Cabriolet by Malcolm Bobbitt
VW Beetle - The Car of the 20th Century by Richard Copping
VW Bus, Camper, Van, Pickup by Malcolm Bobbitt
Works Rally Mechanic by Brian Moylan

First published in 1999, revised reprint 2000. This revised and updated edition first published 2002, reprinted 2004. Veloce Publishing Ltd., 33 Trinity Street, Dorchester, DT1 1TT, England. Fax: 01305 268864/e-mail: info@veloce.co.uk/website: www.veloce.co.uk.
ISBN: 1-903706-73-4/UPC: 36847-00273-2

British Library Cataloguing in Publication Data - A catalogue record for this book is available from the British Library.
Typesetting (Soutane) design and page make-up all by Veloce on AppleMac. Printed and bound in the UK.

Contents

Veloce *SpeedPro* books -

ISBN 1 903706 76 9

ISBN 1 903706 91 2

ISBN 1 903706 77 7

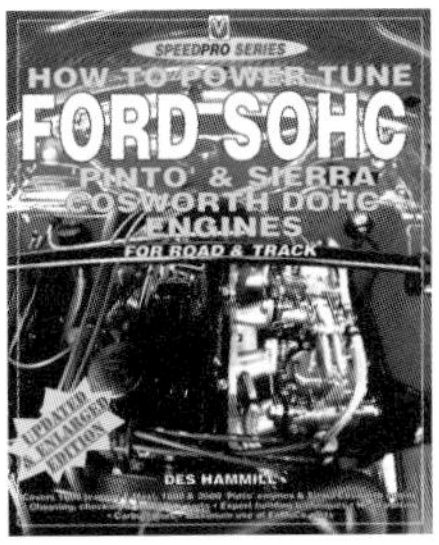

ISBN 1 903706 78 5

ISBN 1 901295 73 7

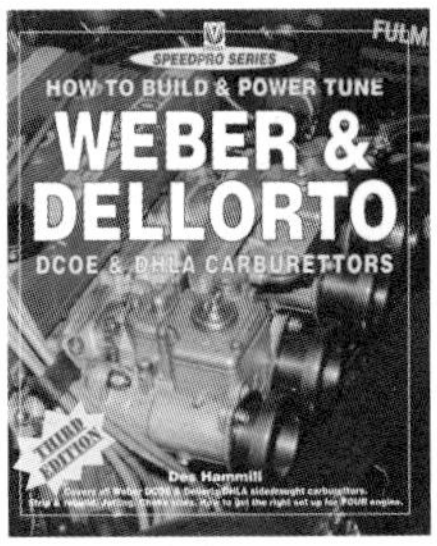

ISBN 1 903706 75 0

ISBN 1 901295 62 1

ISBN 1 874105 70 7

ISBN 1 903706 60 2

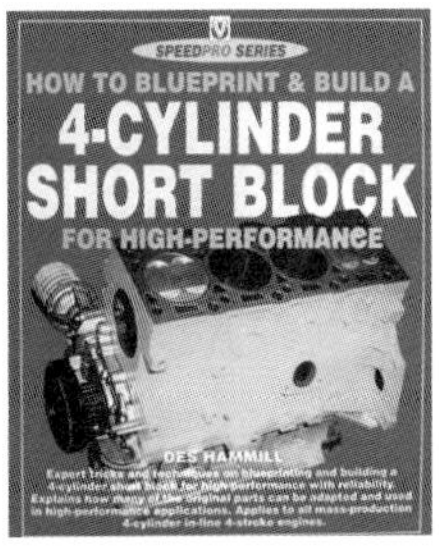

ISBN 1 903706 92 0

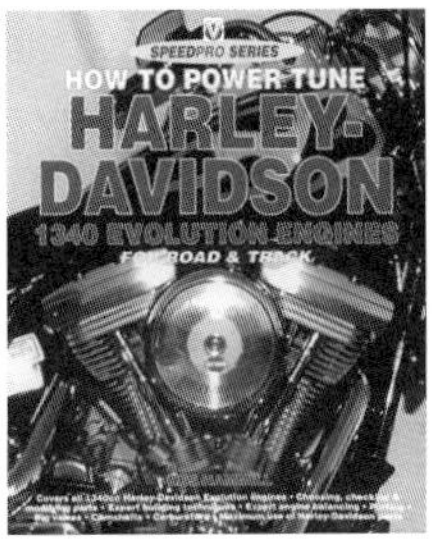

ISBN 1 903706 94 7

ISBN 1 901295 26 5

ISBN 1 901295 07 9

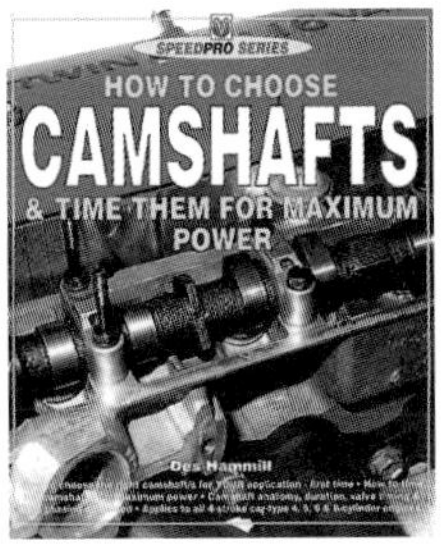

ISBN 1 903706 59 9

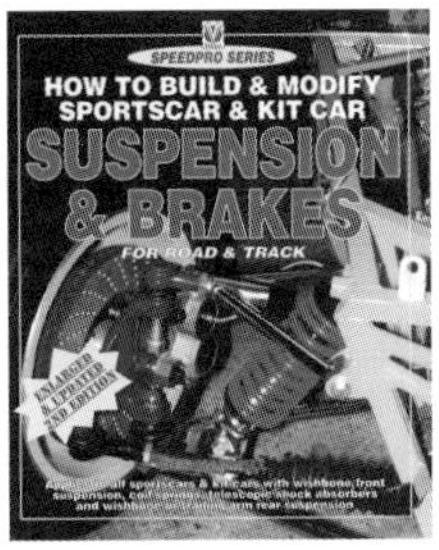

ISBN 1 903706 73 4

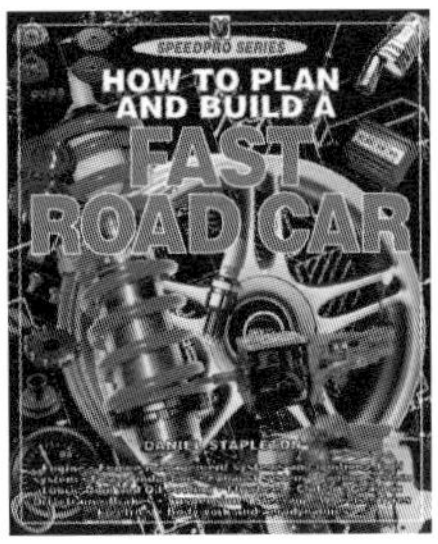

ISBN 1 874105 60 X

ISBN 1 901295 76 1

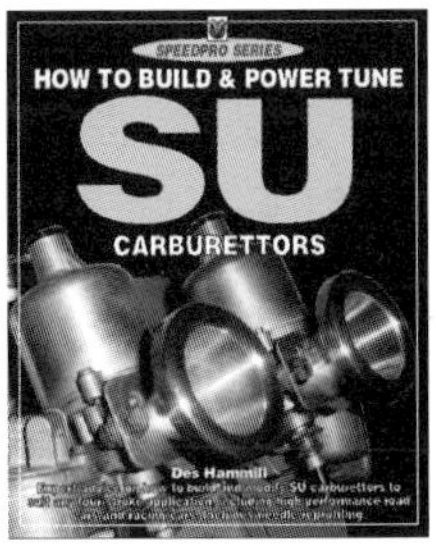

ISBN 1 903706 98 X

ISBN 1 903706 99 8

ISBN 1 901295 63 X

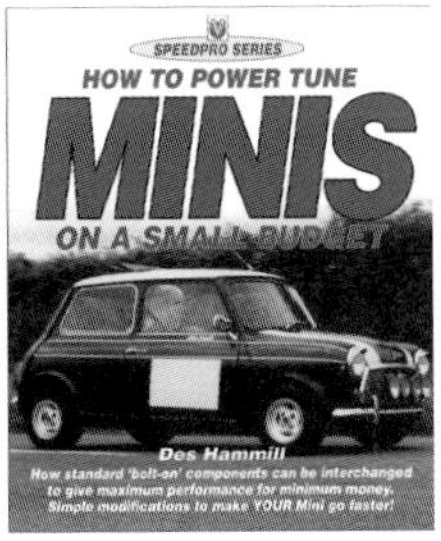

ISBN 1 903706 07 6

ISBN 1 903706 09 2

ISBN 1 903706 17 3

ISBN 1 903706 61 0

ISBN 1 903706 80 7

ISBN 1 903706 68 8

ISBN 1 903706 14 9

ISBN 1 903706 70 X

ISBN 1 903706 72 6

- more on the way!

Introduction & thanks

Some years ago, an associate came to me complaining about the low power output of his 302 cubic inch Chevrolet V8 engine. The engine was rebuilt and, after it had been run and tested, was re-installed in the car.

A track test day was arranged and after the engine had been warmed up, the car was taken for several medium speed circuits of the track. Everything seemed fine, so it was time for some fast laps to test the engine at full throttle. With clouds of rubber smoke pouring off the tyres and engine roaring, the car snaked away from a full power start. The car went through the first turn and then on to the straightway, before tearing off into the distance, leaving behind the mighty sound of a V8 at full bore ... then, nothing. The car didn't come round as expected and silence prevailed ... After what seemed an age, the driver came limping into the pit covered with blood from various cuts and abrasions. When asked what had happened, all he could say to me was that the engine was fantastic, but did I know anything about handling and brakes?

The moral of this story is, of course, that cars are packages, and *all* aspects of a high-performance car need to be given serious consideration and attention (if you value your life, that is). This incident sparked off my interest (obsession actually) in the handling and braking characteristics/capabilities of cars. The handling/braking characteristics of the car you will be driving need to be paramount in your mind and must take priority over increasing engine power.

***

This book is designed to give two-seater kit car and sportscar owners the detailed information that will ensure the car they drive handles properly. Whether the car is front-engined or rear-engined, has independent front suspension and a live rear axle, or fully independent suspension, all aspects of setting-up the car's suspension are covered in this book. The basic information also applies to most other types of car.

Far too many kit cars and sportscars have substandard handling, yet there are simple adjustments that can be accomplished in a very short time, in your own garage (provided the floor is perfectly flat and level), which will rectify the faults and transform the car's handling.

There is a huge range of kit cars and sportscars available and the majority of people who buy them are car enthusiasts. This means that the majority of owners want them to go well and handle well. While the 'go' department may be easier to sort out, the solving of handling problems is often, wrongly, regarded as a complete 'black art.'

If two identical kit cars, for example, are bought by two different people and built-up separately, the chances are that both cars will handle differently. The cars may well be identical in specification yet, if they are set-up without a clear understanding of what is required, what should have been good-handling cars can end up having sometimes quite dangerous handling characteristics. This is not right, and definitely not what the manufacturer intended.

The majority of kit cars and sports cars are well equipped, with many cars having fully adjustable suspension systems (a good thing, although off-putting for some people because choices have to be made which if made without full knowledge of what is involved could result in serious handling problems). Manufacturers of kit cars are often not good at supplying suspension specifications/settings; the very details that will ensure their creation handles well. Often, when they do supply specifications/settings, the results are still less than satisfactory which begs a question or two!

Most kit cars use parts from mass-production road cars. The most common type of kit car is one that uses a single donor vehicle, with all parts coming directly from that vehicle: this type of kit car tends to have the most handling compromises. Other types of kit car use parts from several types of cars because the designers/manufacturers want to use the most suitable parts which are, nevertheless, available at reasonable prices.

Some cars are road going, others are used for track work and some are used for both. Cars used for track work only often have the best parts that money can buy (and for good reason). Track use and fast road use are not as closely related as you might think. A decision about the true end use of the car has to be made **before** time and money is wasted on totally unsuitable components and settings.

Conventional sportscars and kit cars usually feature a front-mounted engine, gearbox, driveshaft and a live back axle. A refinement to this conventional layout is the inclusion of an independent rear suspension (IRS) to offer improvement over a live rear axle set-up (not always achieved, as it happens). Kit cars such as the Westfield, for example, have been available with a live rear or independent rear axle. There are pros and cons for both systems; the live rear axle tending to be lighter overall but, sometimes, creating the handling problems associated with live rear axles; an independent rear axle is heavier, but usually offers better rear end traction and overall handling.

Some kit cars and sportscars have a mid-mounted engine and transaxle combined with rear wheel drive and independent front and rear suspension. Cars such as this are less common (because they are more expensive to build) but there are, nonetheless, plenty of them around, although some of them do not handle as well as you might expect.

The very essence of sporty type kit cars and sportscars is that they should have better handling and performance than more run of the mill cars (a goal not so easy to accomplish these days when manufacturers are producing ordinary cars that have exceptional road-holding). While suspension systems of various cars differ in design, the ultimate aim of every suspension system is the same, that is to give as near perfect handling as possible within the confines of cost and expected comfort. The purpose of the suspension system is to have the wheels follow the contour of the road surface as closely as possible under all circumstances, and for the whole of each tyre's contact area to be loaded (the car's weight acting on the wheel) and in touch with the road surface.

Many cars (including popular sportscars) are made up using components from other production cars and, although this is understandable from a cost point of view, the parts are not always completely suitable and the word 'compromise' enters the equation.

The vast majority of kit cars and sports cars seldom see more than 130mph or 210kph, so the recommendations and advice in this book are to suit cars that will not exceed this speed.

Conclusion

There is something very satisfying about being able to set up your own car. However, to achieve a level of basic understanding that enables you to prepare your own car and know what is causing problems, and then make appropriate changes (if not initially always the right ones, but changes that eventually lead to the right result) takes a bit of thought. Handling problems can be quite frustrating at times, but there is always a logical solution and when you've read this book you'll know that suspension tuning is not a 'black art.' Sporting cars are great fun, and there is virtually nothing that cannot be resolved on the handling front through attention to detail and an understanding of what is actually involved. The ideas and procedures detailed in this book are simple, effective and do not involve high cost items. Simplicity is often the best policy.

Important note

The basis of accurately setting up the suspension geometry of any car is the measurement of all the various factors from a fixed datum point. This means, as a pre-requisite, having an area of floor that is absolutely level and flat and 3ft/1m wider and longer than the vehicle. It **is not possible** to accurately measure and set up suspension systems from an area that is not flat. The sort of accuracy that is required is that the floor be flat to within 0.040in/1mm.

This requirement may seem very strict, but everyday concrete floors are laid to this sort of accuracy and over greater areas than that required for a car. Many concrete garage floors are remarkably flat provided they have been finished properly. Certainly, if a concrete garage floor is being laid, arrangements can be made for the floor to be levelled off with a bit more care than is, perhaps, usual and you'll end up with a floor that meets the requirements. It's fair to say that the average garage floor is probably going to be within 0.125in/3.2mm, which is not really accurate enough: it may be accurate enough to improve the car's suspension settings, but not to get the car 'spot-on.'

Any floor, or any specific area of a floor, can be checked using a Cowley level. Any floor can be levelled, without going to too much expense, by using 'self-levelling compound' (available from builder's merchants). Usually, self-levelling compound is used to level a floor prior to laying tiles and is most certainly not designed for driving a car over, but it will take this sort of weight provided the floor underneath is sound and, most importantly, anyone can use self-levelling compound.

The idea is simply to pour self-levelling compound over the existing floor within shuttering which defines the area to be levelled. The principle of this compound is that, being almost water-like in consistency, after spreading it finds its own level. When the compound sets the area is level and flat.

The thickness of the self-levelling compound need be only 0.125in/3mm at the thinnest point to give reasonable strength. The self-levelling compound surface may not last forever, but, with due care, it can certainly last for a few years.

Alternatively, and what most people will probably do, is find a floor that is known to be flat and level (proven by checking with a Cowley level or, better still, a laser level, which most builder's supply merchants will have) to set up your car's suspension. This may mean transporting your car to the site, but avoids work and expense to create your own 'setting up pad.'

In many instances, where suspension systems are being set up on a regular basis, a specific part of a floor is checked for levelness and flatness and is usually marked off by way of painting a perimeter line around the area. This area is then not normally used for anything other than setting up suspension systems or for storing cars.

It must be understood that all of the measuring and checking suggested in this book **must** be carried out on a truly flat floor and that levelness is very helpful. Failure to comply with this basic requirement will result in errors which will detract from the overall handling of the car.

Note that throughout this book references to "chassis or suspension pick-up points" mean those areas of the car at which the wishbones or trailing arms are attached. No distinction is made between a true chassis and the 'chassis' of a monocoque car.

GLOSSARY OF TERMS

There are several common terms that are consistently used when discussing suspension settings, such as negative camber, negative castor, bottom arm angle, top arm inclination, toe-in or toe-out, to name a few. These terms

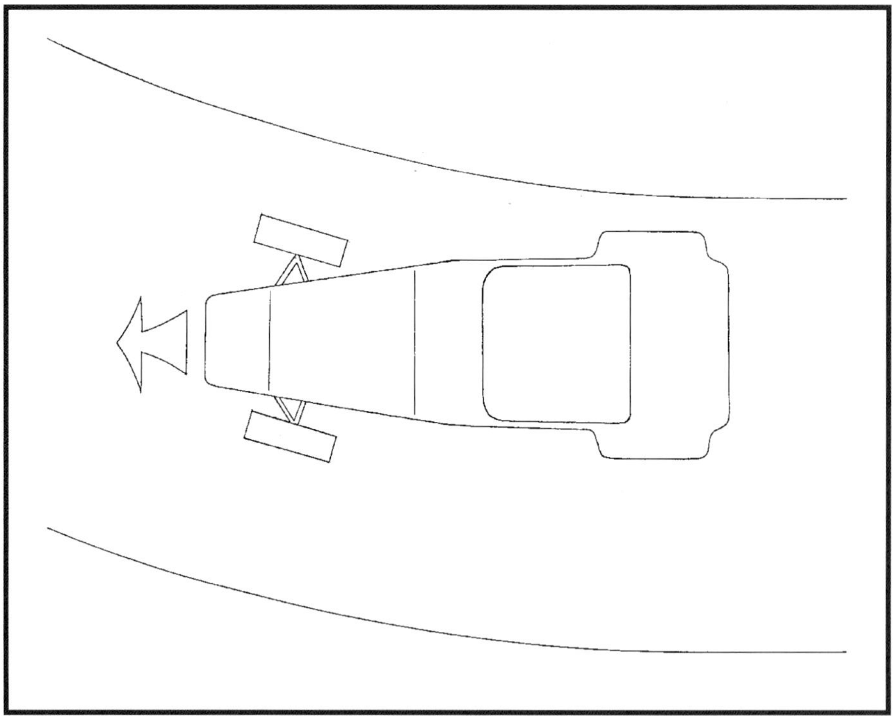

Understeer - the wheels have been turned into the corner, but the car tries to travel straight ahead.

do need to be known and understood. The following is a list of the common terms and a brief description of what each term relates to and, in some cases, a brief rundown on cause and effect.

Understeer

Basically, this is the car trying to go straight ahead when the steering wheel has been turned to make the car turn into a corner (curve). This is a common problem when cars are taken too near the limit of their capability, and sometimes it happens nowhere near what the limit should be!

There are various causes of understeer and, unless the car is seriously at the limit of its capability, many of them can be negated or reduced through adjustments or modifications. Most people will do anything to get rid of understeer because it's disconcerting to drive a car which has chronic understeer. Coping with understeer involves slowing down or driving the car in a manner which minimizes the effect of understeer: both of which mean that the car is probably going slower than it could. There is nothing better than driving a car which never seems to understeer, no matter how wrong you get it in a corner.

In most cases the problem of understeer is caused by tyres that are not being supported correctly (cannot generate enough grip) because the wheels have the wrong attitude. One way or another, this all usually comes back to suspension geometry. Another likely reason is that the front wheels are effectively 'fighting' each other because the wheel on the inside of the curve does not have enough lock on it (see the diagram on page 98).

Oversteer

This problem manifests itself as the car turns into a corner. The car turns into the corner well enough, but the back end feels like it will, or does, swing outward: the car is 'tail happy.' This effect can give a definite cornering advantage in racing and rallying, but there are limits to how much the back end can come out of line before it becomes a problem.

If the oversteer is extreme, the car will almost certainly spin because it is not controllable. One thing that can help here is to fit the best tyres money can buy: tyres that are gripping are not slipping. Also, oversteer can be induced by suspension geometry: certain circumstances cause the wheelbase to change, or a rear wheel to toe-out, because of body roll.

Static negative camber

Camber mostly applies to front wheels, but will also apply to the rear wheels of cars with independent rear suspension. Negative camber means that the top of the wheel's axis is inboard of vertical (positive camber would be outboard). 'Static' negative camber is the amount of negative camber when the car is stationary, at normal ride height and with the two front wheels in the straight ahead position. The amount of negative camber required varies, but for some cars it may be up to 2 degrees and, sometimes, a bit more. There are some specialised racing cars that do have a larger amount (5 degrees) of negative camber for specific

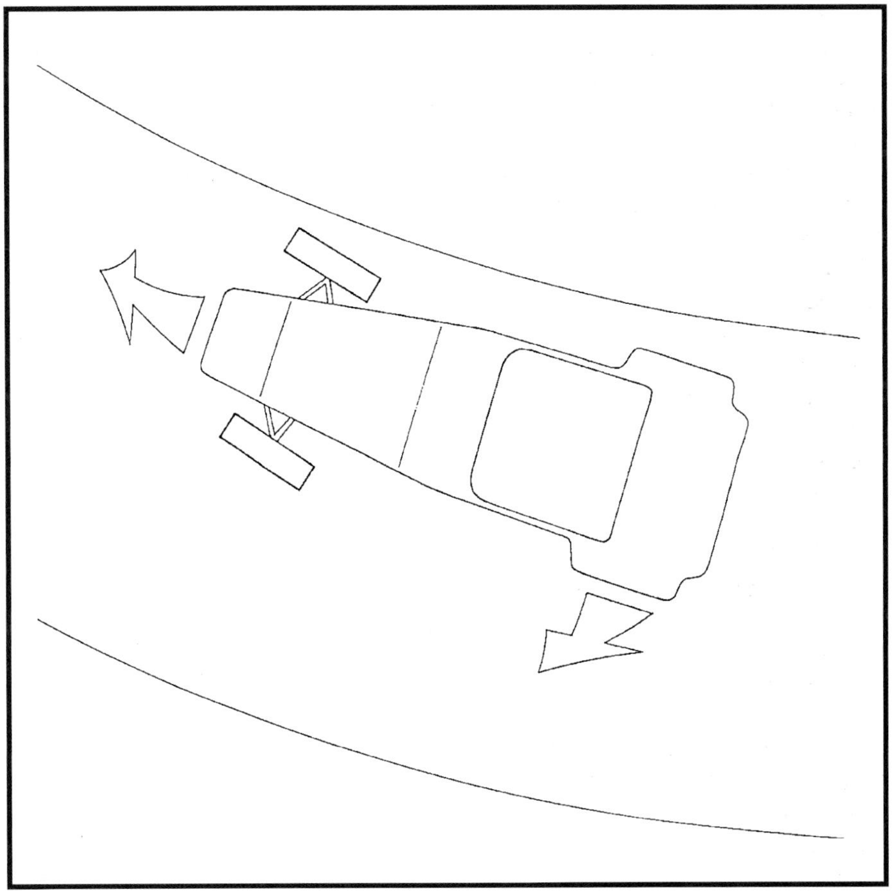

Oversteer - the car turns into the corner, but the back end immediately starts to 'come around' or 'go off line.'

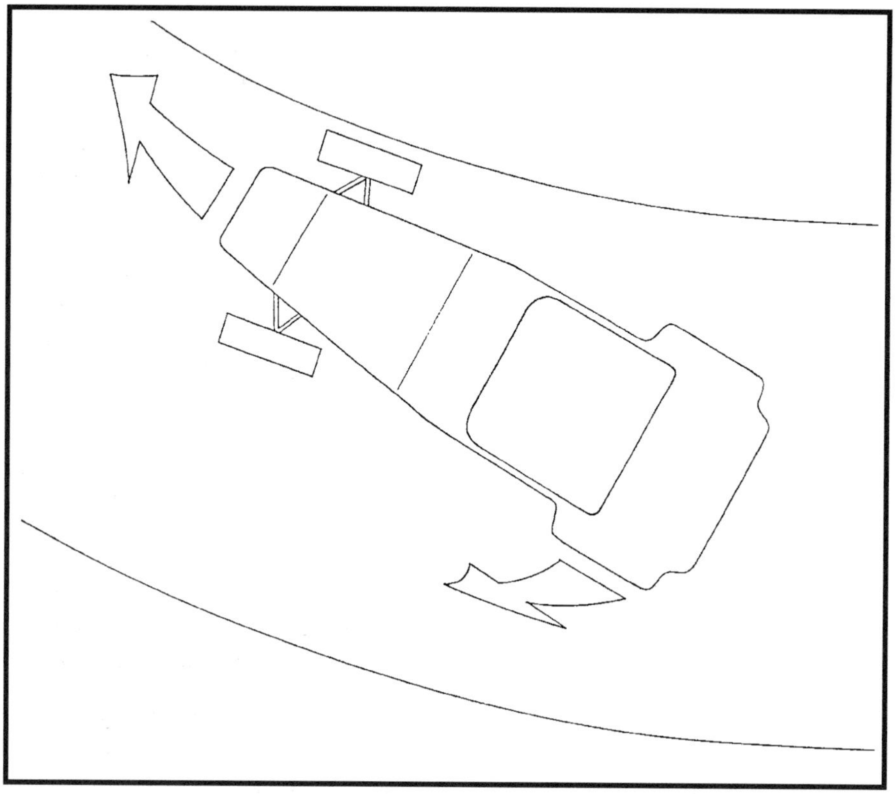

Corrective steering (opposite lock) has to be applied to prevent the car going completely out of control (tailslide, leading to spin).

reasons. Take it that the ideal static negative camber setting of all wheels which have adjustable camber is 0.5 to 1.0 degrees of negative camber. This is the range to consider for all cars that are being used within the speed range defined for this book (see "Using This Book").

Although the car is set up with a specific amount of static camber, it does not mean that during cornering, with some body roll, the settings will remain the same: there's much more to it than this ...

Some static negative camber is usually a good thing, but too much is not.

Dynamic camber

This term refers to the amount of wheel camber present when the car is in motion and, more specifically, when the car is cornering. Three things can happen to the left hand front wheel of a car turning right (and vice versa): it will maintain its static negative camber setting; gain more negative camber than the static amount; or lose negative camber slowly (go towards positive). This is because as the car is cornered hard, and the body rolls, the suspension geometry is making beneficial adjustments to wheel attitude (technically induces more negative camber).

Essentially any sports car turning right, for example, will ideally have between one degree negative to one degree positive camber on the lefthand front wheel (not always easy to achieve as it happens). When turning left, the righthand wheel should have these same amounts of camber.

Any car that exhibits a lot of positive camber (that's 3-4 degrees or more) of the lefthand front wheel of a car turning hard right (or vice versa) has a major geometry problem and is going to require corrective modifications if it's ever going to handle properly.

More often than not, because of the effects of body roll on the suspension geometry, the lefthand front wheel of a car turning right may well have anything from one degree of negative camber to three degrees of positive camber on it, with 1 degree negative to 1.5 degree positive being

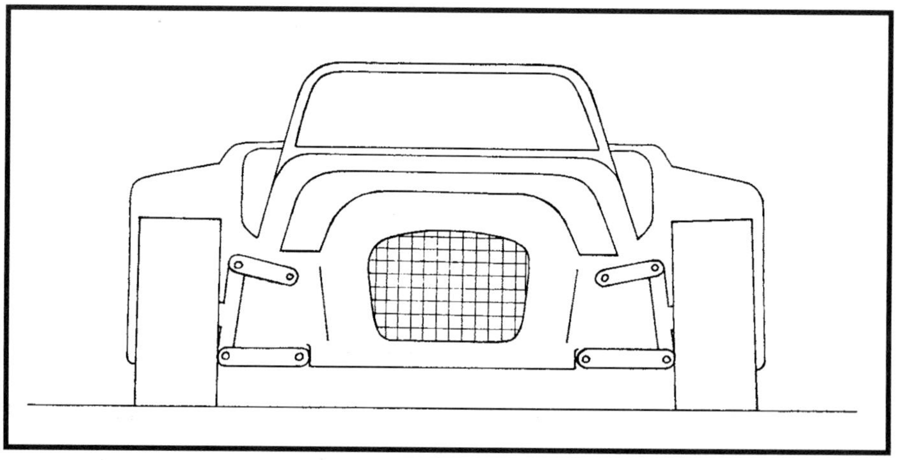

Front wheels set with 2 degrees of negative camber.

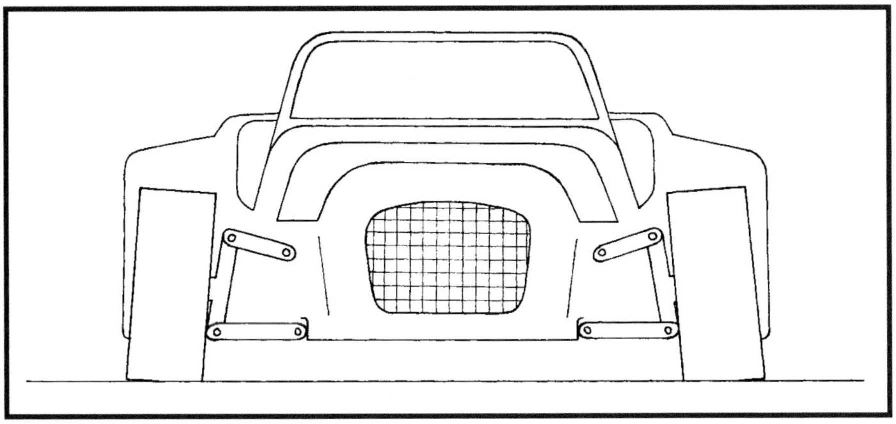

Negative camber taken to extremes at 5 degrees is as bad as it looks.

Car is turning right and exhibiting body roll. Wheel on the inside of the turn, at A, has zero camber, while the wheel on the outside of the turn, at B, has about 1 degree of negative camber: consider this ideal, but not necessarily easy to achieve.

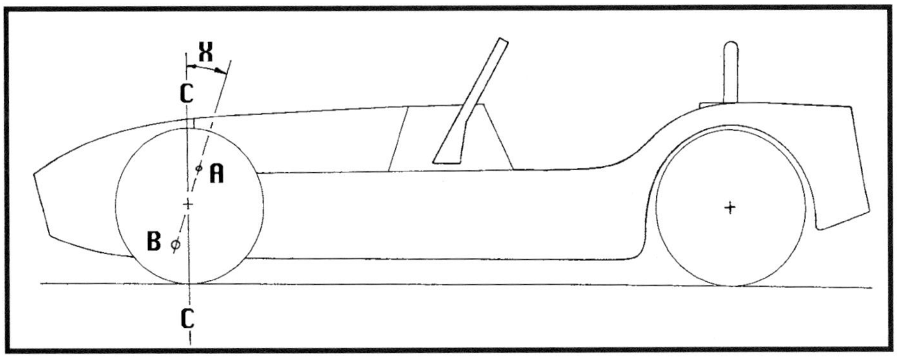

Castor angle (positive) X. Position "A" is the centre of the top balljoint. Position "B" is the centre of the bottom balljoint. "C-C" is the vertical plane.

the ideal range to aim for.

In the right turn situation just described, the righthand front wheel should ideally be as near to having zero camber to 1 degree positive camber on it as it's possible to have. More often than not, this wheel will have anything from 1 to 3 degrees of negative camber on it (or even a lot of negative camber on it: 6 degrees of negative camber is not impossible!)

To summarize, for a car cornering hard right, the lefthand front wheel should have between 1 degree negative to 2 degrees positive camber on it, with 1 degree negative to zero degrees being ideal, though difficult to achieve. 1 to 2 degrees of positive camber on this wheel is acceptable but on the way toward the tyre not being supported camber-wise as well as it might be. In the same situation, the righthand front wheel will usually have zero camber to 1 degree of negative camber, or a difficult to achieve 1 degree of positive camber. Anything up to 8 degrees of negative camber is, unfortunately, more common than you might imagine!

The basic reason for having an amount of static negative camber adjusted into the suspension setting is for tyre support: giving the tyre the best possible attitude when it is under cornering load. The attitude of the tyre is all important when cornering hard. If the left hand front tyre on a car turning right is trying to roll itself off the rim (excessive positive camber such as 5 degrees or more), the car is not going to handle well; if at the same time the tyre on the inside of the turn is angled (negative camber) so much that only 30% of the tyre tread is in contact with the road, the car is not going to handle well as it will understeer. A part of the secret of good dynamic camber is to have the right amount of positive castor.

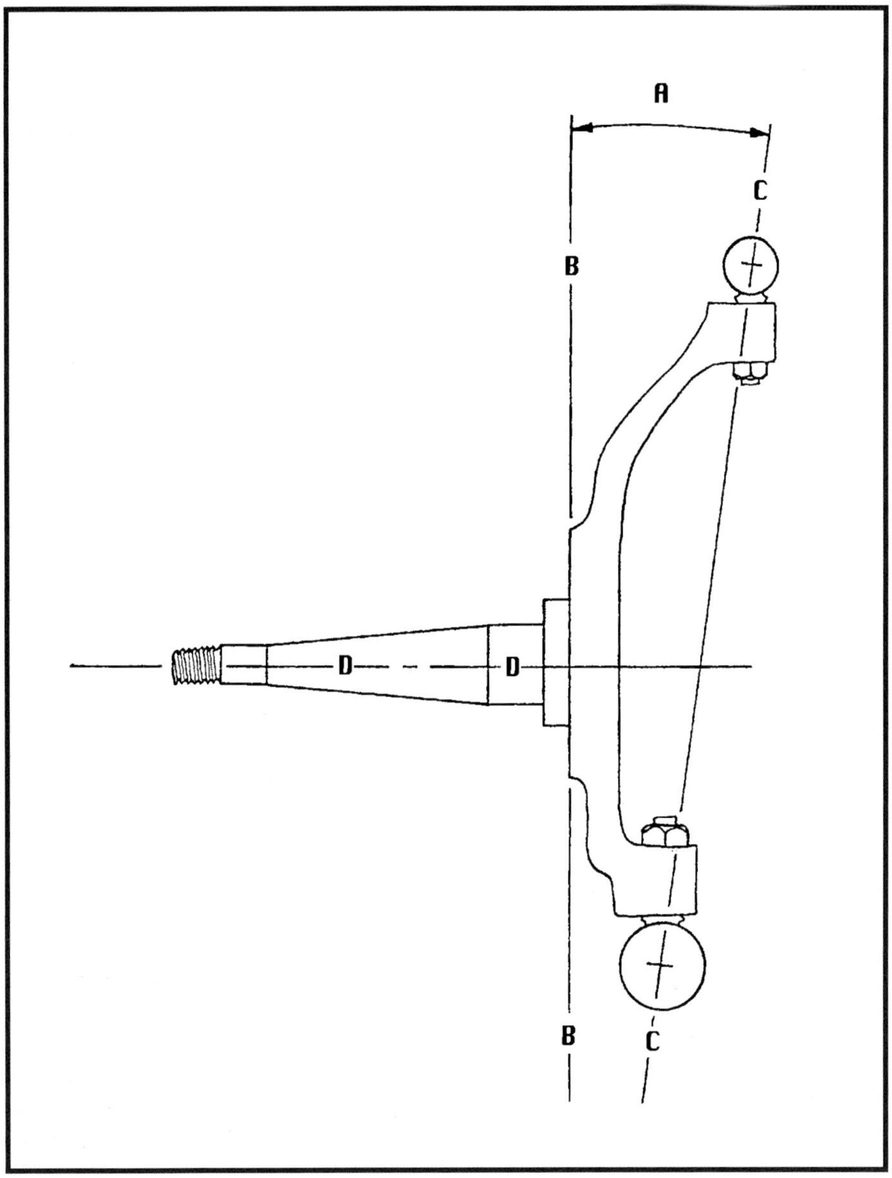

King pin inclination (kpi) is the angle formed between the vertical axis of the wheel "BB" and a line drawn through the centres of the top and bottom ball joints "CC." The king pin inclination angle is "A." The stub axle "DD" is 90 degrees to "BB."

Positive castor

Positive castor is the amount by which the axis of a front stub axle leans backward towards the rear of the car. Stub axles are attached to the wishbones by ball joints. The effective camber angle is the angle of a line drawn through the centres of the two ball joints in relation to a vertical line that intersects that point on the ground.

Consider the range of positive castor angles required to be between 3 and 6 degrees. Any less than 3 degrees will not really be effective, and any more than 6 will almost always be too much. Start with 3 degrees and work up in 1 degree increments; don't start at 6 degrees and work down. The steering wheel will also get slightly harder to turn as the castor angle is increased. The maximum amount of castor angle to ever consider using is 8 degrees.

The effect that castor has is to cause the wheel to lose or gain camber, depending on which way it is turned (it also applies a self-centring effect to the steering). The more castor present in the set up, the greater the camber gain for the same amount of lock on the steering. So, increasing the amount of positive castor is a good method of gaining camber during cornering provided it is not taken too far (too large a positive camber angle). Positive castor is the requirement (never negative castor which is dangerous) with the effect of positive castor being opposite depending on which way each front wheel is turned.

The effects of positive camber on each front wheel are: If the lefthand front wheel is turned to the left, the positive castor (however much it is) tends to cause the wheel to gain positive camber. If the lefthand front wheel is turned to the right, the positive castor tends to cause the wheel to gain negative camber. If the righthand front wheel is turned to the left, the positive castor tends to cause the wheel to gain negative camber. If the righthand front wheel is turned to the right, the positive castor tends to cause the wheel to gain positive camber. Although understanding this may be difficult at first, it is vital.

The larger the amount of positive castor or degrees of positive castor on the front wheels, the greater the gain of negative or positive camber (depending on which way the wheels are turned and how much the wheels have been turned).

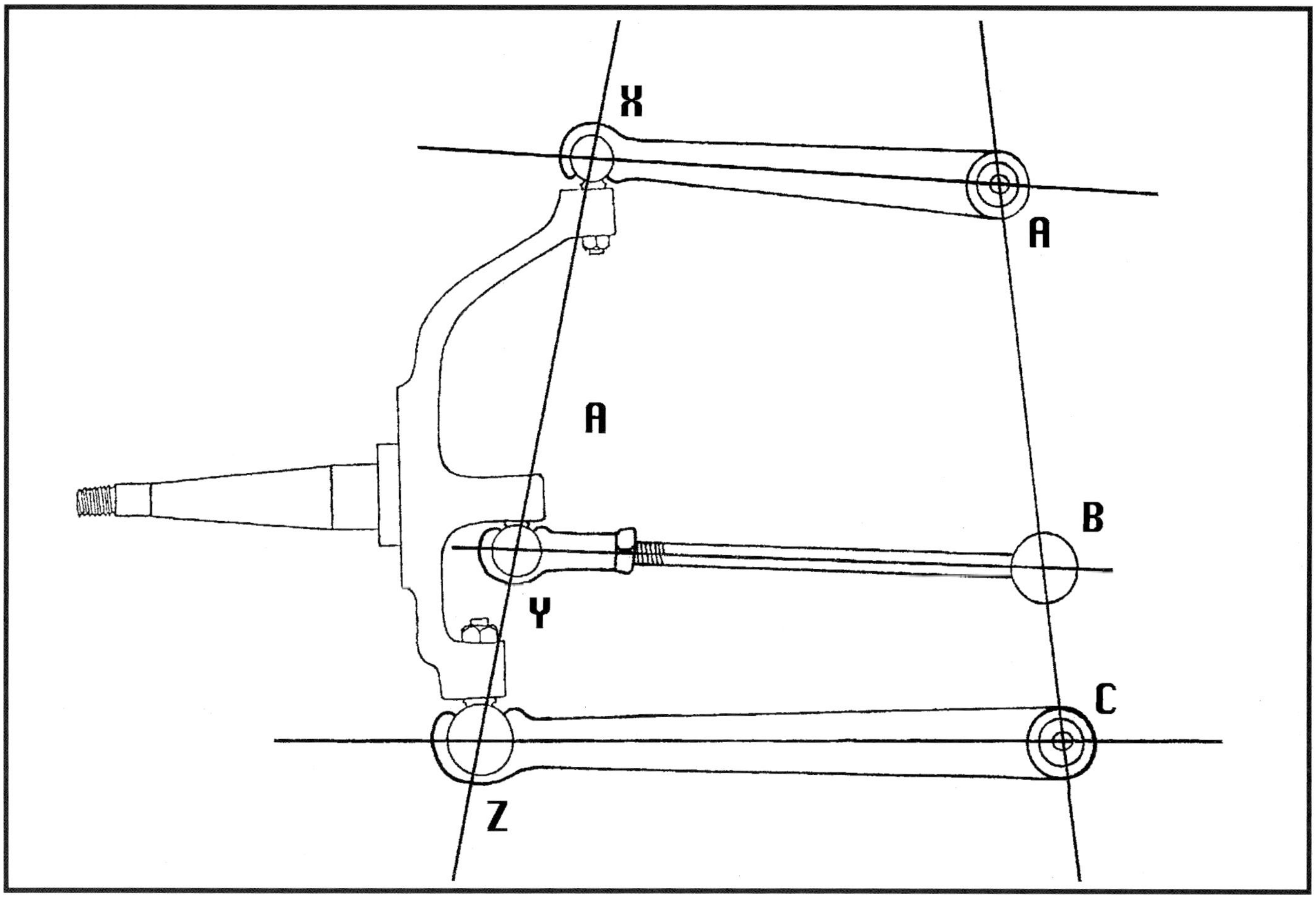

The basic requirement for a suspension which will not have bump steer is (with the two front wheels in the straight ahead position) to have the chassis pick-up points "A" & "C" and the steering rack balljoint "B" in line. Further to this, the top and bottom ball joint centres on the stub axle and the tie rod and chassis pick-up points "X"-"A," "Y"-"B" and "Z"-"C" must be as shown in the diagram (in a similar horizontal plane).

For a car turning to the right, for example, the lefthand front wheel will tend to gain negative camber while the righthand front wheel tends to lose it (could go positive, depending on how much lock is put on the wheel).

The converse of this is also true as all road going sports cars or racing sports car have to negotiate left and righthand turns and corners. The suspensions are set equally side to side of the car (geometry settings such as castor, camber, toe-out). What you don't want, however, is one side of the car to have a different setting from the other side of the car, this is courting disaster!

This is all quite easy to see if, for instance, you stand about 10 feet or 3 metres in front of the car while someone sits in the car and turns the steering wheel (slowly) lock to lock. If the particular car is a Caterham, Westfield or a Marlin, for instance, on which the front wheels are quite exposed it's quite easy to see what is going on as the wheels are turned lock to lock and gain an understanding of what castor does. The one thing that doing this does not show you is the effect that body roll has on the suspension geometry (more on this later).

Note that castor and kpi (king pin inclination) work closely together: each playing their part in altering camber as steering lock is applied. The larger the kpi angle, coupled with a lot of positive castor, the more the loaded front wheel will gain camber - and the unloaded wheel lose it - during cornering. You can 'mix and match' kpi and castor to achieve the required dynamic geometry. For instance, a stub axle with a shallow kpi angle may need a lot of positive castor to provide effective dynamic geometry.

If the car is set up with the minimum amount of castor (3 degrees of positive castor) but does not have enough negative camber to support the tyre under hard cornering, increase the positive castor on both front wheels by 1 degree at a time until the tyre has the right attitude; don't increase negative camber. **Warning!** - The castor angles **must** be identical side to side of the car (except perhaps for cars which only corner in one direction).

King pin inclination (kpi)

Although new road going cars are no longer fitted with true king pins, they all have designs which still use the principle of a king pin and its inclination. True king pins (the pins about which the wheels pivot) were used on beam axle cars in years gone by. Many specialist racing cars, particularly those used on oval circuits (sprint cars and midgets), still use a beam front axle and still have actual king pins. These cars have been perfected over the years for the application and no other form of front suspension has displaced this 'old fashioned' system. The term "king pin inclination" has now been universally shortened to "kpi."

Kpi determines, in part, static wheel camber. As kpi is relatively difficult to adjust, it's usually better to adjust castor to get the required dynamic wheel camber.

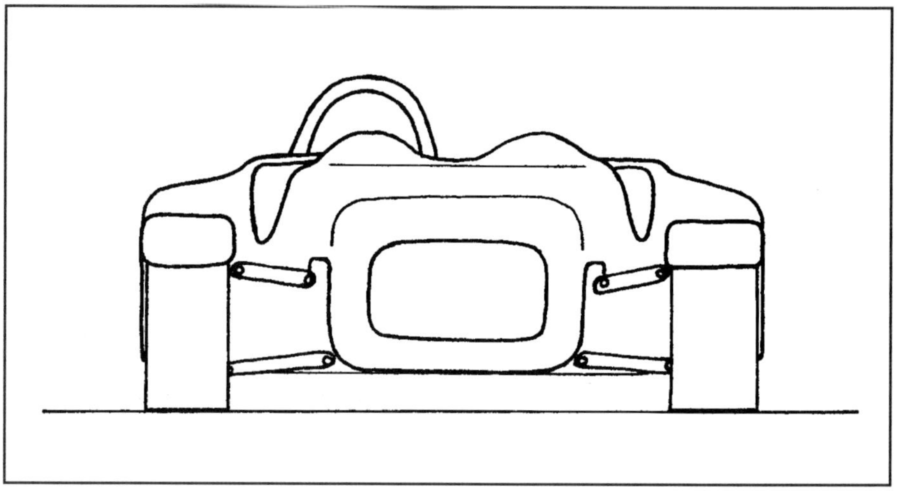

The front wheels are steering straight ahead and have virtually no camber on them.

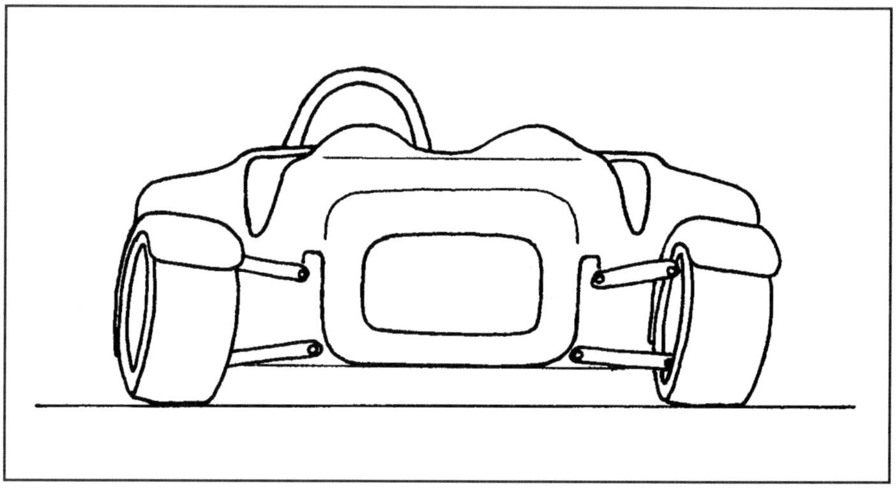

The steering wheel has been turned to the left. The wheel on the left of the diagram has gained negative camber, while the one on the right has gained positive camber. Of, course, the opposite will apply if the steering wheel is turned to the right. These gains are solely due to the kpi of the stub axle and the castor angle set into the front suspension geometry.

Bump steer

Bump steer is the effect created when one, or both, front wheels toe-in or toe-out in reaction to undulations in the road surface. This leads to the car being unstable (darting from side to side) when the steering wheel is stationary. The problem of bump steer can almost always be removed by geometry adjustment or component modification.

Bump steer can be used to advantage to a small degree by inducing toe-out on the wheel that is on the inside of the turn (body roll present and that wheel in droop). The wheel on the outside of the turn remains unaffected. What this means is that if the suspension has to have a small amount of bump steer (can't be totally adjusted out), it is better to have toe-out bump steer when the suspension is in the droop position, rather than when it's in compression. It is not always possible to get rid of bump steer by adjusting the height of the steering rack so, if it cannot be adjusted out, at least have the bump steer working for you rather than working against you.

Using this book & essential information

USING THIS BOOK

Throughout this book the text assumes that you, or your contractor, will have a workshop manual specific to your car to follow for complete detail on dismantling, reassembly, adjustment procedure, clearances, torque figures, etc. This book's default is the standard manufacturer's specification for your car so, if a procedure is not described, a measurement not given, a torque figure ignored, you can assume that the standard manufacturer's procedure or specification for your car needs to be used.

You'll find it helpful to read the whole book before you start work or give instructions to your contractor. This is because a modification or change in specification in one area may cause the need for changes in other areas. Get the whole picture so that you can finalize specification and component requirements as far as is possible before any work begins.

ESSENTIAL INFORMATION

This book contains information on practical procedures; however, this information is intended only for those with the qualifications, experience, tools and facilities to carry out the work in safety and with appropriately high levels of skill. Whenever working on a car or component, remember that your personal safety must **ALWAYS** be your **FIRST** consideration. **The publisher, author, editors and retailer of this book cannot accept any responsibility for personal injury or mechanical damage which results from using this book, even if caused by errors or omissions in the information given. If this disclaimer is unacceptable to you, please return the pristine book to your retailer who will refund the purchase price.**

In the text of this book **"Warning!"** means that a procedure could cause personal injury and **"Caution!"** that there is danger of mechanical damage if appropriate care is not taken. However, be aware that we cannot foresee every possibility of danger in every circumstance.

Please note that changing component specification by modification is likely to void warranties, therefore absolving manufacturers from any responsibility in the event of component failure and the consequences.

It is also usually necessary to inform the vehicle's insurers of any changes to the vehicle's specification.

The importance of cleaning a component thoroughly before working on it cannot be overstressed. Always keep your working area and tools as clean as possible. Whatever specialist cleaning fluid or other chemicals you use, be sure to follow - completely - manufacturer's instructions and if you are using petrol (gasoline) or paraffin (kerosene) to clean parts, take every precaution necessary to protect your body and to avoid all risk of fire.

Chapter 1
The 'chassis'

Note that in the context of this book the term "chassis" can be taken to mean a true chassis (comprised of metal tubes) or the 'chassis' created by the rigid box sections of a monocoque body - both serve the same purpose.

The chassis/relevant structure of a monocoque body must be straight in the sense that all of the suspension pick-up points are in the correct positions relative to the car's structure and each other. If the chassis pick-up points are wrongly positioned (faulty manufacture/crash damage), the suspension geometry will be wrong and this cannot be worked around. All of the pick-up point centres for each pair of pick-up points on each side of the car have to be an equal height from a known datum (a perfectly level, flat floor). Even if the car is fully assembled, it can still be measured satisfactorily without too much trouble. Checking the alignment of the suspension pick-up points is the first step to improving a car's handling.

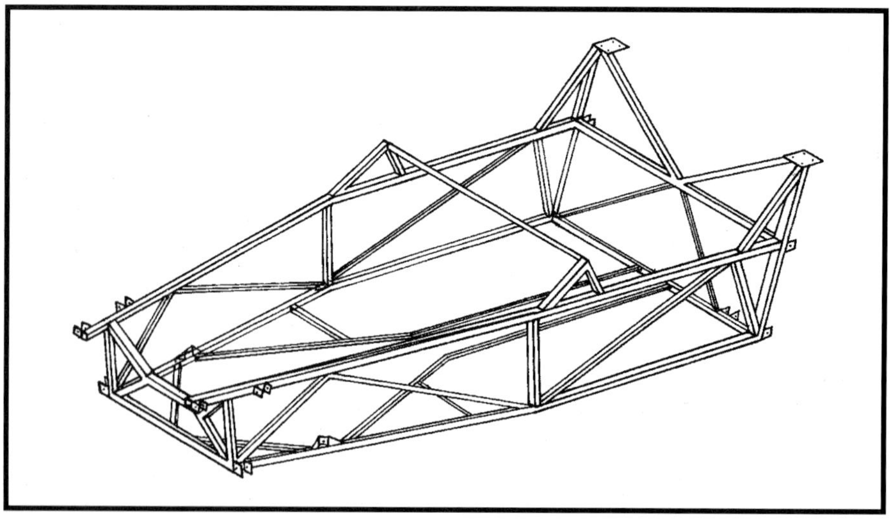

A tubular chassis with no protrusions below the lower rails can sit dead flat on a flat floor.

METHODS OF CHECKING CHASSIS INTEGRITY

Bare true chassis

If the car has been stripped for a rebuild it's relatively easy to check it for straightness. This is the ideal time to check a chassis as, if it is found to be incorrect, it can be repaired and then rechecked before being built up. The ideal accuracy on any chassis is to have all of the suspension pick-up point positions within a tolerance of 0.040in/1mm, but up to 0.080/2mm is just about acceptable. Any chassis that is bent and proven to have more error than this, is never going to be able to be set up to handle well. It is unreasonable to expect perfect handling from a car with so much in-built error.

The odd bit of damage, such as slightly bent tubes or body structure, is

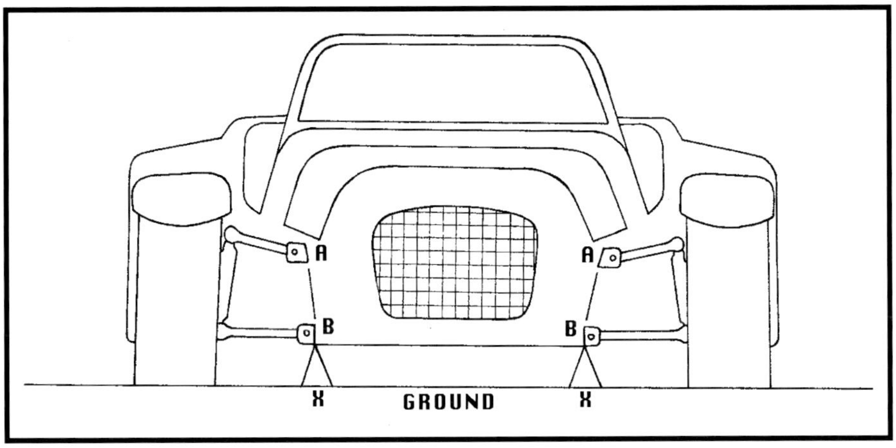

With the two lower front suspension points set at equal heights from the ground ("X"-"B" both sides of the car), the rear of the car can be lifted (see following picture) to measure the rear suspension pick-up point heights.

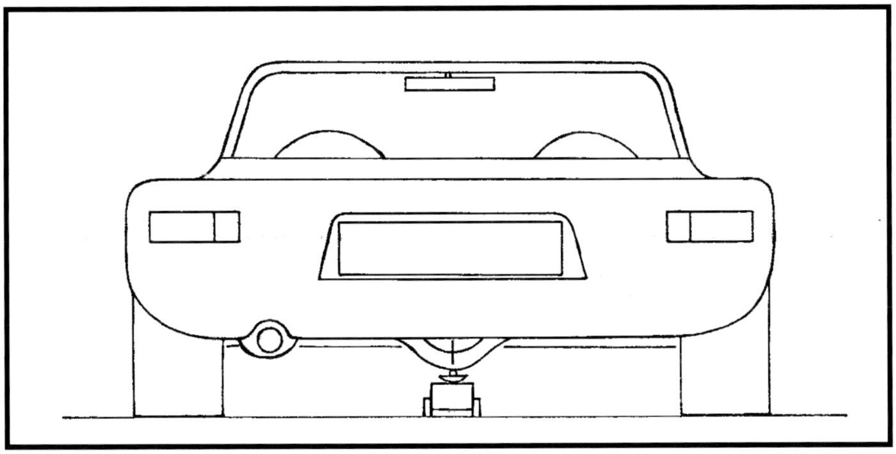

Prior to lifting, with a socket set extension bar on the trolley jack's lifting pad: the fact that the extension bar is round (and strong) ensures point contact. The bar must contact the differential casing centrally. The exact centre point is found by measuring.

not of any consequence, provided the pick-up points are not affected. Naturally, in the interests of having a perfect chassis, it's ideal to have no damage of any description. Relocate the suspension pick-up points if necessary.

The chassis is placed on the level floor and measurements are taken from the floor to the suspension arm pick-up points/bolt holes. If the chassis cannot be rested on the floor because the lower chassis rails are not the lowest point of the chassis, it will have to be raised to clear the floor with packing pieces (usually pieces of planed wood such as 2in by 2in/50mm by 50mm).

Irrespective of whether the chassis is on the floor or packed up to clear the lowest part of the chassis, the measurements taken will show whether the chassis is straight.

On some chassis the front suspension is part of a separate subframe to which all of the suspension wishbones are mounted. In this case, with the subframe bolted firmly onto the chassis, treat the subframe and chassis as one. If the subframe is mounted to the chassis via rubber bushes, it's recommended that the rubber bushes be removed and aluminium spacers made up and fitted in their place, using through bolts so that the subframe is rigidly mounted. This means that the subframe and the chassis are now, to all intents and purposes, one unit. This modification also provides an adjustment feature: slight chassis re-alignment (front to rear) can be affected by altering the thicknesses of the aluminium bushes. Any reduction in movement within the chassis usually results in better handling; the downside is an increase in road noise as the rubber is not there to dampen it, but this is a minor detail.

Monocoques and fully assembled cars

If the car is a production type monocoque sportscar or a kit car (with a true chassis) which is fully assembled, it can still be checked in this condition. The car is set level by jacking and placing blocks under suitable chassis points so that the bottom front wish-bone or wishbone centre points (as measured up from the floor) are at equal heights: a steel rule is usually most suitable for measuring this. Next, the rear of the car is jacked up in the centre of the differential casing. This must be done accurately to ensure that the jacking point is in the true centre point between the rear wheels. The exact centre of the rear axle must be measured using a tape measure and marked for easy identification. The easiest way of ensuring that the centre point is accurately located and used is to place a 1/2in drive socket set's extension bar (or any 0.5-0.625in/12-16mm diameter round bar) across the top of the trolley jack's lifting pad.

Warning! - **Always** place axle

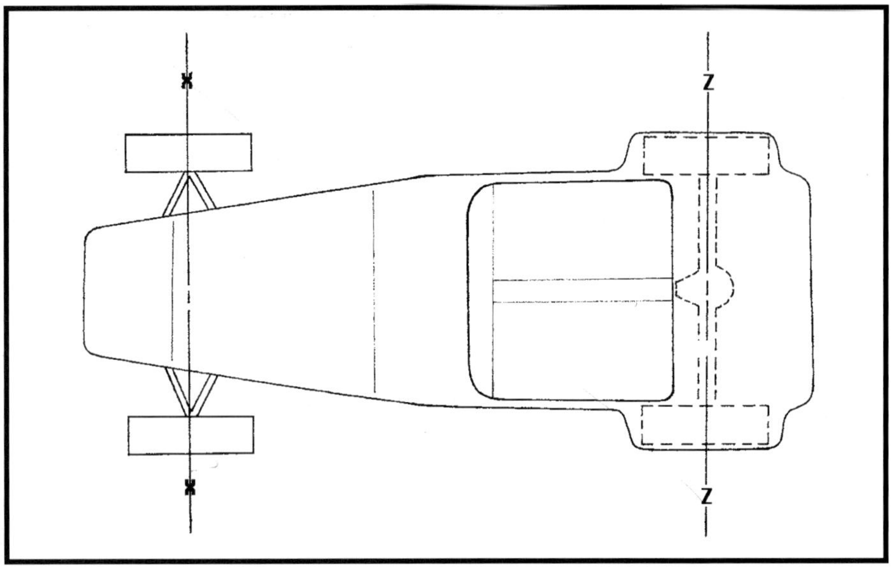

Parallelism of the planes "X"-"X" and "Z"-"Z" is required.

stands under the car as a safety precaution before going underneath. **Never** trust a jack.

Measure from the floor to the rear suspension pick-up points. The dimensions for each matching pair of points must be the same.

CHECKING CHASSIS INTEGRITY

Squareness

Squareness, in this instance, relates directly to the parallelism of the front and rear axles' axes (theoretical, in the case of the front suspension and for independent rear suspension). If the car has a live rear axle, measurements are taken from the axle and transferred to the front of the car. If the front and rear axle axes are not parallel the car will 'crab' (travel slightly sideways) as it goes down the road or track. The more the error the greater the 'crab' effect. Also the car will tend to turn better one way than the other due to the fact that the wheelbase is different on the car side to side.

There is a further consideration regarding squareness and that is the positioning of the car's wheels about the centreline of the vehicle. The front and rear track widths of a car can be different, but both have to be displaced equally about the centreline of the car. If the chassis is bent or twisted in some way, the wheels may well be parallel front to rear but not in line on the basis of the left rear wheel being in the same position behind the left front wheel as the right rear wheel is in relation to the right front wheel.

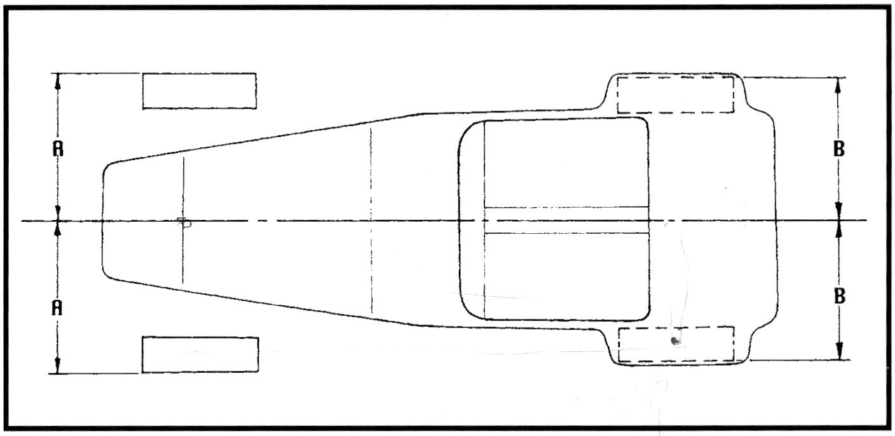

Wheels on each axle should be equal distances from the car's centreline.

There are two ways of checking axle parellelism. The car can be positioned on a flat and level floor area and the chassis pick-up point locations transferred down to the floor using a set square; the car is rolled away and then the points can be connected by lines drawn on the floor. Alternatively, accurate lines are drawn on the floor and the car accurately positioned over them, a set square is then used to transfer the pick-up point locations to the floor. Use the method that best suits the car concerned.

In the first instance the chassis is checked by relating the pick-up points of the front and rear suspension to each other. The average wheelbase is between 90-98in/228-249cm long and this length can pose a problem of scale when absolute accuracy is required. The solution to this is to use a three-four-five triangle (any right-angled triangle is subject to this mathematical principle - see diagram overleaf).

For greater accuracy, the proportions of the triangle (its second longest side) can be increased so that it is nearly the length of the car's wheelbase. For instance, the measurements used to construct the triangle can be 6 by 8 by 10 feet/180 by 240 by 300cm (or any size triangle

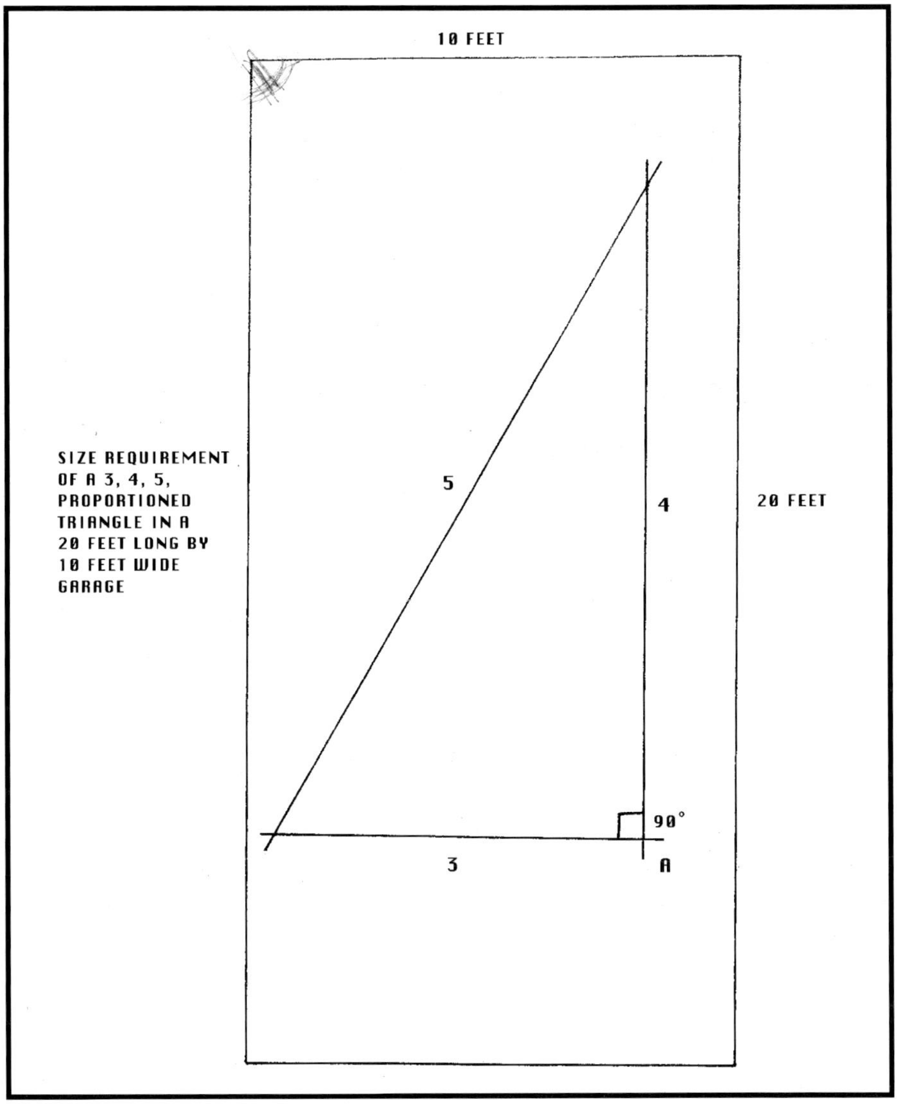

Any three lengths in the proportions shown result in a right angle being formed at A.

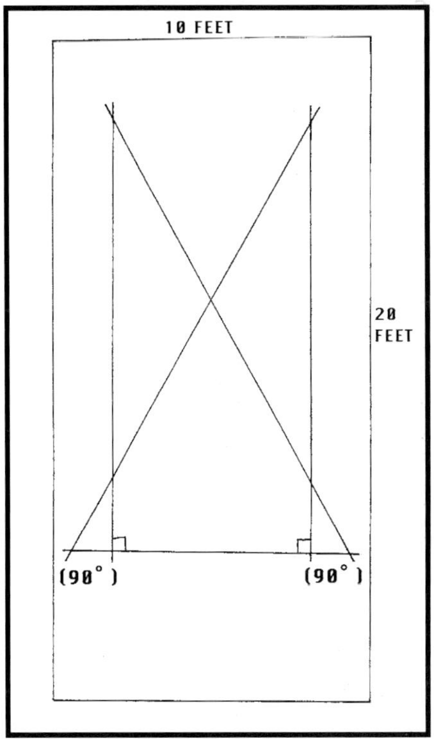

Two triangles drawn on the floor with the short side of each triangle common to both.

using the 3 - 4 - 5 proportions). So, if the as-measured distance from the front bottom pick-up point to the back edge of a live axle casing is 99in/ 251.5cm, this dimension can be used in the following formula and a triangle of the exact size drawn on to the floor.

If the distance from the front suspension pick-up point to the rear of the live axle's casing is 99inches/ 251.5cm, this dimension is, in the first instance, divided by 4. The result of this is a common denominator - in this case 24.75in/62.8cm - which is, in turn, multiplied by 3 and by 5. This results in 74.25in, 99.0in and 123.75in/188.6cm, 251.5cm and 314.4cm as the lengths of the sides of the triangle.

In fact, two triangles are drawn so that a rectangle is constructed on the floor. In this way the car is accurately measured for wheelbase and the position of the wheels in relation to each other (side to side, front to rear).

The triangles drawn should match the car's wheelbase accurately, but will be well past the width requirement of the suspension pick-up points (the distances to the suspension pick-up points will be measured inward from the sides of the rectangle formed by the two triangles).

A suitably-sized set square is then used to measure from the lines of the triangle to the chassis' suspension pick-up points which have been transferred to the floor. Any error will be quite plain to see and will be measurable. In the case of a live rear axle vehicle, for example, the trailing arms and Panhard-rod may well be adjustable while the front wishbone pick-up points are fixed. In this case the rear axle is aligned with the non-adjustable front suspension pick-up

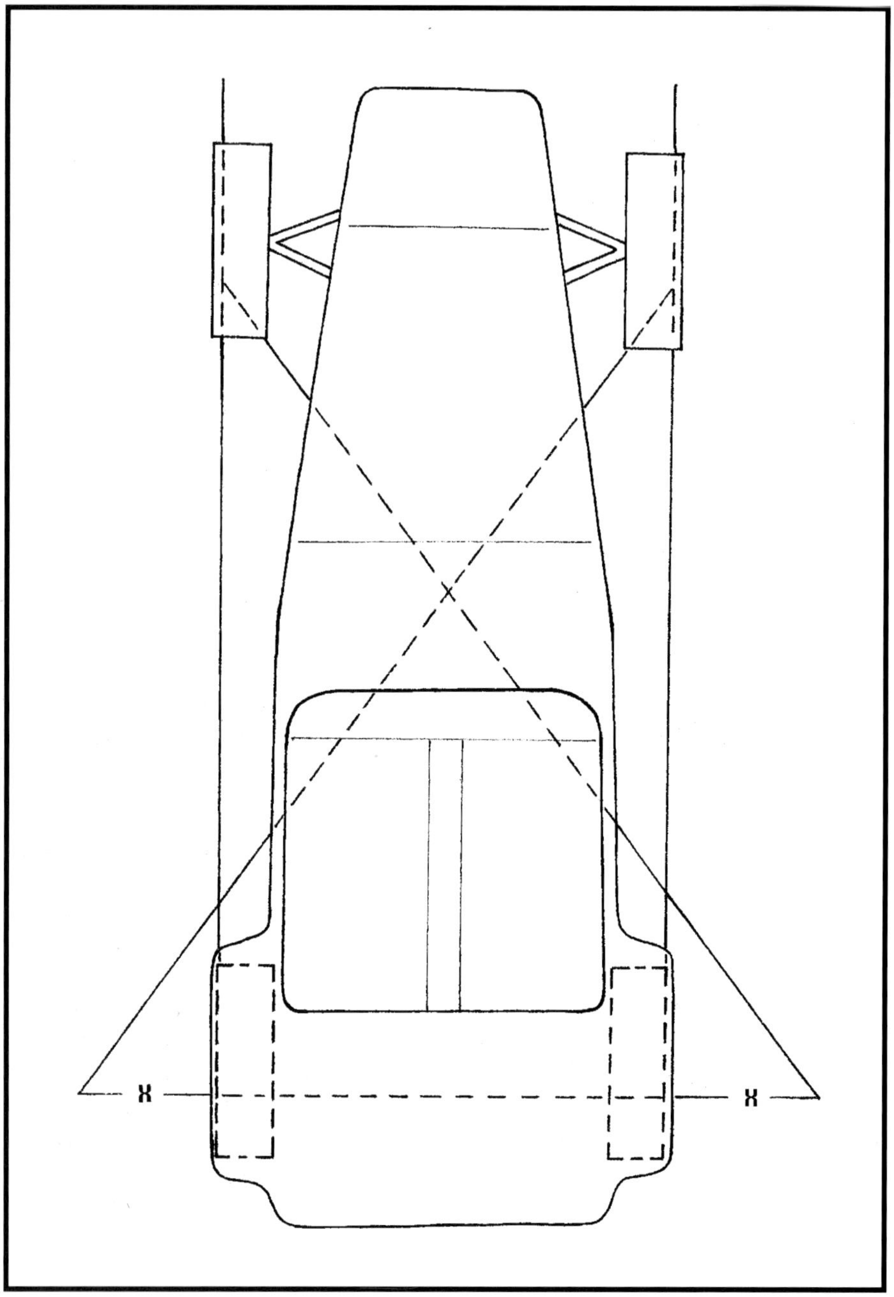

Position the car over the triangles and, using a set square, transfer the measuring points to the ground.

points. The trailing arms may have to be shortened on one side or adjusted both sides to bring the wheelbase to size: shortening or lengthening the Panhard-rod is the way to move the axle laterally.

Warning! - When adjusting Rose joints, you should always check how much thread is actually in the suspension component. Insufficient thread in the wishbone, trailing arm or Panhard-rod could result in suspension failure. Consider one and a half times the diameter of the thread as the **minimum** amount of (lengthwise) thread screwed into the component.

Start at the front of the chassis. Measure from the floor up to the lower wishbone pick-up point bolt holes. The pick-up point holes **must** all be an equal distance from the floor. An ideal tool for measuring this dimension is a large set square graduated in imperial or metric units. This will allow direct measurement from the floor surface to the centre of the pick-up hole, with the knowledge that the measurement is being taken in the vertical axis (note that the set square must be kept vertical in the plane at 90 degrees to its baseline; you can use a second, smaller set square to ensure this is the case).

If the lower front wishbone is of 'parallel'-type, all four pick-up point measurements are going to be the same. If the suspension has anti-dive geometry, the two rear pick-up point holes are going to be higher than the front two. In this case, the two front pick-up point holes **must** be an equal distance from the floor, and the two rear pick-up point holes **must** be an equal distance from the floor.

If the pick-up point bolt holes are not at equal heights, the likelihood is that the chassis is bent.

True chassis

If you are dealing with a bare true chassis which is sitting flat on the floor, measure all around the lower chassis rail using a hacksaw blade (0.025in/ 0.65mm in thickness): if there is no distortion in the rails, the hacksaw blade will not be able to pass between the floor and the lower side of the chassis rail. If the chassis is not bent, the chances are that one side's brack-ets are bent or have, perhaps, been

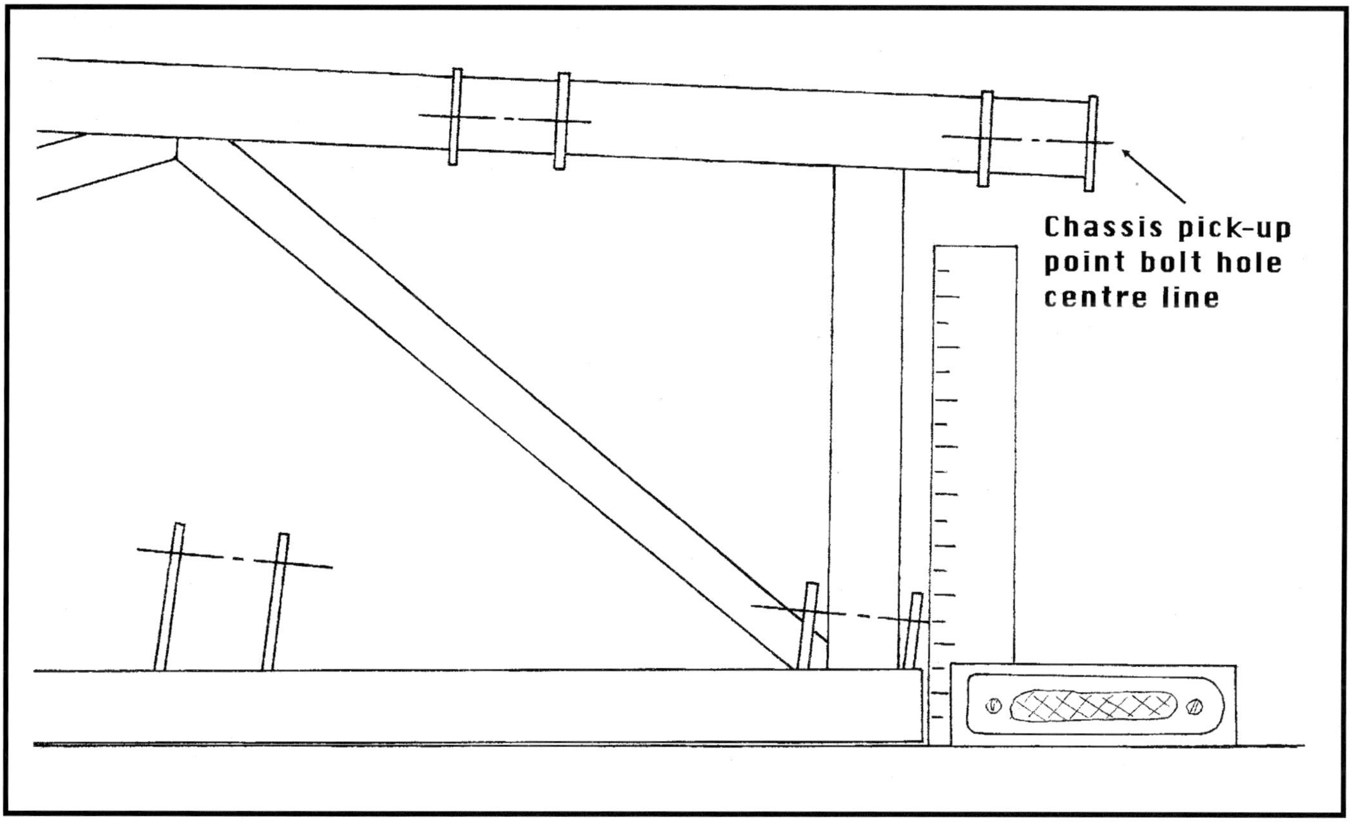

Graduated set square being used to measure directly from the floor to the centre of the lower pick-up point on this bare true chassis.

replaced at some stage and fixed in the wrong position. The solution in this situation is to remove the offending bracket/s and reposition them, or make new ones and position so that the lower pick-up points are identical in distance from the floor to the bolt holes.

It is almost always possible to identify which brackets have been repaired, replaced or repositioned, as the welding is usually not as good as the original and there is usually some surrounding damage to the chassis. Try to identify the correctly positioned original brackets and then alter the other side to suit.

If the chassis is bent, the exact starting points of the bent area must be found, and the exact amount of bend calculated. If the chassis is sitting flat on the floor, normally the bend will manifest itself as that part of the chassis that raises up off the floor. The distortion will usually be progressive and start from a reinforced part of the chassis. If 80% of the chassis sits flat on the floor without any rock, the bent part of the chassis will easily be found by pushing a hacksaw blade, or feeler gauges, under the chassis rail to ascertain the amount of distortion that is present in the chassis.

If the car has had several accidents, the chassis may well be so bent that it rocks so much it is difficult to tell which parts, if any, are straight. In some instances, it can be more expedient to find a good chassis and discard the original because the amount of rectification work will be substantial and costly.

If the distortion is too great (more than 0.060in/1.5mm), the chassis will have to be cut at the point where the bending starts and a new section incorporated, or the original tubing repositioned after cutting, so that alignment is restored. This is almost always major work and quite time-consuming, but it is necessary if the suspension geometry is to work correctly.

If the chassis is not bent too much (up to 1.5mm/0.060in), one or both brackets can be removed and repositioned so that the pick-up point bolt holes are perfectly in line with each other. The chassis is still slightly bent, but the pick-up points have been restored to their correct relative positions. Whilst not being a perfect solution, this is a lot better than pick-up points that are out of position. The car will not exhibit any bad handling characteristics if the suspension pick-up points are relocated slightly.

Monocoques and complete cars

If the 'chassis' is an all-steel monocoque, or you are checking a fully built car, checking for distortion will be a little more difficult.

Once again, the floor must be completely flat and level. If the car has a handling problem (turns right better than it turns left, for instance), a thorough inspection of the chassis may well reveal the cause.

Warning! - Do not go beneath the car unless it is safely supported and completely stable: **do not** rely on jacks alone, use axle stands/blocks of wood.

With the fully assembled car positioned on a level floor, the front suspension pick-up points can be checked. This is often best achieved by resting the front subframe, or chassis rails, solidly on wooden blocks of **equal** height. The car is jacked up at the front only and the blocks placed under the front of the car. The jack is then lowered until the car rests on the wooden blocks, which must be in identical positions on both sides. Next, the jack is placed dead centre under the rear axle assembly and the rear of the car raised approximately 2in/50mm to remove most of the static weight from the rear suspension (see diagrams earlier in this chapter).

With the car resting solidly on the blocks of wood, the distances from the front suspension pick-up points to the floor are accurately measured. If the measurements of each individual pair of matching (side to side) pick-up points are the same, the front of the car can be considered to be correct. If these measurements are not equal, in order to complete the overall measurements, it will be necessary to add thin packing pieces (sheet aluminium or suchlike) to the wooden blocks until the front suspension mounting points are at equal heights. The measurements involved here must be completely accurate and the same within 0.040in/1mm (0.80in/2mm maximum).

With the car assembled, the pick-up point mounting bolts will all be in place and it will be difficult to determine where the exact centre of the bolt head is (though a very good estimation can be made). Another way is to measure to the lower edge of the flat of a hexagon nut or bolt. This is a remarkably accurate datum, unless the bolts heads are of differing sizes (not impossible). The nuts or bolts can be easily turned so that one flat is parallel with the level floor, which makes measuring easier and more accurate. The measurements from the floor to the chassis pick-up points do not necessarily have to be taken from the centres of the bolts, but they do have to be from the exact same point (anything associated with the bolt or centre point of the pick-up point) on each side of the car.

With the front of the car resting on blocks of wood, and the individual front suspension pick-up points on both sides of the car proven to be positioned an equal distance from the level floor, attention is now focused on the rear of the car. The next step is to check that the rear suspension chassis pick-up points are at equal distances (side for side) from the floor. This is the acid test. The ideal situation will see all of the matching rear suspension pick-up points at equal heights or within 0.040in/1mm (0.80in/2mm maximum).

If there is a bigger difference than this, either the front suspension subframe mountings or rear suspension subframe mountings, or both, will have to be 'packed' until the front and rear suspension pick-up points are within tolerance side to side. This process will entail unbolting the subframes and placing packing pieces between the subframes and the monocoque. Some cars have only a front subframe, in which case it alone can be packed. These cars will have the rear suspension pick-up points precision drilled into the moncoque structure.

Irrespective of what type of car, or how the pick-up points are arranged, the front and rear suspension pick-up points need, ideally, to be in the same plane and within 0.040in/1mm (0.80in/2mm maximum).

A rubber bushed car (subframe to monocoque chassis mounting, that is) can be converted to a solid bushing and any discrepancy allowed for in the thicknesses of the new bushes that are made up (note that solid bushings will inevitably result in more noise and vibration).

Note that rubber bushings (if fitted) between the monocoque chassis and a subframe must be in good condition, as any movement will certainly cause the pick-up points to be inaccurate when the car is cornering hard, with all the usual forces acting on the car.

Upper wishbone/top arm mounting points

The procedure for checking the location of the top suspension arm pick-up points is similar to that for the lower arm pick-up points. The two front pick-up point bolt holes on each side of the chassis should be the same distance from the floor. The same applies to the two rear pick-up point bolt holes.

If there is any discrepancy between the pick-up points on the two sides of the car, the reason/s for the discrepancy must be found and adjustments made. This may mean repositioning the bracket/s or chassis repairs to bring everything back into alignment.

At this point the distance in the vertical plain from the floor to each of the pick-up points of the front suspension will be known. Any errors need to be recorded as, after all the other measurements have been taken, they will need to be taken into account in relation to other errors which may be discovered.

There is no substitute for accurately positioned suspension pick-up points, and this applies equally to top and bottom pick-up points.

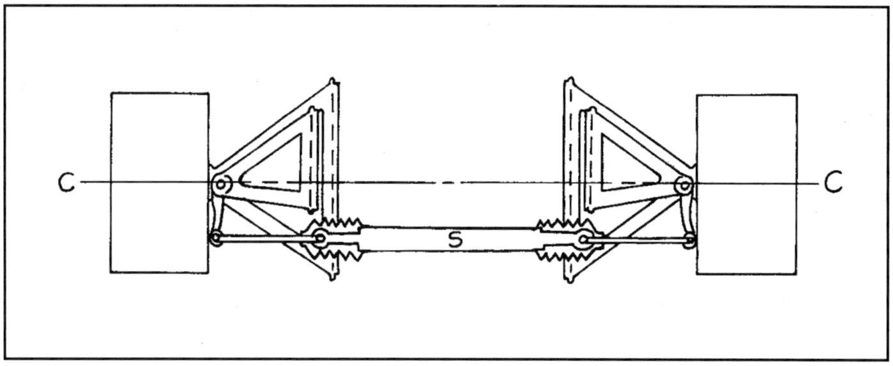

The steering rack must be parallel to the front suspension pick-up points across the car when looking down on the chassis. Regardless of whether the rack is front-mounted (as shown here) or rear-mounted, it should be as parallel as possible with the centre line of the two front wheels (CC).

STEERING RACK POSITIONING

Although it may seem obvious to some, it's important that the steering rack is positioned correctly in the chassis. Many handling problems can be directly attributed to how the rack has been fitted to the car. Essentially, the rack must be parallel to the front suspension top and bottom A arm pickup points, when viewed from the front and from above the car. This means that the axis of the rack must be parallel in two planes.

It's actually quite easy to get the fitting of the rack quite wrong, especially on kit cars which often have a bit more latitude to the fitting arrangement of the rack (for reasons best known to the manufacturers). When the rack is in a set position, or is non-adjustable, it can mean that there is less trouble all round. This presumes, of course, that the rack is positioned in the correct position in the first place.

If the rack is fitted incorrectly in one or both planes, the result can be better 'turning in' in one direction (left as compared to right, for example), or turning could be poor in both directions. Avoid any possible complications from this source by checking that the rack is correctly fitted in both these planes in the first place.

This aspect of rack positioning has nothing to do with the precise height requirement to eliminate 'bump steer', which I'll come on to shortly, it's just a 'fitting' criteria which is often not taken into consideration. One side of the car can end up with perfect steering geometry while the other side is incorrect.

It's not impossible for a steering rack to be up to 5 degrees out of alignment in one or both planes, and the owners of the car could be completely un-aware of the situation, other than knowing that something is not quite right somewhere. Any good test driver can spot an incorrectly fitted rack more or less instantly. Cars that are not driven fast don't always show up rack positioning problems, although in most instances the owners of such cars may have noticed that the car tends to steer better in one

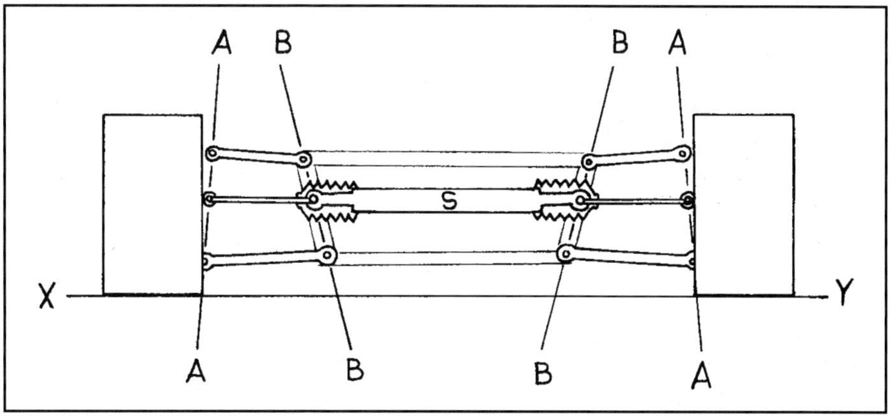

The steering rack (viewed here from the front) must be parallel to the ground (X-Y). On kitcars or specials, making good choices with regard to parts (such as stub-axles and the rack), and then making the chassis to suit is essential if the car is to handle properly.

direction than the other. The problems (potentially dangerous) can be quite disproportionate to the amount of effort required to actually fit the steering rack correctly.

With the steering rack parallel in both planes, it can now be located in its correct position on the chassis to eliminate any bump steer. Positioning the rack parallel in both planes in the first instance, before any other remedial work is undertaken, may seem somewhat strange since you may have to move it a considerable amount afterwards. This is quite true, but you have to start somewhere, and it is possible, of course, that the rack could be approximately in the right position in the chassis but just not parallel in the two planes. If the rack needs repositioning, you'll have pack up or out one of the rack mounting positions to achieve an ideal position across the car.

The steering rack must also be correctly positioned laterally across the car. To find the correct position, take the rack out of the car and hold it in a vice (use work protectors to avoid marking the rack and don't squeeze it too tight). Turn the rack by hand through its travel by the splined shaft. This will prove easier if a flanged joint or a universal joint is fitted on to the spline. Take the rack through its travel and count the number of full turns and part turns that it takes to achieve this. Divide the number of turns by 2 and, with the rack at its full travel in one direction, count it back to the true halfway position. There will now be an equal number of full and part turns to get the rack to full lock in either direction. Mark the splined spindle and the main body of the rack with a white felt tipped marking pen (two lines that are easy to align) so that the true halfway position won't be lost as the rack is being fitted into the chassis.

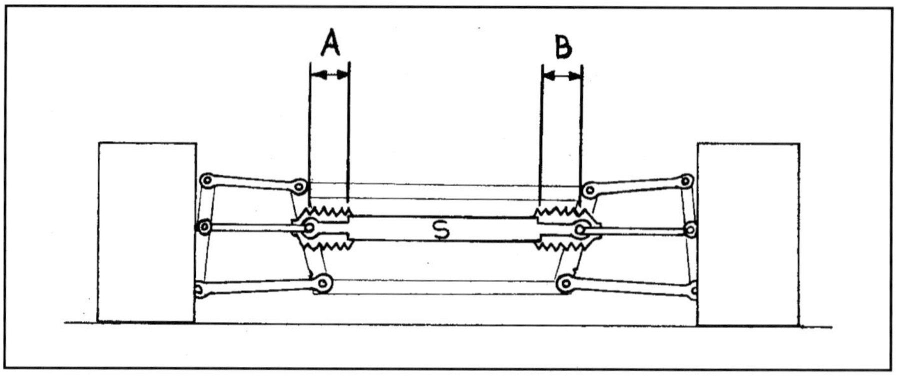

The steering rack (S) sits precisely in the centre of its left and right travel, and the ball joints of the rack are on the same axis as the pivot points of the top and bottom wishbones. Rack movement at A equals that at B.

Next, remove the clips that hold the two 'boots' onto the rack body and measure the exact distance between the centres of the ball joints. It's possible to get an extremely accurate measurement without disturbing the rack 'boots'. If you have trouble getting this right, though, you'll have to remove the 'boot' clamps and slide the 'boots' along the tie rod arms and out of the way. Whatever this distance is on your particular rack, this is the distance that must be equally dispersed about the true centre of the front suspension A arm chassis-mounted pickup points (that's the top and bottom A arm pick up points, of course). The steering rack **must** be in the central position.

Summary

When repositioning the steering rack for optimum steering geometry you have to start somewhere, and just getting the steering rack parallel in two planes is the first step on the way to achieving this. The next step will involve getting it central to the chassis.

Removing or minimising bump steer requires adjusting the height of the rack in the chassis. (For more information on bump steer, see Chapter 6).

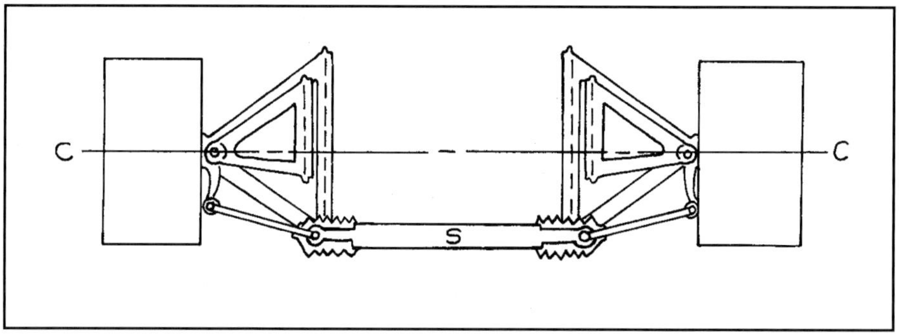

Although not ideal, positioning the rack well forward of the centre line of the two front wheels is permissible, and not as bad as it might at first appear.

Chapter 2
Ride height

Every car has a ride height that suits its suspension geometry. If a car is very low and it is decided to raise the ride height to increase the ground clearance, the actual suspension geometry may well be unacceptably altered (especially the front because of the steering) and, likewise, if it is decided to lower the car the suspension geometry may well be unacceptably altered. Unfortunately, the ride height of cars is often altered without taking into account suspension geometry and, in many instances, this does not matter if the intended speeds will not be great

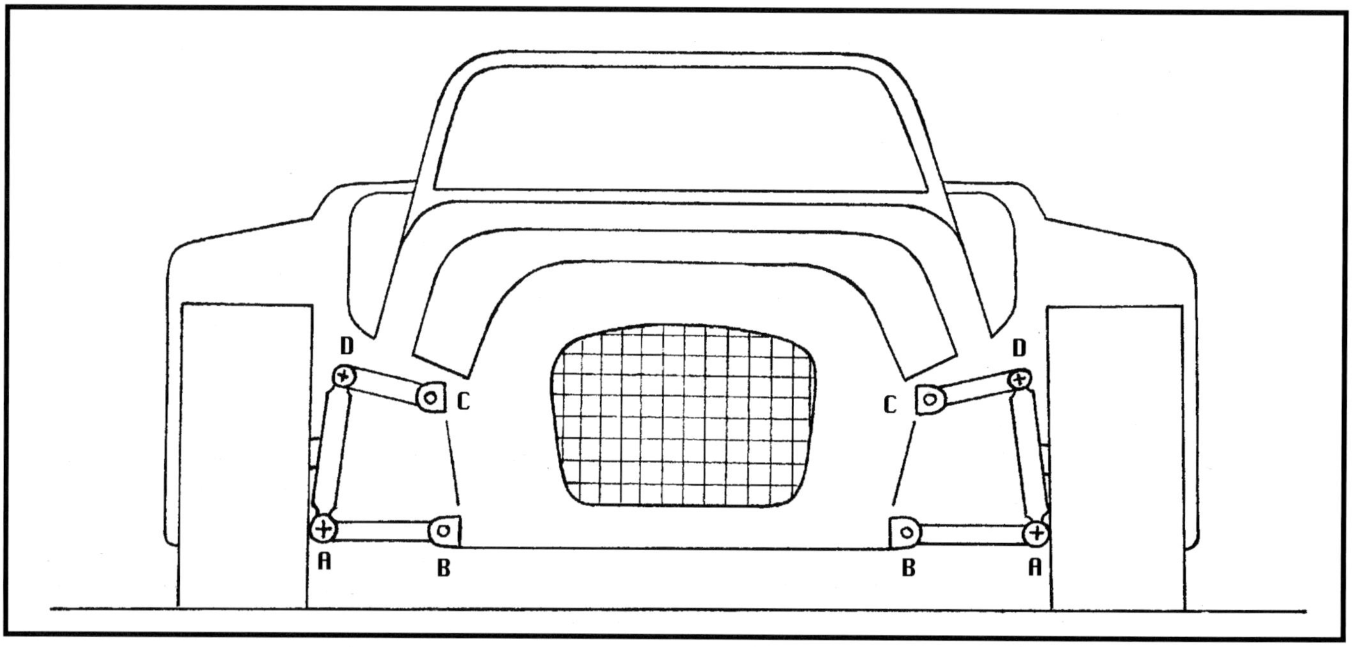

The bottom chassis pick-up point centre (B) and the bottom ball joint centre (A) are an identical distance from the ground. The top chassis pick-up points (C) are lower than the top ball joint (D) by 1-1.5in/ 25.5-38mm. The wheels have 1 degree of negative camber. Consider this to be good basic suspension geometry.

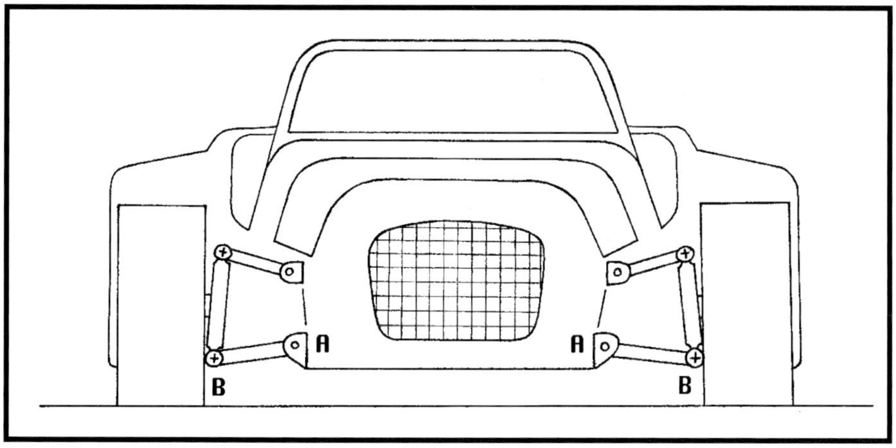

The bottom wishbone chassis pick-up points (A) are higher than the bottom balljoint centres (B) by 0.25-0.625in/6.3-16mm. The top wishbone chassis pick-up points are lower than the top balljoint centres by 1-1.5in/25.5-38mm. Wheels have 1 degree negative camber. Consider this to be good basic suspension geometry.

enough for there to be any noticeable affect (poor handling). At high speed with high cornering forces being generated it is, however, very likely that incorrect suspension geometry will be noticed!

FRONT SUSPENSION

The first two diagrams in this chapter show the recommended attitude of an unequal length dual wishbone independent front suspension system if the car is to handle well.

There is a slight alteration possible in the ideal scenario. This sees the bottom chassis pick-up points higher, which means that the bottom ball joints and the chassis pick-up points are not parallel with the ground. The chassis pick-up points are higher. The effect of having this set-up is that, during cornering, the bottom of the wheel is pushed out further (gains negative camber), but it can work against other aspects of the car's handling, such as during very hard braking.

Of course, it is possible that by lowering or raising the ride height of a car the suspension geometry will be improved (it depends on the particular car). There have been instances where cars have been raised to improve the attitude of the bottom suspension arm and the top wishbone repositioned so that overall geometry is improved.

On some cars the top wishbone pick-up point on the chassis is repositioned lower down (a new bracket welded onto the chassis/new holes drilled) to effect better geometry.

Improving wishbone geometry for some cars could be as simple as turning the mounting bracket of the wishbone upside-down (thereby lowering the chassis pick-up point of the wishbone).

There are several factors that can lead to a need for suspension geometry changes. If the wheels are changed for larger diameter ones, for instance, the car may be raised off the ground by an extra 0.5in/12.5mm, or more. With the car higher off the ground, the first reaction is normally to lower the ride height back down to what it was. This is achieved by adjusting the spring platforms on the shock absorbers or altering spring length. The three accompanying diagrams (page 26) show the same car, the only difference being the raising and lowering of the chassis in relation to the ground. In the diagrams the camber of the wheels has been adjusted so that all wheels have 1 degree of negative camber.

On average, lowering a car by 0.5in/12.5mm will alter the angle of the (usually shorter) top wishbones by approximately 3 to 3.5 degrees and the (usually longer) bottom wishbone by 2 to 2.5 degrees. You should note that such changes to true wishbone angles are not easily seen, especially on some bottom wishbones. The wishbone pivots at the chassis end are almost always on the centreline of the arm when viewed front-on, and so is the top wishbone ball joint, but the bottom wishbone ball joint is often not. This means that the true angle of the bottom wishbone (a straight line between the centre of the pivots and the centre of the ball joint ball) is often not easily seen in relation to the actual plane of the lower wishbone. Always bear in mind that when reference is made to wishbone/suspension arm angles, it is the **true angle** that is being discussed - **not** the apparent angle.

Raising a car's ride height by 1in/25mm to effect more ground clearance or, more specifically, sump clearance, may well alter the angle of the (usually) shorter top wishbone by up to 7 degrees and the (usually) longer bottom wishbone by up to 5 degrees. This is a significant change and is almost always unacceptable.

It would be useful if manufacturers of kit cars and some sportscars gave the distance from the ground to the centre of the wheels and the distance from the ground to the bottom chassis rail. With the correct dimensions known, it would not matter what wheels and tyres were fitted to the car as the relationship between the two measurements could

Car's ride height set correctly for the suspension geometry.

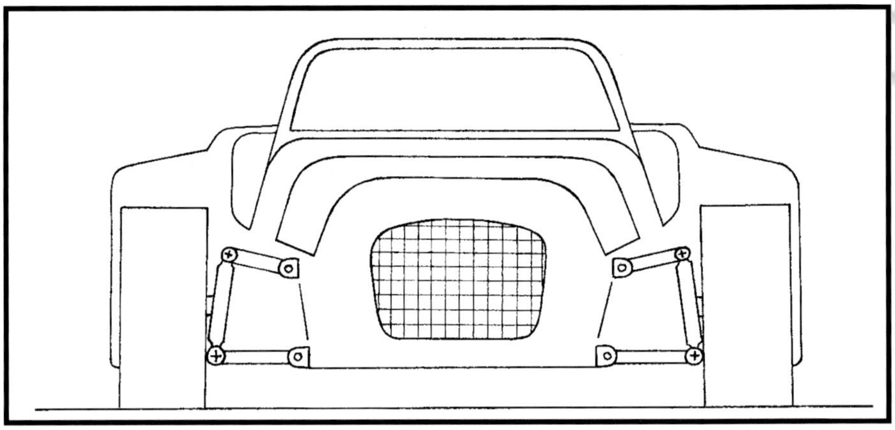

The same car's suspension when it has been lowered to original ride height after bigger diameter wheels have been fitted. Not ideal.

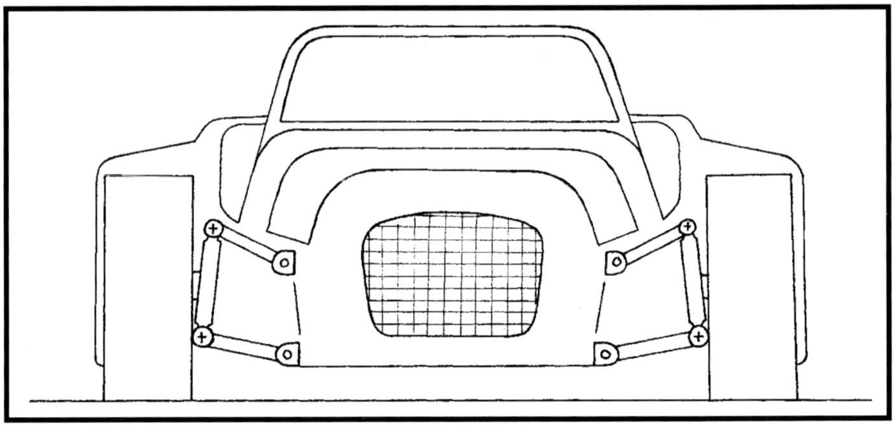

The same car's suspension after ride height has been raised to increase ground clearance to stop the sump getting continually knocked. Not ideal.

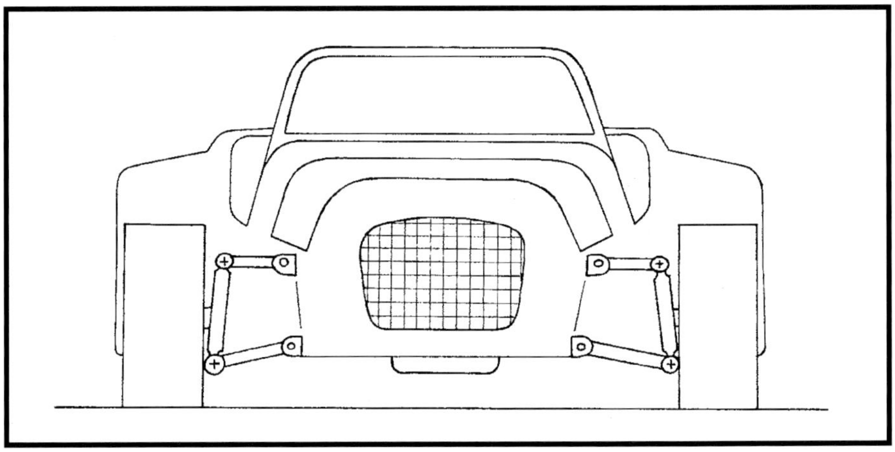

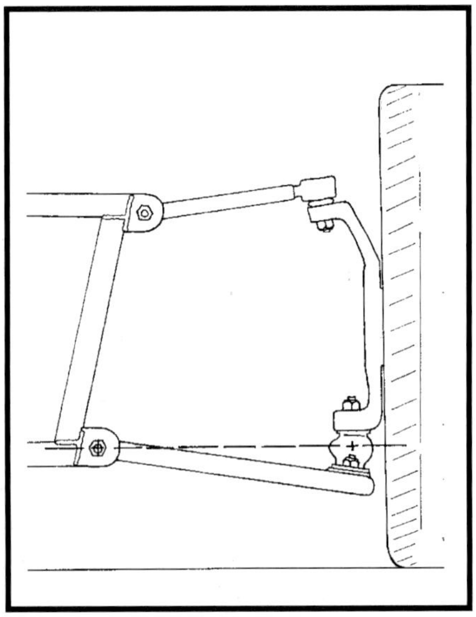

This wishbone has its balljoint bolted to it and the balljoint centre is well above the wishbone. The dotted line shows the true attitude of the suspension.

still be maintained.

As a general rule, consider 0.25in/ 6.3mm (up or down) to be the limit of adjustment from standard ride height that can be accommodated by the suspension geometry without resorting to geometry modifications.

REAR SUSPENSION

Live axle rear suspension

The majority of live axles on kit cars, for instance, are located by four trailing arms, with the lateral location of the axle via a Panhard rod or some other means. (The Panhard rod is a simple and effective means of locating the rear axle laterally, with no problems relating to good handling.) It's really not possible to make the rear axle suspension any simpler than the system just described. Some cars do feature alternative arrangements to locate a live axle but, generally, they are complicated in comparison and offer little, if any, improvement over the four trailing arm/Panhard rod suspension system.

There are other types of trailing arm suspension systems, but the same criteria apply in that the centre points of the trailing arm pick-up points, and rear axle pick-up points, should be equal distances from the ground. The trailing arms (usually metal pressings) are often not straight by design, and this can be confusing, so go by the bolt hole centres of the axle pick-up points and the chassis or subframe pick-up points. Measure up to the bolt hole centres from a level floor.

Ideally, the trailing arms are set parallel to the ground, as is the Panhard rod. This ensures a minimum of change in the effective length of the arms as the body of the car rises and falls. The arms travel through an arc as the body rises and falls, but it can be

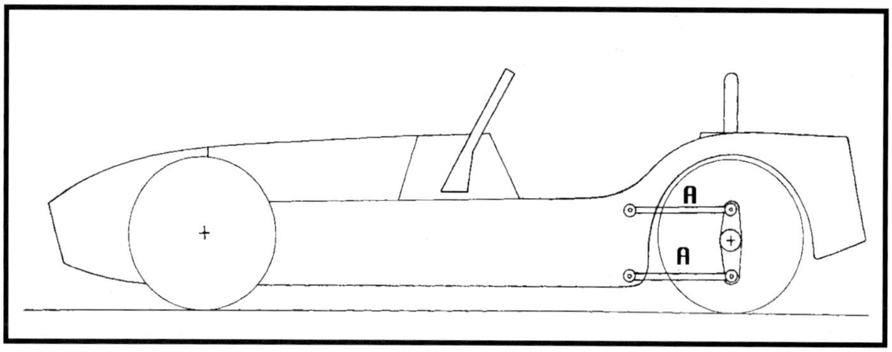

Trailing arms (A & A) and the Panhard rod are normally set parallel to the ground. The Panhard rod should be as long as possible within the constraints of the design.

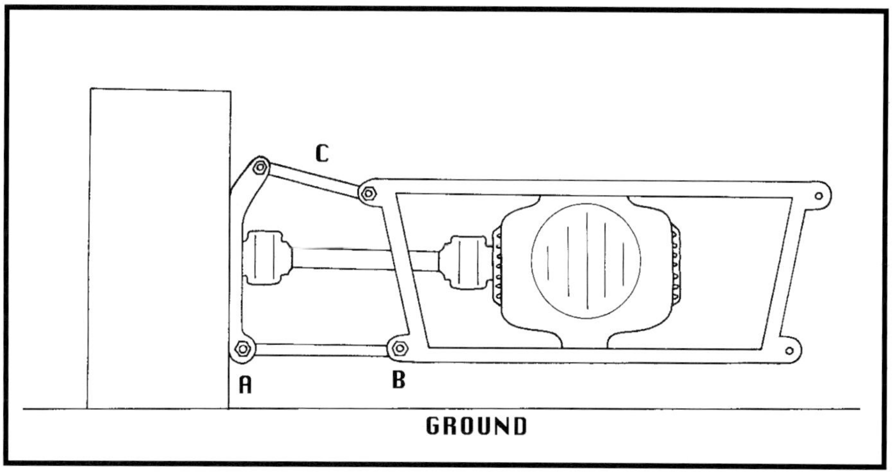

Left hand rear suspension shows the upright's lower pivot point centre (A) is the same distance from the ground as the lower chassis pick-up pivot point (B). Top arm (C) is inclined.

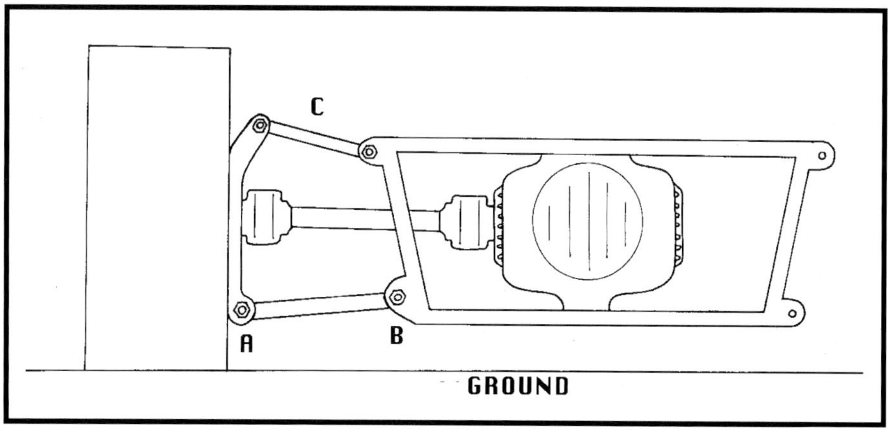

Left hand rear suspension shows the lower chassis pick-up point centre (B) higher than the upright's lower pivot point centre (A). Top arm (C) is inclined.

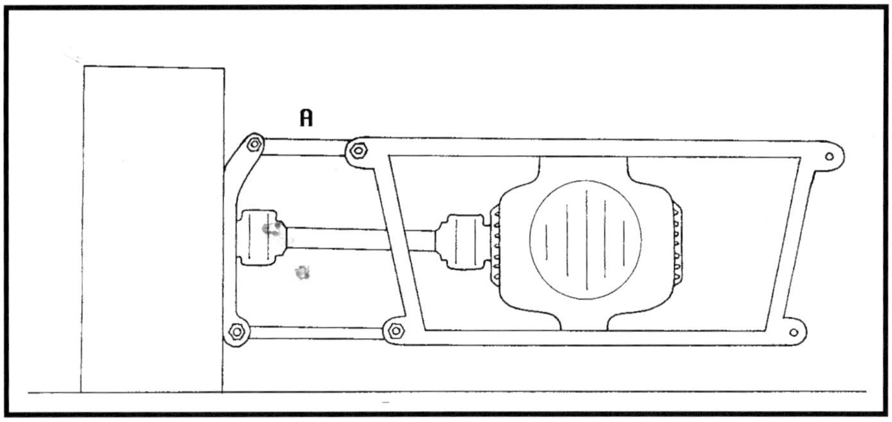

Some cars have chassis and upright pick-up point centres an identical distance from the ground. Wheel camber change is dependent on the top arm (A) being shorter which will pull the top of the wheel inward because of its short working radius. Such settings seldom give ideal geometry.

assumed with confidence that, if the arms are parallel with the ground when static, the suspension movement will, for the main part, be equally displaced about the ride height. This, in turn, will mean that the rear axle will remain in as constant a position as possible within the framework of the design.

The longer the trailing arms, the more stable the position of the rear axle. This is why, on many sportscars, the trailing arms seem to start almost at the longitudinal centre of the car, which is all well and good for many applications, but is not necessarily the best set-up for all cars. Short trailing arms do have their place and for very good reason, it just depends on the application. Short trailing arms, angled 5 degrees upward as they go back to the rear axle, will lengthen the wheelbase slightly on the outside and shorten it on the inside during body roll. This behaviour can be used to advantage in certain circumstances to prevent or reduce power oversteer.

As a general rule, take it that long trailing arms (12in/30cm, and more) are desirable for use on suspension systems that have the live rear axle going through a lot of up and down travel (not many sportscars need this), while short arms (8-12in/20-30cm) are normally quite acceptable for a rear suspension system that has a total travel of up to 4in/100mm.

The ideal basic setting of trailing arms is with their pick-up points parallel with the ground. This, and nothing else in the first instance, is the criteria which sets the rear suspension ride height.

Dual wishbone rear suspension

The more sophisticated types of sportscar suspension have a rigidly mounted, centrally situated differential centre section with jointed driveshafts to the rear wheels. The rear wheels have 'uprights' which are located by a bottom and top wishbone (four wishbones in total).

The geometry of the more sophisticated type of rear suspension system is usually set up similarly to that of the front suspension wishbones. The bottom wishbones' chassis and upright pick-up points all being parallel to the ground or, sometimes, the chassis pick-up points are set slightly higher (0.25-0.375in/6.3-9.5mm) than the upright's bottom pick-up point.

The top wishbone arms' chassis pick-up points are set lower (by 1-1.25in/25.5-38m) than the uprights' top pick-up point.

The advantage of having rear suspension which has a bottom chassis pick-up point higher than the upright's bottom pick-up is that it induces slightly more negative camber under suspension compression during cornering (the right rear wheel on a car turning left, or vice versa). When the arm is level with the road or track, it pushes the bottom of the wheel outwards (not a lot but enough to make a difference). Under braking, such geometry tends to pull the bottom of the wheels in, but not a lot, and seldom to the point of causing instability (reducing negative camber).

Swing arm rear suspension

The majority of modern swing arm independent rear suspension systems have a single swing arm on each side of the car positioned parallel with the ground. A small amount of negative camber (0.5 of a degree) is usually built into the swing arm, so that at the true ride height the wheel has slight negative camber. By lowering the car, negative camber is increased. If the car's ride height is increased, negative camber will be reduced to the point where the wheels have positive camber.

With this type of suspension, the negative camber angle of the wheels is a pretty good indication of what the true ride height should be. Where, for example, 0.5 degree of negative camber is standard, it can usually be increased to a maximum of 1 degree, but this may entail structural changes to the arm or arm mounting points.

Swing axle suspension

Swing axles are rarely used on modern cars. With this form of suspension the axles (driveshafts) are used as swinging arms, each having a universal joint at the differential end upon which the

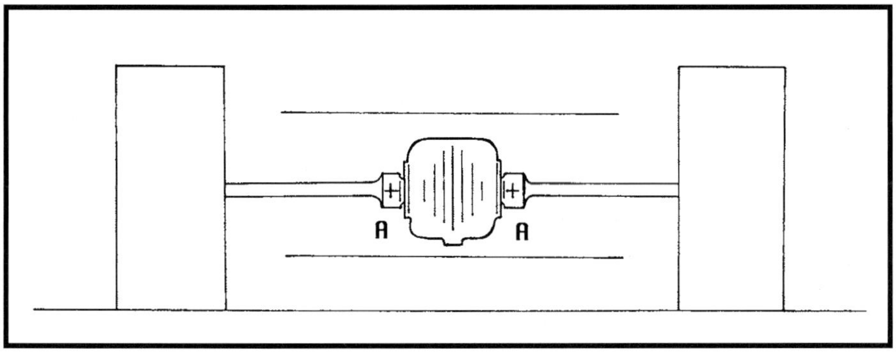

Swing axle rear suspension pivots from universal joints (A) on each side of the differential. The wheel axis and the axle axis are the same (no compliance between the two. Diagram shows wheel attitude at the correct ride height, 0.25-0.5 degree negative camber).

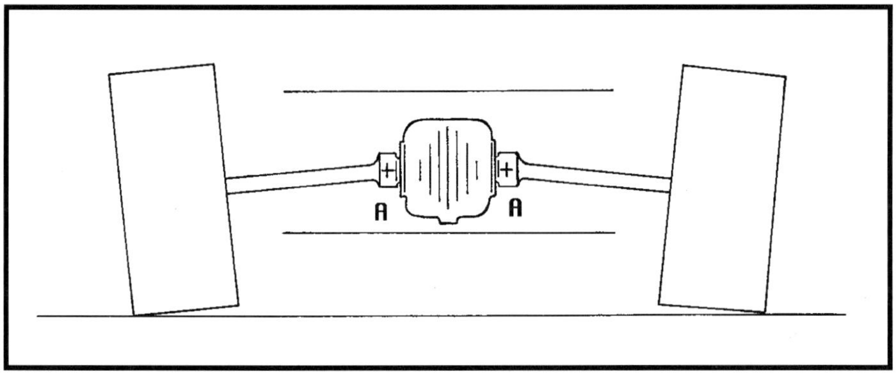

Swing axle rear suspension in 'droop.' Suspension travel needs to be limited so that the suspension does not allow the wheels to move more than 2.5 degrees of negative or positive camber. The wheels camber in the right directions for cornering purposes, it's just that they camber far too much.

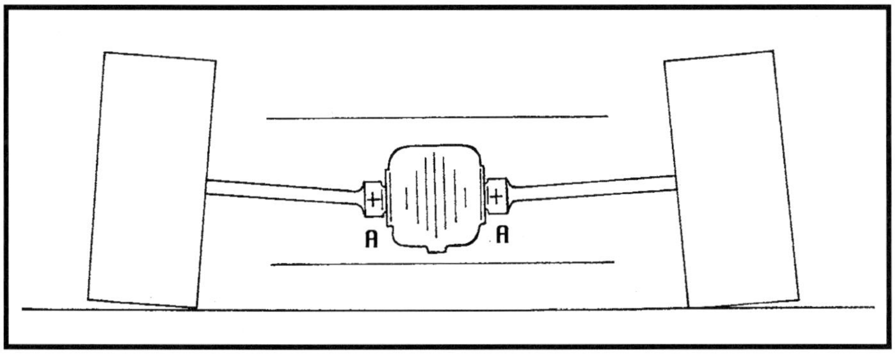

Swing axle rear suspension in compression. Tyres are not in good contact with the ground. The more suspension travel there is, the more the suspension goes negative. The only thing to do is limit the suspension travel using strong springing and, perhaps, an anti-roll bar.

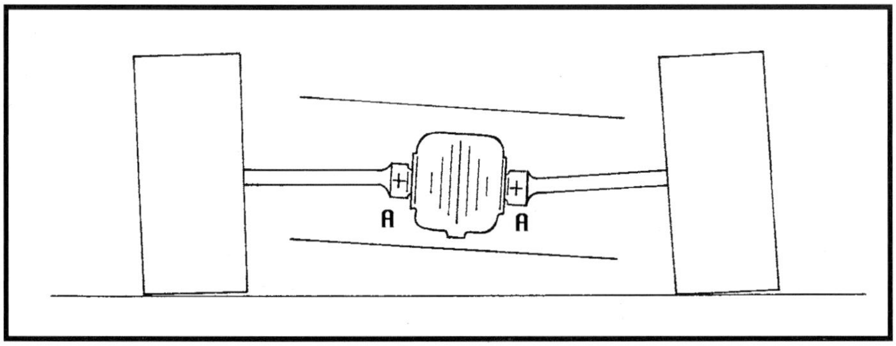

Car is turning left and has 3 degrees of body roll. Wheel on the right has too much negative camber, while wheel on the left has too much positive camber. This view is from the rear of the car. Axles pivot at (A) and (A) only.

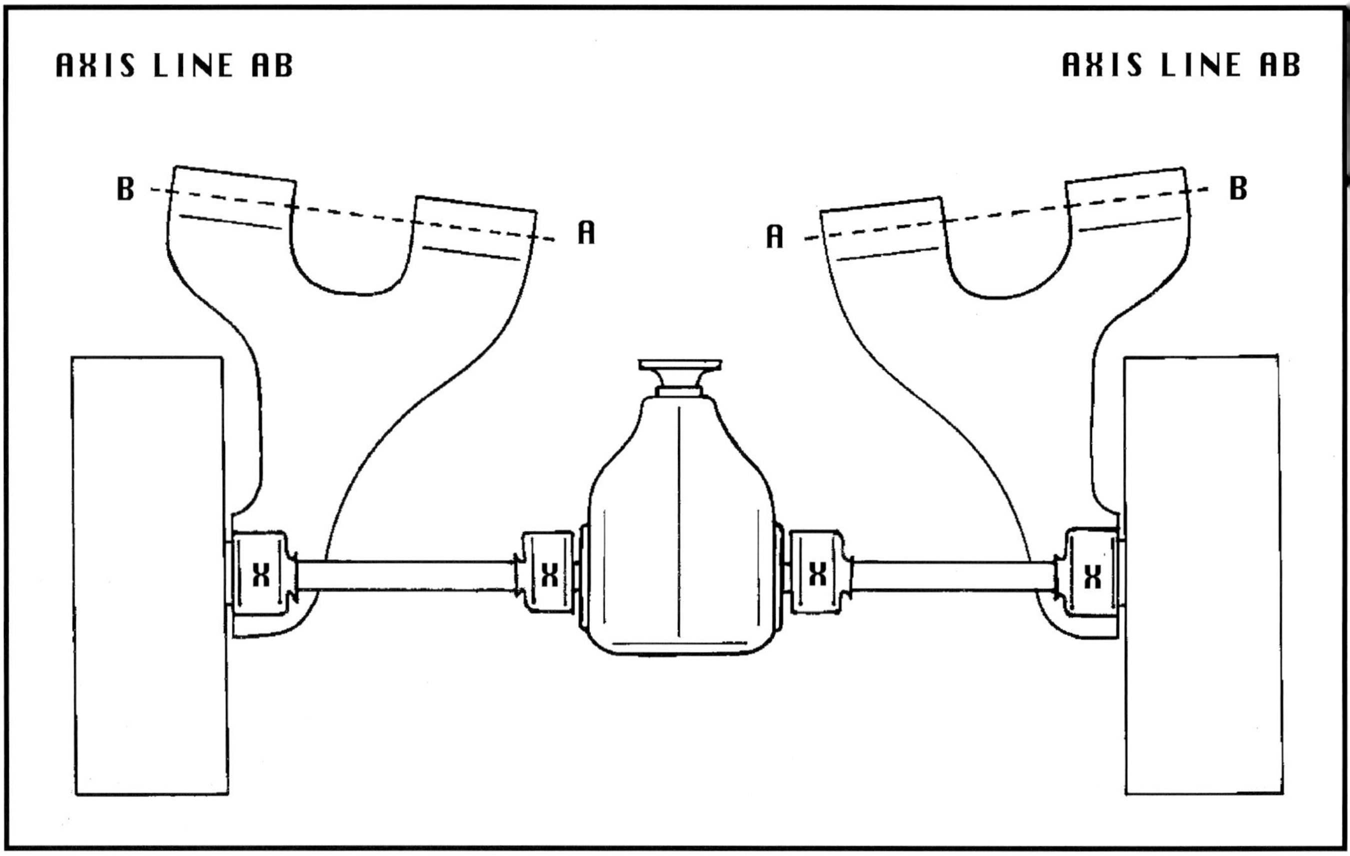

Universal joints or constant velocity joints are marked "X" and there are four of them. There is axle compliance to compensate for the axle length variation required. Swing axle pivot lines are marked "A"-"B." The steeper the pivot angle (points "A" moved closer to the differential assembly) the greater the geometry alteration and wheel camber for a given amount of suspension travel.

wheel pivots during suspension movement. The theory of this design is okay, but there are a few associated problems in practice.

The geometry is not ideal because the wheels gain and lose camber excessively during normal body roll. A heavily loaded vehicle, or one that has been lowered, may exhibit an increase in negative camber. Conversely, if the car's ride height is increased, for example, the negative camber would be reduced to the point that the wheels could have positive camber on them when the suspension is in full 'droop'. In most instances this type of suspension will not exhibit more than 1 degree of positive camber in this full 'droop' situation. The main advantage of the 'swing arm rear suspension' over the older style 'swing axle suspension' is the reduction in wheel camber for the same amount of wheel travel.

With this form of suspension the only way to control excessive camber is to limit the suspension travel, which will deliver a substantial improvement in handling at the expense of a smooth ride. Travel should be limited so that the wheels cannot go beyond 2.5 degrees of negative or positive camber. Suspension travel can be limited by fitting stronger springs and/or using a Z-bar (if possible): the fitting of very firm shock absorbers is not necessarily the best way around this problem.

Independent suspension - general

Note that independent rear suspension geometry that allows the rear wheels to toe-out during cornering will cause the car to oversteer to a degree: the amount of oversteer being commensurate with the amount of toe-out.

For example, if the left hand rear wheel toes-out by a significant amount when turning right, or vice versa, oversteer will result. The reason for this is that when the highly loaded rear wheel toes-out during cornering, it effectively steers the back of the car in

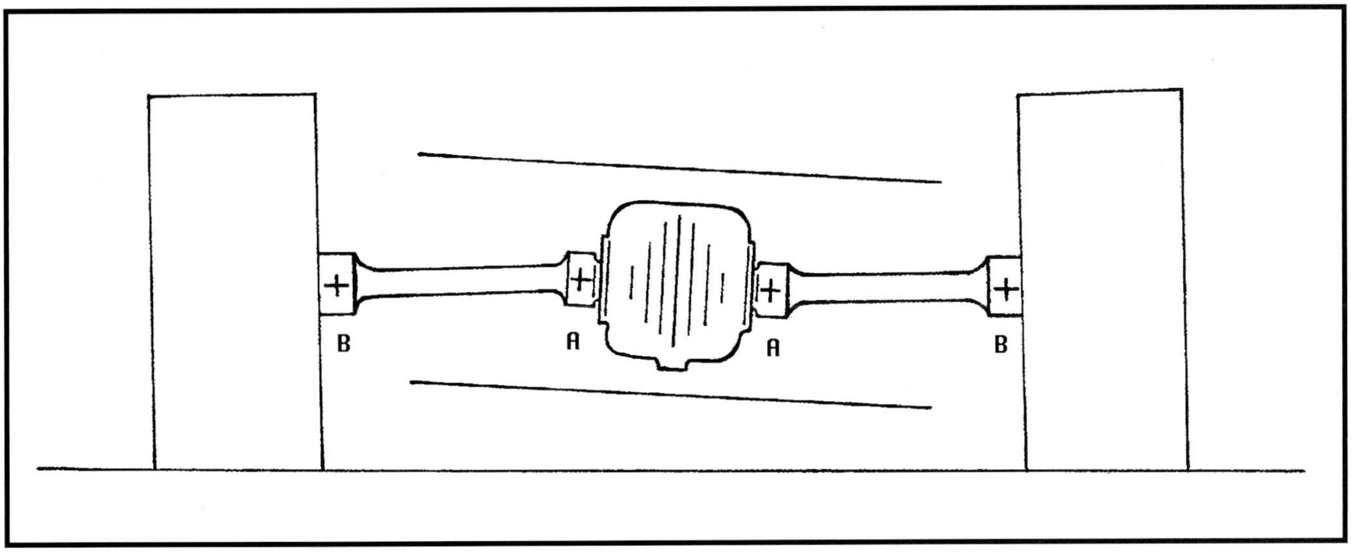

The body has 3 degrees of roll. Right hand wheel has 1 degree negative camber, while the left hand rear wheel has 0.5 degree positive camber. View is from the rear of the vehicle and the car is turning left.

that direction.

Some cars have geometry that works perfectly in a straight line, with no toe-out ever being present. The problem only arises when the car is in a body roll situation and cornering hard (the very time you need the geometry to be correct!). When the car is at its normal ride height, toe-in will be present. However, when the rear suspension is in compression, coupled with some body roll, this situation frequently alters to an unacceptable degree: what was 0.040in/1.0mm toe-in can become 0.040in/1.0mm or more of toe-out!

DE DION REAR AXLES

The De Dion rear axle idea is still being used in kit cars, and for very good reasons. They can be very simple or very complicated in their construction (stay away from a complicated system).

There are several advantages in using a De Dion rear axle: the unsprung weight of the rear axle assembly as a whole can be reduced considerably, over that of a live rear axle. This happens because the centre section of the differential, the drive shaft (from the engine/gearbox), and a portion of the two side axles are unsprung as opposed to sprung weight. This means that the weight of these components is acting on the rear wheels as opposed to being part of the rear wheels (a very significant difference!). This results in more traction and better handling generally, provided the other aspects the De Dion rear axle assembly are set correctly. The rear wheels can have some negative camber built into the geometry, if required, and they can (and should) also have an amount of 'toe in' built in. These last two aspects of the set up of a De Dion rear axle assembly (and especially the last one, the 'toe in') can really make a difference to the general handling of the vehicle.

The rear of most sports cars (especially kit cars) is usually quite light, and the more weight that is acting directly on the rear wheels the better. There will rarely be an overall weight reduction when fitting a De Dion rear axle assembly. In fact, it may even be slightly heavier than the standard live rear axle.

On a reasonably smooth road or track surface, the De Dion rear axle system will be very good. However, the fact that the two rear wheels are linked together by a bar does have a few drawbacks. For example, because the wheels are connected, the De Dion system will not handle undulations as well as a properly sorted fully independent rear suspension system. If one rear wheel goes into a dip or hole in the road surface, for example, the other wheel will be affected. As the term suggests, however, a fully independent rear suspension system will not be affected in the same way.

A live axled vehicle doesn't have 'toe in' on the axle. The De Dion axle, however, can and should have 'toe in', in much the same way as independent rear suspension. This means having 2mm of collective 'toe in' equally dispersed about the centre line of the car. De Dion axles also allow the possibility of having up to 1 degree of negative camber built into each rear wheel at the normal suspension ride height. This can either be directly built into the De Dion 'tube', or the rear suspension 'tube' can be made adjustable using shims, for example).

It's important to avoid having rear wheel 'toe out' when exiting a corner. If the car is exiting a lefthand corner or bend, for example, what you don't want is for the right rear wheel to have 'toe out' on it as this will tend to steer the back of the car in that direction (oversteer). The lefthand rear is not quite so critical in this situation as it's almost always less loaded with weight in this situation. The opposite is also true for a righthand corner.

CONCLUSION

Methods of setting suspension geometry vary considerably. In the case of a kit car, find out before the kit is bought - not afterwards. Find out from the car's manufacturer what the recommended ride height is and the criteria for measurement. If the manufacturer is not helpful, don't worry; the best settings can be arrived at by testing on your own account. The manufacturer's recommendation may be as simple as saying that the lower wishbones of the front suspension are set parallel to the road, as are the trailing arms/wishbones of the rear suspension. This is easy to check relatively accurately using a tape measure and a flat level floor.

The basic settings for independent front and rear suspensions, as already described, are recommendations that, if realised, will ensure your car exhibits good handling characteristics. With regard to front suspension, in reality there is rather more to it than this (such as kingpin inclination (kpi) and castor), but more on this later in the book. With regard to rear suspension, there are also further considerations (such as the all-important toe-in, which is required throughout the suspension's travel).

Never set ride height - high or low - at the expense of good geometry.

Irrespective of which company or person designed and built the car, the suspension system can be measured at strategic points and the optimum settings for good all-round handling worked out. There are well known parameters and design considerations for suspension systems and, if the basics are followed, any car can be set up as close to optimum as possible. Be aware that some cars are built with such poor geometry that some small structural changes may have to be made before any significant improvement in the handling of the car can be realised.

Chapter 3
Suspension geometry

Good suspension geometry requires that the centres of the points about which all of the components of the suspension pivot are correctly positioned. The geometry parameters are sorted out at the car's design stage, and it is then that the overall efficiency of the suspension system is set.

Most front suspension systems use wishbones or track control arms of one sort or another, which can be mass production car-type metal pressings or specially made tubular items. As far as mass production car-type live rear axle systems are concerned, expect to see four trailing arms with the two top arms angling in towards the centre of the differential to effect lateral location; alternatively, four parallel trailing arms and a Panhard rod or Watts linkage for lateral location. More sophisticated independent rear suspension systems will have wishbones, swing arms or trailing arms which are usually pressings though, sometimes (especially on kit cars and competition cars) two wide-based tubular wishbones per side. On some racing only sportscars, you'll find two single independent trailing arms, one top link and a reversed wishbone to locate each rear upright (but not always).

Irrespective of what type of suspension a car has, there will be suspension geometry of some description (good or bad). Each car's suspension points can be measured and then an assessment made about how good, overall, the handling can be expected to be.

FRONT AND REAR SUSPENSION BASICS

There are various forms of suspension design, but the most common front suspension system for kit cars and sportscars is the unequal length wishbone system, which sees the top wishbone shorter than the bottom wishbone. The wishbones can be parallel with the bottom chassis rail or angled in relation to the chassis centreline. It's more common for the wishbones of kit cars to be parallel to the chassis rails as this simplifies the construction of the car.

The rear suspension is slightly simpler because it does not have wheels that turn to steer the car left or right. However, on the basis of the camber changes required for cornering, front and rear systems are quite similar in principle.

Note that wishbones from mass production cars are almost always metal pressings and, as a consequence, quite bulky when compared to tubular, specialist-manufactured items, but the actual geometry provided by both types can be identical - looks can be deceiving!

The precise pick-up points at the chassis end for all types of wishbones, or other swinging arms, are the centres of the pivot bolt holes. The pick-up points at top and bottom of the front stub axles are the centres of the ball joints .The pick-up points of the rear uprights (trailing arm systems) are the centres of the pivot bolt holes. Accurate measurement of these precise points, from a flat and level floor, is essential if a reasonable assessment of the status of the suspension geometry is to be made.

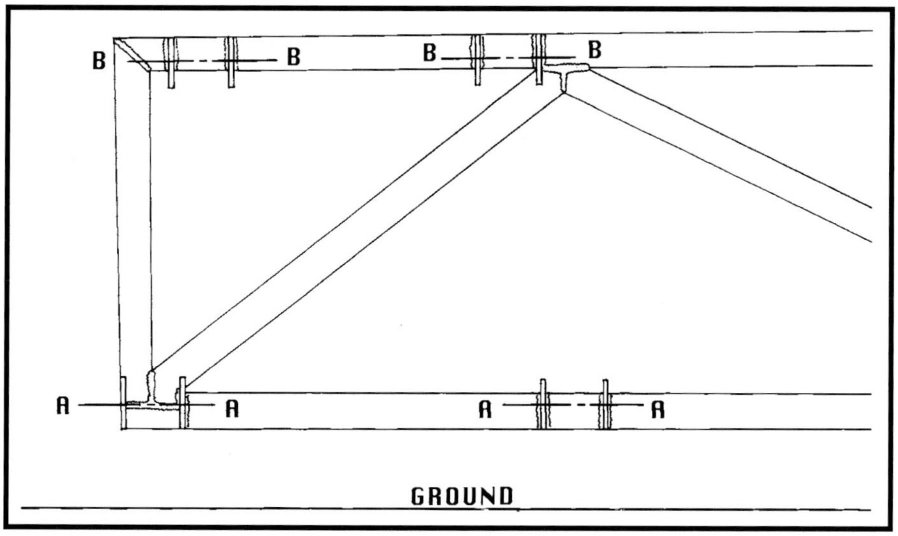

Side on view of this chassis shows the bottom front wishbone pick-up points (AA) parallel with the chassis longitudinal axis and the ground. The top wishbone pick-up points (BB) are also parallel to the ground.

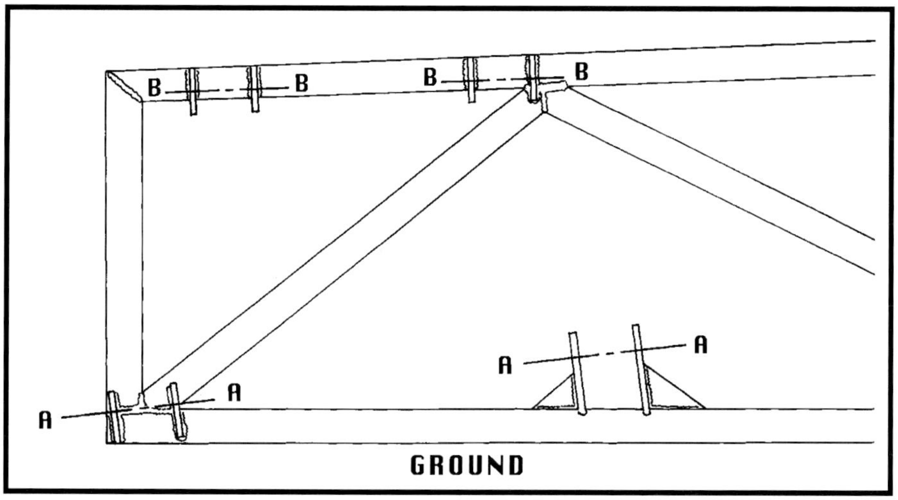

Side on view of this chassis shows the bottom wishbone pick-up points (AA) inclined and not parallel with the ground. The top wishbone pick-up points (BB) are also slightly inclined. This sort of wishbone inclination is for anti-dive geometry.

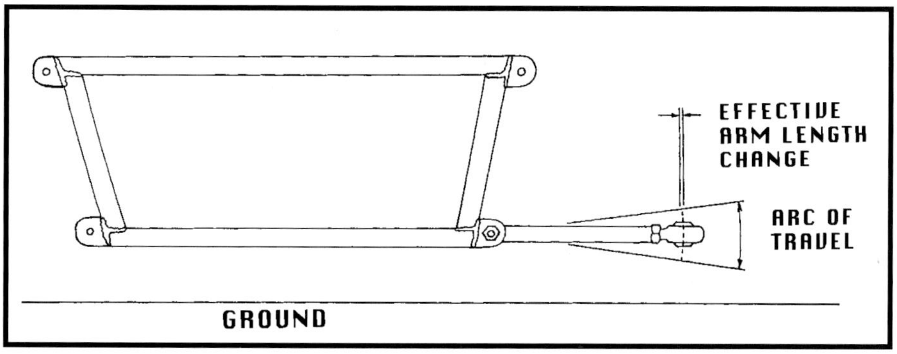

Bottom arm's arc of travel creates minimum change of arm length when the pick-up point centres are set parallel with the road surface.

The precise centre points of the ball joints have to be accurately estimated, which is not actually all that easy, although by lifting the rubber dust cap a reasonable assessment (of the actual ball's centre point) (within 0.06in/1.5mm) can be made.

FRONT WISHBONES (LOWER)

Consider that when the centre of the bottom ball joint and the bottom wishbone pick-up points (on both sides of the car) are an equal distance from a level flat surface, the ideal starting point has been achieved. Average suspension travel is approximately a total of 2.5-4in/63-101mm, but, irrespective of this, if the chassis pick-up point and the centre of the ball joint are on a parallel line in relation to the road, the wishbones effective length will be as constant as possible under all operating conditions. This type of design/setting has no real disadvantages.

Some suspension systems are not designed with wishbone pick-up points parallel to the bottom ball joint and, instead, have the chassis pick-up point centre higher, by around 0.25-0.625in/6.3mm-17mm, than the ball joint centre. There is some advantage with this set-up in that, when the car is cornering (exhibits body roll), in effect the bottom arm lengthens whilst the arm on the other side of the car shortens. This has the effect of pushing the bottom of the tyre out on one side of the car and bringing the bottom of the tyre in on the other side of the car: this is all about wheel/tyre attitude while cornering. The slight disadvantage of this design is that when travelling on a straight but undulating road, when the suspension is in compression the wheels display more negative camber. In the same situation, during suspension rise the negative camber is reduced, but this seldom goes too far or causes the wheels to have positive camber. Avoid having the chassis pick-up point higher by more 0.75in/19mm than the stub axle's bottom ball joint centre.

FRONT WISHBONES (UPPER)

The chassis pick-up points should always (if possible) be lower than the centre of the top ball joint of the stub axle. The reason for this is that, when

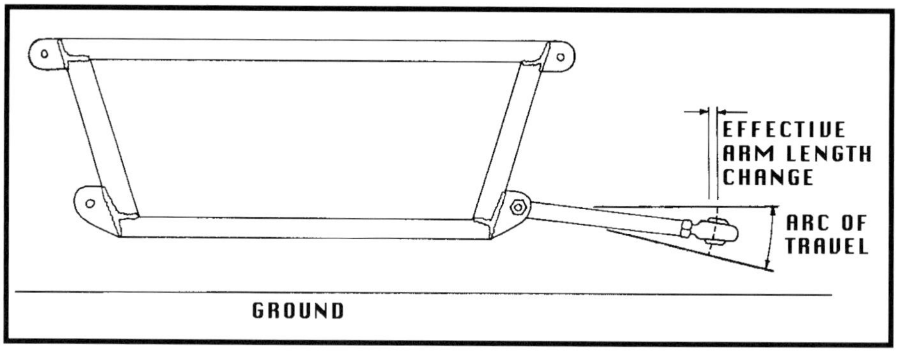

Bottom arm's arc of travel causes effective arm lengthening in suspension compression and shortening in droop because the chassis pick-up point is higher than the bottom stub axle balljoint centre.

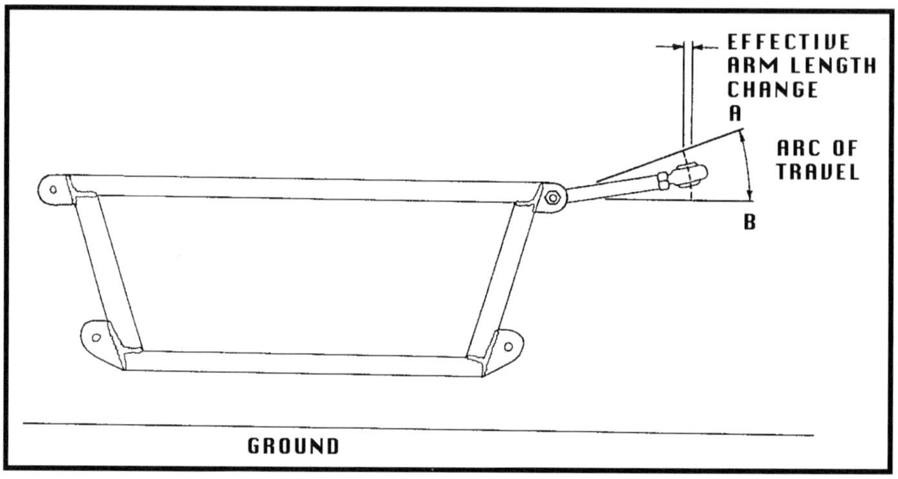

Top arm is inclined at the ride height. Suspension arm has maximum possible effective arm length alteration as the suspension goes through its arc of travel (A-B).

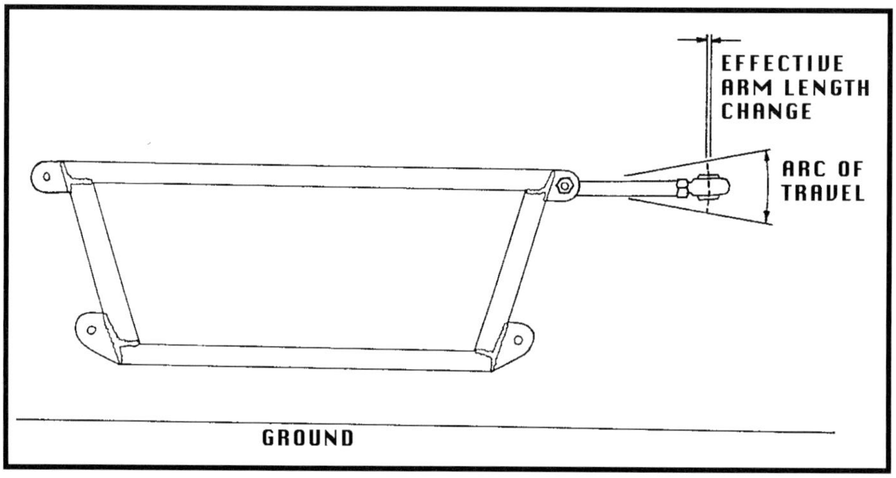

Top arm parallel to the ground at ride height. Arm moves through an arc of travel as the suspension compresses or droops. Suspension arm has minimal length alteration.

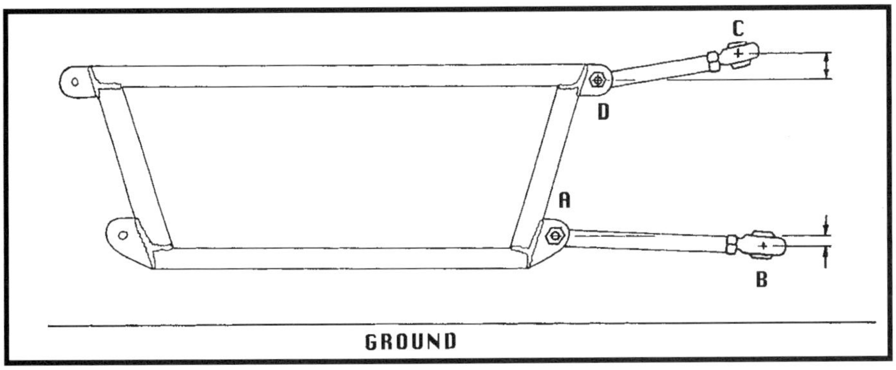

Lower suspension pick-up point (A) on the chassis is higher than the centre of the stub axle's balljoint centre. The top chassis pick-up point (D) is lower than the stub axle's top balljoint centre (C) at the car's ride height.

Bottom arms are parallel with the ground and the top arms are inclined down from the chassis to the top ball joint. This is not an ideal suspension layout at all.

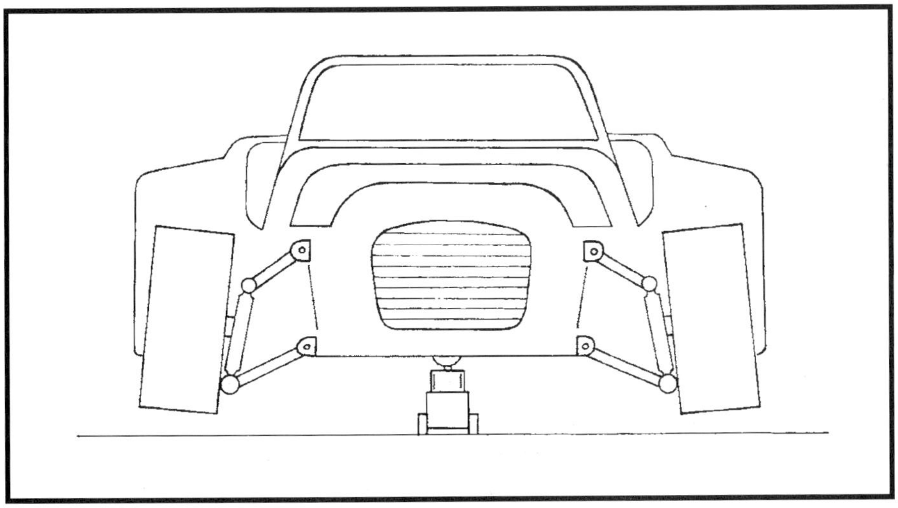

the suspension is in compression during cornering (body roll), the arm effectively shortens and pulls the top of the wheel/tyre in (induces negative camber). On the other side of the car the suspension is in droop and the arm effectively parallel with the road surface (the ideal situation), meaning that it is as long as possible - which tends to push the top of the wheel/tyre away from the car (reduce negative camber).

The geometry associated with the top arm in the position just described, in conjunction with the bottom suspension pick-up point and ball joint centre line being parallel with the road surface, causes the wheel to have negative camber when the suspension is in compression and minimal negative camber when the suspension is in droop. This means that with a car turning left, for example, the right front tyre tends to adopt negative camber, while the left front tyre tends to remain near vertical or moves towards positive camber.

The difference in height between the top wishbone's chassis pick-up points and stub axle ball joint centre will vary, but consider the minimum difference to be 0.5in/12.5mm (on average 3 degrees inclination down towards the chassis from the top of the stub axle) and the maximum difference to be 1.5in/38mm (on average about 10 degrees of wishbone inclination from the ball joint inwards). 1in/25.5mm is the recommended starting point as a height difference

With the front wheels in the straight ahead position, jack the car at the front until the front wheels are clear of the ground and the front suspension is at full droop. If the front wheels adopt an attitude of negative camber, as indicated in the diagram do not expect the car to have good handling (expect understeer).

between the two upper wishbone datum points.

Some cars (several current kit cars, for example) are not built with optimum upper wishbone angles and have chassis pick-up points higher than the centre of top ball joint (by as much as 2in/50mm). This sort of design promotes understeer and really has no place on a sportscar. The camber angles of the wheels are heading in the opposite direction to what is required during cornering!

It is reasonably easy to tell what sort of suspension geometry a car has without measuring anything. Simply place a jack in the middle of the chassis at the front and jack up the car until both wheels are off the ground. Now stand back a bit and note the attitude of the front wheels. If the wheels in full droop exhibit a lot of negative camber (5 degrees or more) don't expect the car to be a brilliant handler. If, on the other hand, the wheels exhibit 2 or 3 degrees of positive camber with the suspension in full droop, expect the car to have suspension geometry conducive to good handling.

Car turning right and with 3 degrees of body roll. The left front wheel has positive camber and the right hand wheel a lot of negative camber. Cars like this understeer and are not nice to drive (unstable, to say the least, at speed).

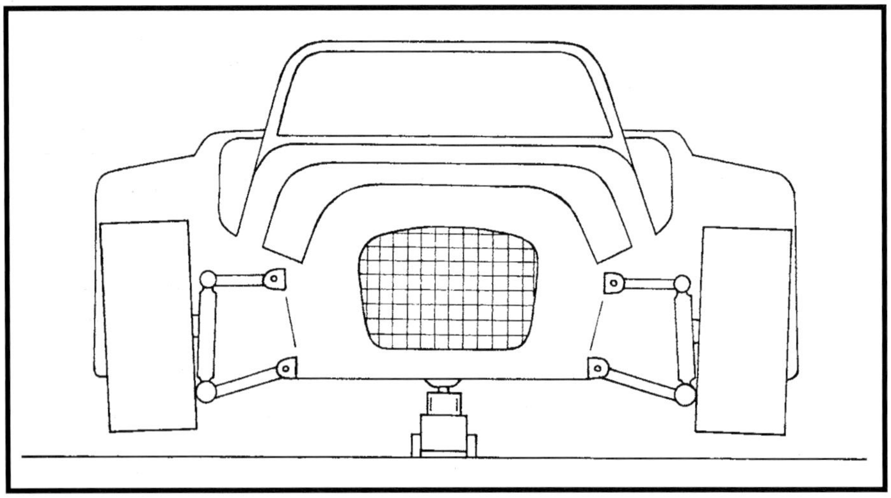

With the front wheels in the straight ahead position, jack the car at the front until the wheels are clear of the ground and the front suspension is in full droop. If the front wheels adopt an attitude of positive camber, as indicated in the diagram, expect the car to have good handling.

The difference between these two examples of front wheel attitude in a corner is like night and day. The car with negative camber in the full droop position will, when turning right, exhibit positive camber on the left-hand front wheel and a lot of negative camber (to say the least) on the right-hand front wheel. Expect such a car to have understeer and generally poor handling characteristics.

The car with positive camber in the full droop position will, when turning right, usually exhibit 0.5 to 1 degrees of negative camber (depends a bit on the amount of steering lock used - more lock, more negative camber) on the left hand front wheel and have 2 to near-zero degrees of negative camber on the right hand front wheel. Expect such a car to have good handling characteristics.

INDEPENDENT REAR SUSPENSION

There is a considerable variation in the design of independent rear suspension systems, especially in kit cars. Some kit cars have the complete rear end assembly from a mass-production donor vehicle, while others will feature selectively used mass production parts. The car may be front engine and use a conventional gearbox, driveshaft and differential assembly which is rigidly mounted into the chassis, or it may have a rear mounted engine that uses a transaxle of some description. Either way, the basic suspension design and suspension settings will be similar. All independent rear suspension systems need to be thoroughly checked to ensure that, at no time in the travel of either side's suspension, does a wheel have toe-out. Toe-out on an independent rear suspension system is not conducive to good handling.

An independent rear suspension system must have an amount of toe-in throughout suspension travel. The toe-in of each wheel must also be equally dispersed about the centreline of the car. Toe-out causes rear end instability, and cars that have this feature tend to wallow when they go over an undulating surface and the back end moves around. When a rear wheel moves into toe-out, that wheel effectively steers that corner of the car in its direction of travel. This problem is always very easy to see. Consider the optimal minimum collective (that of both sides of the car added together) amount of toe-in to be 0.080in/2mm and the maximum amount 0.120in/ 3mm.

Many cars are set with toe-in at the ride height, so when the car goes down a smooth level road it handles perfectly well. The problems arise when the road surface is undulating and the car is being driven quite fast. When the rear suspension is in compression or droop (body roll), the rear wheels either toe-out or toe-in. The toe-in does not really cause a problem, but the toe-out will cause that wheel to steer in that direction. This problem is almost always felt by the driver (and perhaps passengers) of the car as a perceptible sideways movement at the back every time the car goes over a rise or bump. This situation is caused by that side of the car only having toe-out. The other side of the car may well have toe-in. The car may have toe-in when it is measured at ride height, but the toe-in is not equally dispersed about the centreline of the car and this is the problem. One wheel is effectively always in toe-out, whilst the other wheel has a considerable amount (far too much) of toe-in. What must be established is whether the car has toe-in, and whether it is equally dispersed about the centreline. The way to do this is to establish the level of squareness of the rear wheels relative to the front wheels.

The importance of squareness of each rear wheel to its opposing wheel in relation to the chassis, and the squareness of the front pair of wheels in relation to the rear pair of wheels, is often overlooked. This can be the cause of handling problems with fully adjustable independent suspension cars (too many choices of things to alter).

In a hard cornering situation with a car that has toe-out and is exhibiting body roll, a rear wheel toes-out and will steer in the direction of the toe-out. In many instances, this problem will make the car oversteer and, at worst, cause the car to spin. It doesn't take too much toe-out to result in this sort of instability. There can be several causes of this problem: the rear suspension subframe could be misaligned with the chassis, or the wishbones out of alignment (incorrectly made or bent), to name a couple.

There is a degree of complication with independent rear suspension systems which means they should be frequently checked to ensure that nothing is out of alignment. The higher the speeds the car is used at, the more critical the settings become. When independent rear suspension systems are designed and set correctly, they give unmatched handling but, if they are not, they can be inferior to a well set up live axle. Many cars fitted with a live axle seem to handle better than their independently suspended counterparts. The comparatively straightforward installation of the axle, and easier setting up plays a part here. Independent rear suspension cars are also frequently heavier than their live axle counterparts.

The rubber (or other compliant material) bushings of independent rear suspension systems need to be in as-new condition; this will prevent excessive movement that could cause toe-out. If the system uses Rose joints, they need to be checked for wear quite frequently. Rose joints do not last that long and are really not suitable for road cars. The advantage of Rose joints (when in perfect condition) is the accuracy of the joint's movement about its centre, and its ability to swivel. Rose joints can be made to last longer if they are covered with a rubber boot to keep the dirt out, but no matter what is done they'll wear relatively quickly and are not inexpensive items!

ANTI-DIVE GEOMETRY

The better thought out independent front and rear suspension systems incorporate anti-dive geometry, but this adds a degree of complication when making the car. The main point being that the coil-over shock absorbers have to have swivel joints or Rose-type joints at each end. In short, this involves angling the arms of the front suspension through the centre of gravity of the car (longitudinally) which prevents the car from nosediving under heavy braking. In fact, if the angles are correct (meaning they do actually go

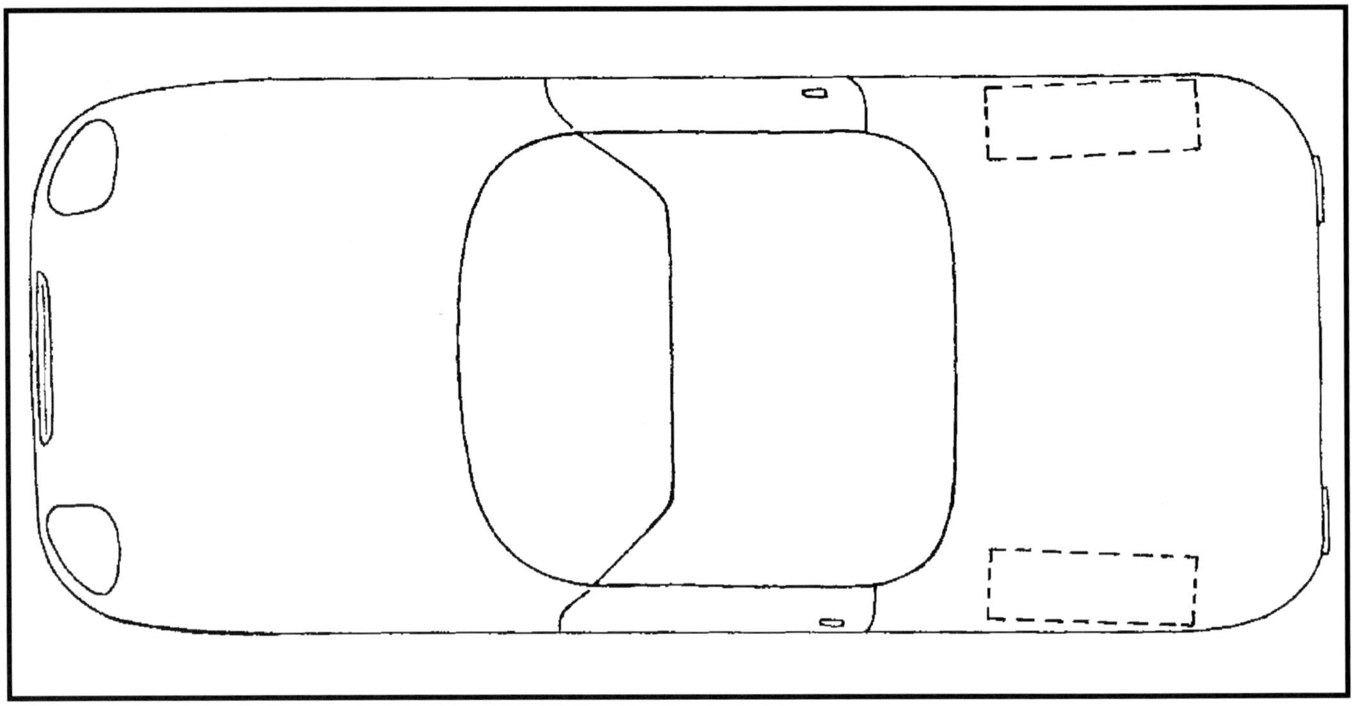

Rear wheels (dotted in) with toe-in equally dispersed about the centreline of the car.

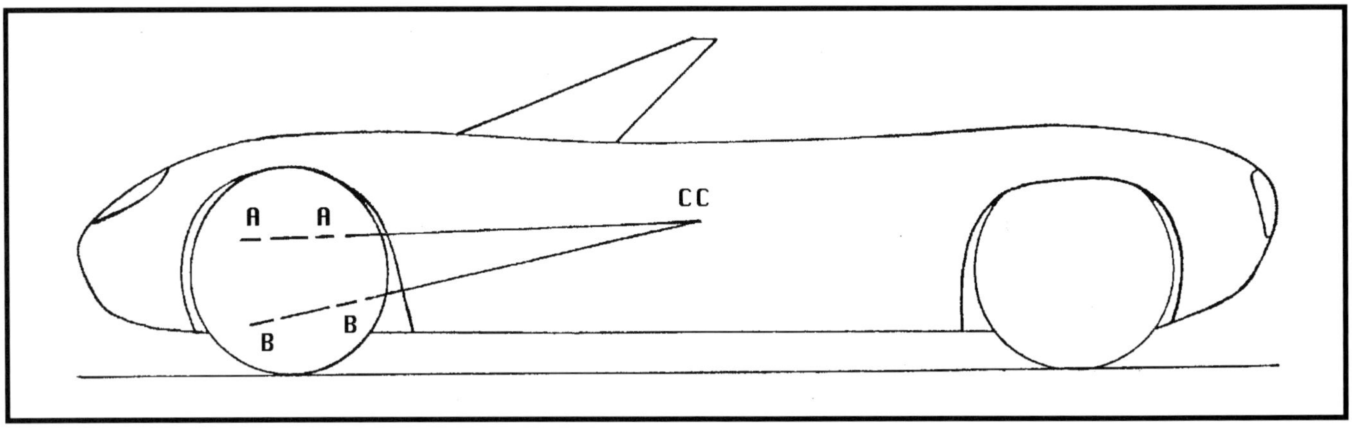

Cars with anti-dive geometry may well be able to use softer springing, which means that the wheels will follow the road better. "A"-"A" are the top wishbone chassis pick-up points, "B"-"B" the lower wishbone pick-up points. CG is the position of the car's centre of gravity.

through the true centre of gravity and not just near it), the front of the car hardly dips at all, even under the heaviest braking. The advantages of this system are that no extra spring pressure is required in the front suspension to prevent nosedive, and it avoids alterations in the geometry caused by excessive nosediving (such as camber changes and excessive toe-out) which make the car unstable under heavy braking. Needless to say, anti-dive geometry is well worth having despite the complications involved, especially when the car is front-engined and the engine relatively heavy (over 300lb/135kg).

TRAILING ARM LIVE REAR AXLE LOCATION

The most common method of longitudinal axle location is by trailing links with lateral location controlled by a

Panhard rod (five link suspension). The trailing arms (links) may be of equal or unequal length. The trailing arms should, if possible, always be set parallel with the ground, but if they are angled (0.187in/5mm) from the chassis up to their fixing point on the rear axle, this will be acceptable.

Do not have the trailing arms angled down from the chassis to their fixing point on the axle. The reason for this is that the wheelbase on one side of the car will shorten slightly in body roll, promoting oversteer.

The reason why parallelism of the arms is desirable is because as the trailing arm swings through its arc (when above or below parallel), it effectively shortens, and this feature (wheelbase shortening) is to be avoided as far as possible. If the arms are parallel to the ground at the ride height of the car, the arms will swing up and down through their arcs an equal amount, and effective shortening of the arms will not be excessive in either direction. The

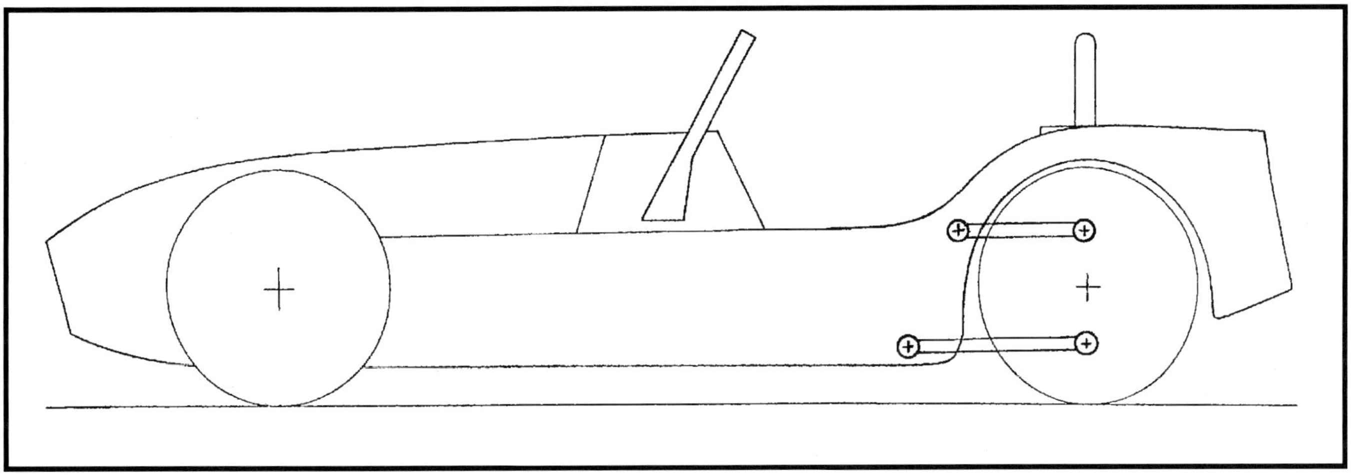

Unequal length trailing arms set parallel with the ground.

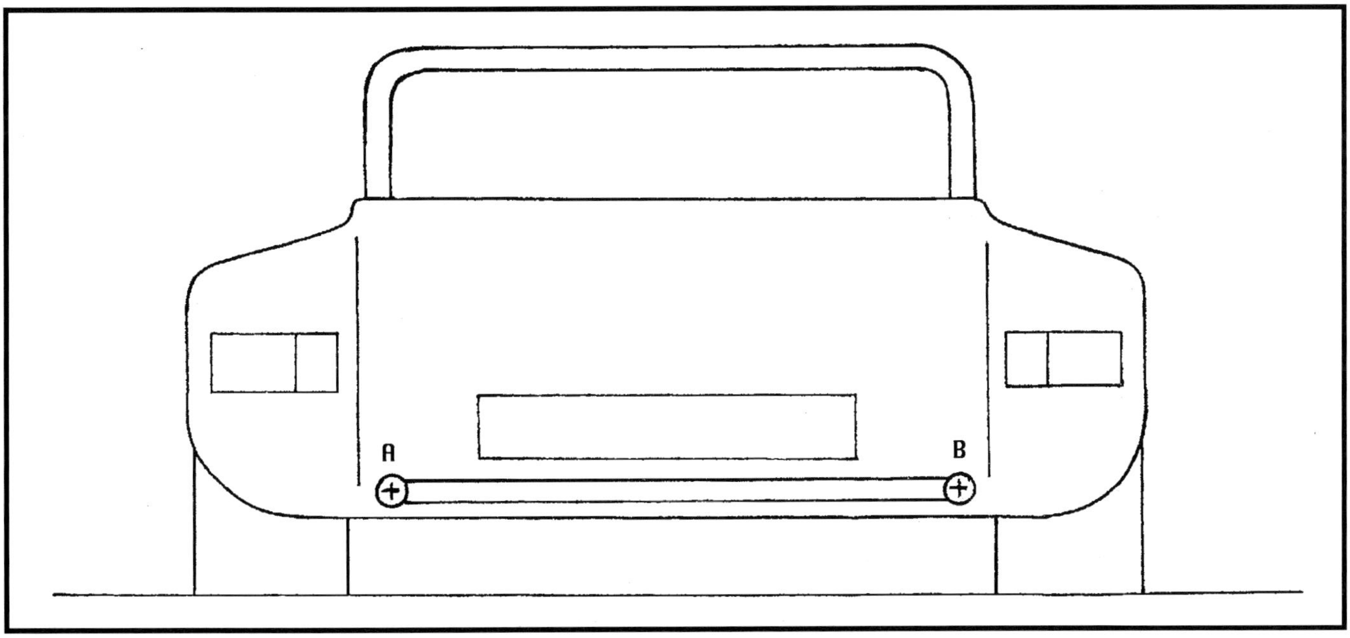

Position of the Panhard rod, which is as long as possible and set parallel to the ground. The Panhard rod is connected to the rear axle at "A" and the chassis at "B" (could be the other way around).

whole idea is to ensure that the car's wheelbase stays as constant as possible. The axle moves backwards and forwards of course, but, essentially, as suspension travel is not all that great, the axle's normal ride height longitudinal position is pretty well maintained.

Chapter 4
Springs & shock absorbers

COIL-OVER SHOCK ABSORBERS

These are the most common type of device used to effect vehicle springing and shock absorbing, and rightly so: they are compact, easy to install and it's easy to change the springs, adjust the ride height and shock adsorbing rate. Coil-over shocks are the most commonly used suspension medium for kit cars and some modern sportscars and specialist sportscars.

Ride height adjustments are carried out by screwing the adjustable spring platform plates up to increase ride height and down to reduce it. Note that to effect adjustment, you'll usually need two pin spanners to undo and lock the two spring platforms and turn the plates. Jack up the car to take the spring pressure off the shock absorber's adjustable spring platform plates. This way the spring platforms are not under load and are much easier to turn.

Frequently, spring platform notches become badly damaged, which is totally unnecessary. They get damaged when the spring platforms are turned using a screwdriver or chisel (unbelievable as it may sound) against the full spring pressure or when the two spring platform plates are still locked. All that is really required is to unlock the two spring platform plates, jack up the car and then turn the platforms separately in the right direction.

Pin spanners or 'C' spanners are what are required to adjust spring platforms.

SPRINGS

Many modern production sportscars feature coil-over shock absorbers of one sort or another.

Some cars have the shock absorber mounted inside the spring, even though there is no direct physical connection between the two components. With this type of set up, even if the standard spring platform is

Typical coil over shock absorber.

Shock absorber adjustment screw.

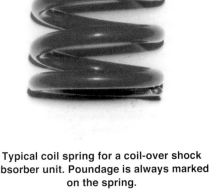

Typical coil spring for a coil-over shock absorber unit. Poundage is always marked on the spring.

not adjustable, there are usually ways around the problem and invariably uprated shock absorbers are available. So, even if not as easy as with a coil-over shock absorber featuring an adjustable spring seat, both spring/ride height and damping rates can still be modified.

Other cars will feature suspension systems with the spring and shock absorber completely separate. Even so, the principles of the suspension system are the same as are modifications to spring height/strength and shock absorber damping rates.

From the point of view of convenience, coil-over shocks featuring spring seats are the easiest type to adjust/modify. It may be possible to substitute this suspension type for other systems (sometimes kits are available), but look at all the options for the existing system before opting for a radical change.

A spring is a spring no matter how it looks. There are various types, ranging from coil springs (the most commonly used) to torsion bars, leaf springs, and so on. This book only refers to coil springs in the given examples as they are so common: all other forms of springing have been virtually superseded. However, the principles for other forms of springing are the same.

Essentially, the springs are what hold the car up at the required ride height and allow sufficient movement above and below this point. The springs also act to resist excessive body roll, while allowing the wheels to follow the road or track surface. The springs must not be so hard that they do not allow the wheels to follow the contour of the road or track surface, or

This shock absorber is fully adjustable in damping action and spring platform height. The knob is used to adjust damping. There are Rose-joints at each end of the shock.

be so soft that they allow the car to have excessive body roll.

If the springs are too hard the car will not handle well on a bumpy undulating surface, and certainly not as well as a similar car which has been set up for these conditions. If the springs are too hard, the car is not easy to control. A softer sprung car, on the other hand, will exhibit more body roll (3 or 4 degrees) than the firmly sprung car (1 or perhaps 2 degrees), but its tyres will remain in contact with the road and be able to 'soak up' the undulations of the road surface. The result on a race track, for instance, will be noticeably faster times, even though the car will look to be rolling around a lot. A car can certainly be sprung too hard or too soft.

On a road car if the springs are too hard the ride is so uncomfortable that there seems to be no suspension. Also, the car seems to 'float' on slightly undulating or corrugated surfaces. In such cases, the tyres are not able to follow the road surface and, effectively, lose contact on an intermittent basis, or become so lightly loaded as to be ineffective (rolling over the road surface, but with no downwards car weight acting on them). The car is controllable but usually doesn't feel as controllable as you would like it to. There is, to all intents and purposes, a noticeable loss of control. If a front wheel is momentarily off the ground the car becomes a three-wheeler and all of the steering is then being done by one wheel (not good). There is no substitute for having all of the wheels firmly in contact with the road, although each wheel may have varying amounts of the car's total weight actively holding its contact patch against the road surface.

The springs are too soft if the suspension bottoms out in a dip (solid sounding noise), or there is just too much body roll. When the suspension bottoms out, for instance, there is no suspension except from tyre compliance and most cars become quite unstable in this situation. Suspension that has bottomed out is no longer effective (no suspension).

Overall, the application denotes the amount of spring pressure that can be used, but the ideal is to run just as much spring pressure as is necessary to avoid excessive body roll (more than 3 to 4 degrees). If you, as a driver, think the ride is too hard for the sort of speeds that you travel at (the car pitches and seems to follow every hump and hollow in the road) a reduction in spring pressure will result in a better ride and, almost always, improved handling. Every car is different, but the optimal springs for the particular application can always be found by testing.

Road cars do not normally need springs as hard as those used for the same type of car prepared for circuit racing. Using the same car for different applications could mean that different springs may have to be substituted. Springs that are just too hard and resist any movement mean that the car has little or no suspension. Very hard springs may well be acceptable on dead smooth surfaces but, in reality, there are not too many of these around. Avoid fitting springs that are too hard as they resist movement and the wheels do not follow the road or track surface 100%, whereas, if the springs were slightly weaker, the wheels would follow the road surface 100% and be fully loaded while doing so. The trade-off of softer springing is increased body roll which, within limits, has to be accepted.

Body roll is not really a problem unless it progresses to the point where the car is really leaning (5-7 degrees plus of body roll) meaning the springs are too soft. If the body rolls during cornering (any corner) and assumes a set stance of a certain amount of body roll (2 to 3 degrees) in any cornering situation (and does not go further), the springs are correct. Sorting out the springs may mean having to try a selection, but it's common to find that one rating (that is, spring rate poundage) of spring for the front and one rate of spring for the rear covers 95% of requirements.

There is no point in having a coil spring fitted to a car that achieves the desired ride height, but is nearly coil-bound while doing so. The problem will then be that the spring will bottom out easily, at which point that corner of the car ceases to have suspension, which is not good at all. This situation can arise when a coil spring is installed which has insufficient poundage rate but enough resistance - even though nearly fully compressed - to give the desired ride height. This is always easy to see because the spring's coils will have virtually no clearance between them (as little as 0.156in/4.0mm) and the spring will be about half of its original free-standing height at ride height.

Springs that are too soft allow too much pitching and body roll movement (especially pitching); the driver usually knows when the car is going to bottom out when a dip is approached unexpectedly and braces him/herself accordingly. It may well be that only the front springs need to be uprated. Also, a car with a heavy engine needs harder springs than that same type of car fitted with a lighter engine.

Choose springs that, when installed in the car and with the full weight of the car on them, have a **minimum** gap of 0.25in/6.5mm between the coils. The fitting of the softest springs possible (without too much body roll) is a well founded principle: always fit the softest springs you can get away with. Fitting the hardest springs possible, on the common presumption that hard springs give less body roll and better handling, is almost always incorrect.

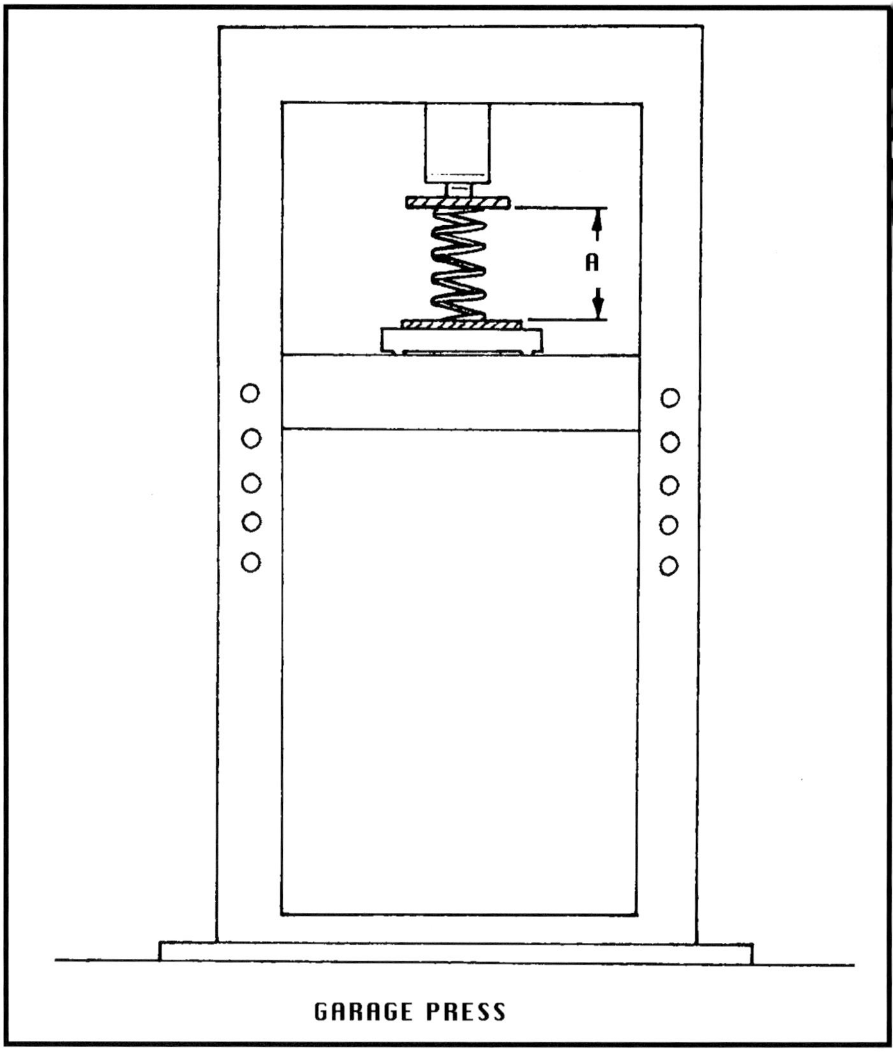

Spring sitting on a set of scales ready to have tension applied. A tape measure is used to measure the free length of the spring (A).

Checking what spring rate a particular spring has is usually confined to reading the code or numbers painted or stamped on it. In spite of what is displayed on the spring as the spring rate, check **all** springs for actual spring rate. The problem is usually one of not having anything suitable to check the springs on, but there is a way of getting quite a reasonable reading and it involves nothing more than a set of bathroom scales and a garage press. The usual measure of a spring's rate is the pounds of force exerted when the spring is compressed one inch. This is often not outside the capability of a set of bathroom scales but, if it is, use 0.5in of travel to measure the poundage and then double the reading. This method gives the spring rate poundage (within a few pounds).

Warning! - Take sensible

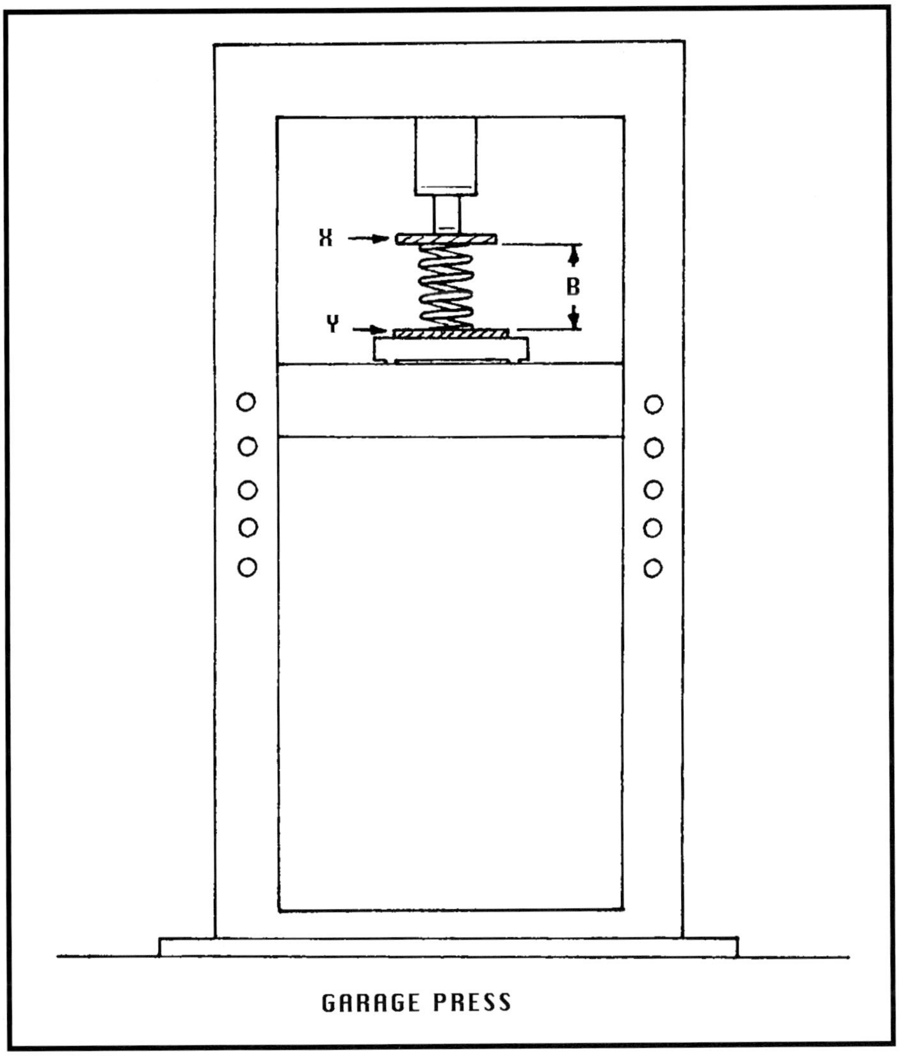

Plywood (X) is placed between the coil spring and the scales and (Y) the coil spring and the press's arbour. The coil spring is then compressed 1 inch (B) and a reading taken from the dial of the scales.

precautions to avoid injury to yourself or others if the following method is used - the spring could jump a long way if pressure is suddenly released and it, or the plywood, is free to fly. With the scales set on the platform of the press and a piece of 0.5in thick plywood placed on the scales, place the spring on top of the scales and beneath the hydraulic ram of the press. Measure the height of the spring at its freestanding height.

The garage press is then activated and the spring compressed. With the spring compressed 1in/25.4mm (measured with the tape measure), the reading on the dial of the scales is taken. Older scales are in stones (14 pounds to a stone) but the poundage can still be easily calculated. Most scales measure up to 280 pounds, but some will go higher. **Caution!** - Monitor the spring's progress during compression because if the weight limit is exceeded, the scales will almost certainly be damaged. Use a half inch of travel if the spring looks like it will be too much for the scales. No claim is made that measuring springs in this manner is dead accurate, but it does give a very good indication of what the true rating of a spring is (variable rate springs excepted).

All coil springs are rated in pounds. So, if your springs are rated at 180, it means that when an individual spring is compressed 1 inch, it will exert 180 pounds of resistance at that point. If your springs are rated at, say, 400, then bathroom scales will not take this pressure: in such cases, compressing the spring by half an inch should yield half of the resistance (200 pounds) that would be present at 1 inch of compression (400 pounds).

UNSPRUNG WEIGHT AND SPRUNG WEIGHT

Every car has a total 'sprung weight' which is dispersed pretty much equally to the wheels side to side of the car. The weight on the two front wheels should be equal and the weight on the rear two wheels should be equal. The weights front to rear can, of course, be quite different. The static weight acting on each wheel is a proportion of the total weight of the car. This is part of the basis of the setting up method described in this book.

To clarify this situation, the total weight of a car comprises the sprung weight and the unsprung weight. 'Unsprung weight' comprises the wheels and tyres, hubs, brakes, stub axles, a portion of the wishbones, coil-over shock absorbers and springs and, at the rear of the car, the whole rear axle (if a live axle) and a portion of the driveshaft and suspension arms. On a car with independent rear suspension the unsprung weight comprises the

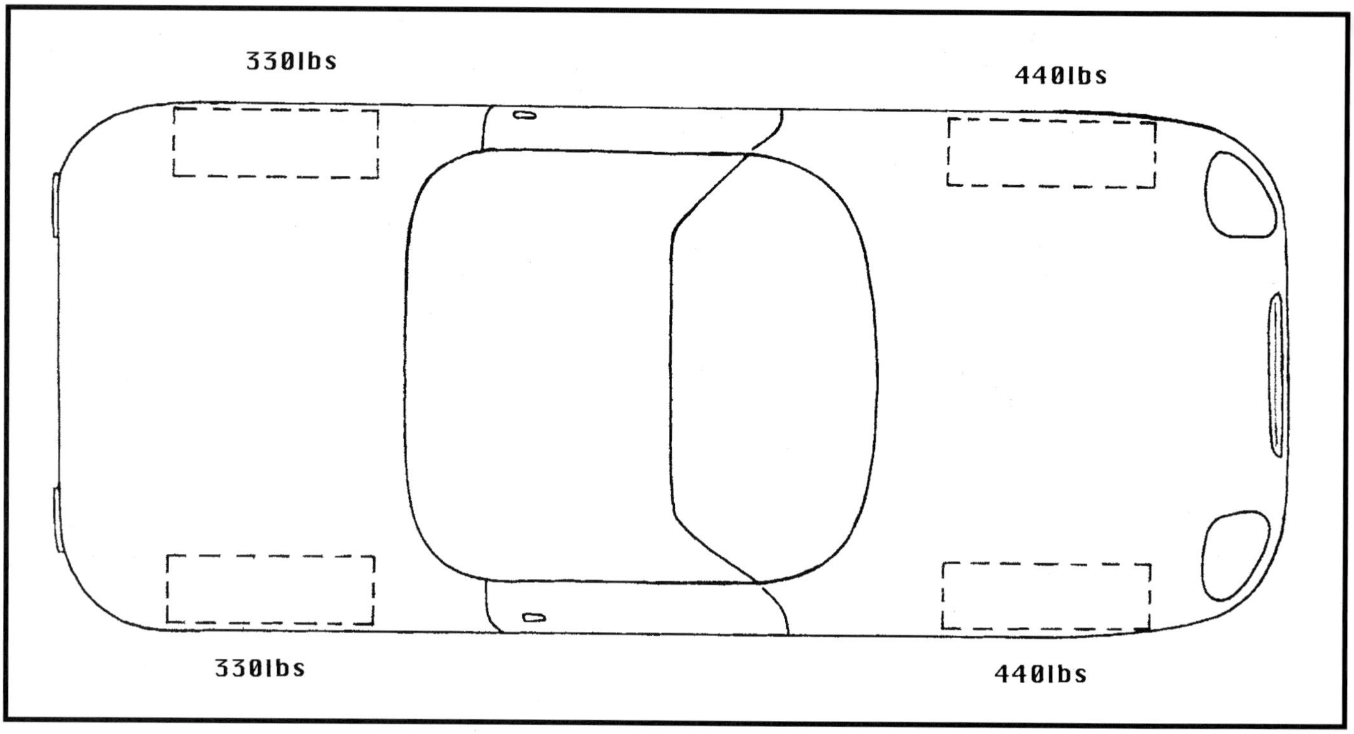

The total weight of this car is 1940 pounds. 880 pounds of SPRUNG weight is acting on the front two wheels and 660 pounds of SPRUNG weight is acting on the rear two wheels. The weights are further divided equally so that 440 pounds is acting on each front wheel and 330 pounds on each rear wheel. The component of UNSPRUNG weight of this car is 400 pounds. Sprung weight is *never* the absolute total weight of the car.

rear uprights, hubs, brakes, a portion of the driveshafts, wishbones and coil-over shock absorbers and springs.

Note that it is not strictly necessary to know the actual weights of the unsprung and sprung elements of any car. Perfectly satisfactory setting up can be achieved without weighing anything, although scales are often used. The setting up methods suggested in this book **do not** require knowledge of the actual corner weights or the total weight of the car: this may sound odd but, in practice, it isn't.

SHOCK ABSORBERS

Shock absorbers basically do one thing: control the action of the spring. Springs have kinetic energy which has to be damped (controlled). The travel of the shock absorber must always be as much as the required total amount of suspension travel or, ideally, slightly more. The last thing wanted is for the shock absorber to reach the end of its travel or compress sufficiently to bottom out: once this happens, the car has no suspension!

Always ensure that the shock absorber is in the middle of its travel when the car is at the correct ride height. This way, there will be an equal amount of suspension travel above and below the normal ride height and the least possibility of bottoming out or topping out the shock absorber. Buy shock absorbers that are the right length for the application. If the existing shock absorber is not in the middle of its travel with the suspension geometry set correctly, move the top or bottom shock absorber mounting bracket so that the shock absorber is in the middle of its travel, or make and fit a new longer/shorter bracket.

Various types of shock absorber have been available over the years, but the most common type now is the telescopic one almost universally found on suspension systems that use coil springs. All of the examples in this book are of the telescopic type, but the end result of all shock absorber control is the same so, if a different shock absorber type is fitted to your vehicle, the principle remains the same.

Shock absorbers which are set too hard do not allow a car to handle as well as it could, because they do not allow the wheels to follow the road surface, and the ride can be very hard (you'll feel every bump). There's a fine line between too much and too little shock absorber damping. The shock absorbers are there to control the rate of change in the car's attitude (body roll, for instance), not to prevent a change of attitude altogether, or offer no control at all. Many shock absorbers are not adjustable and will frequently also be too soft.

The coil-over shock absorbers, as found on most kit cars, are frequently adjustable just by a turn of the screw found on the side of the unit. On some shock absorbers, adjustment is made by removing the top mounting bolt, removing the coil spring, compressing the shock absorber fully, engaging serrations in the bottom of the shock absorber and then turning appropriately to increase or decrease the amount of shock resistance.

If the shock absorbers are adjustable, set them with the least amount of resistance for the smoothest possible ride compatible with the best possible overall handling. Initially, set all four shock absorbers to the minimum setting and test the car: expect this setting to allow plenty of suspension movement and the car to give a very smooth ride. Next, adjust all four shock absorbers to the medium or middle setting of the adjustment scale and test the car: on a road going car the ride should become noticeably firmer, but not to the point of being uncomfortable, and there should be a noticeable reduction in suspension movement. Now, set all four shock absorbers to the maximum setting and test the car: the ride should

Shock absorber adjustment knob.

be very firm, even to the extent that there is very little suspension movement, with the ride becoming harsh to the point of being uncomfortable.

After trying the three settings, the overall effect of each will be known. The next step, depending on the application and driving style, is to narrow down the amount of shock absorber resistance to suit the application.

If the shock absorbers are set too soft, the car will tend to roll a lot (visibly exhibit a lot of body roll) in corners and have too much suspension movement when being driven on an average undulating road. The springs are not being controlled in this example: the shock absorbers must be set with enough resistance to remove all excess spring movement.

Set up the shock absorbers (if adjustable) on the basis of having the minimum amount of resistance possible, but with just enough resistance to control the action of the springs in all situations. This may mean different settings front and rear (but **not** side to side) to suit the car and the application.

A car used for circuit work will have shock absorbers adjusted to the minimum resistance, just enough to damp the action of the springs in all circumstances. To little resistance will cause the car to be unstable with too much suspension movement. That said, **never** set the shock absorbers so hard that the wheels cannot follow the track surface. Shock absorbers set too hard cause the tyres to lose good contact with the road surface (tyres in contact with the track surface, but not loaded with the available weight of the car) and, at worst, completely lose contact with the track surface. Reduce the amount of shock absorber resistance to correct this situation.

For best all-round handling, all four wheels must be in contact with the track surface at all times (not always possible on some circuits) and each wheel must have the correct attitude in every situation.

If a car is equipped with springs that are too soft for the car/application, and the shock absorbers are set very hard to compensate, it will lean in during sweeping bends and will continue to roll as the shock absorbers slowly compress. In this situation it is really the spring rate at the heart of the problem and no amount of shock absorber adjustment will compensate.

Chapter 5
Negative camber, castor & kingpin inclination

NEGATIVE CAMBER

The front wheels of virtually all cars are set with negative camber, but the usual question is how much negative camber would be ideal? Frequently, sportscars and other high performance cars are seen with large amounts of negative camber because it is deemed necessary to improve handling and, more specifically, cornering. Negative camber is built into the geometry of the front suspension to improve the attitude of one wheel during cornering. This wheel is the left hand front wheel of a car turning right or the right hand front wheel of a car turning left. The wheel is highly loaded in this situation and, if it has the right amount of negative camber, the tyre will be supported correctly.

Support of the highly loaded front tyre is quite important. To take the concept of tyre support to what should be an extreme (unfortunately, it is a reality on some older cars), take the right front wheel of a car turning left as an example. The suspension geometry causes the front wheel to exhibit between 5 and 7 degrees (or more) of positive camber. During hard cornering the tyre looks as though it is going to roll off the rim, and the car is definitely not handling well. Suffice to say that, with some alteration to the geometry and suspension (increased castor to promote negative camber, increased static negative camber, stronger springs to reduce body roll, reduced ride height to possibly allow better geometry, altered top 'A' arm position - to name a few), that same car will have a very different attitude at the same speed and in the same corner. The car will be quite controllable and, in fact, will handle much better than it did originally.

Car with excessive negative camber under hard braking does not have the tyres 'in touch' with the road or as evenly 'loaded' as they would be if the tyres were vertical or near vertical.

Many sportscars with a lot of static negative camber (2.5-3.5 degrees) are, in fact, not always good handlers and wear the inside edge of the tyre treads quite rapidly. Frequently, these cars understeer when a reasonable amount of steering lock is applied. The reason for this is that the front wheels have too much negative camber and the tyre patch in contact with the road surface of the most heavily loaded wheel reduces the more the steering wheel is turned. This effect is more pronounced on very light sportscars with very wide tyres.

Further to this, take a sportscar under hard breaking. The front of the car dips and the suspension geometry almost always creates more negative camber. So, just when the largest possible tyre patch in full contact with the road is needed for stopping, the tyres are angled to the road surface. For maximum braking efficiency, the best results are obtained when the wheels and tyres are as near vertical as possible and with no toe-in/ toe-out, but this ideal is never realised.

Consider the usable range of static negative camber to be between 0.5 and 1.0 degrees, and up to 1.5 degrees to the absolute maximum.

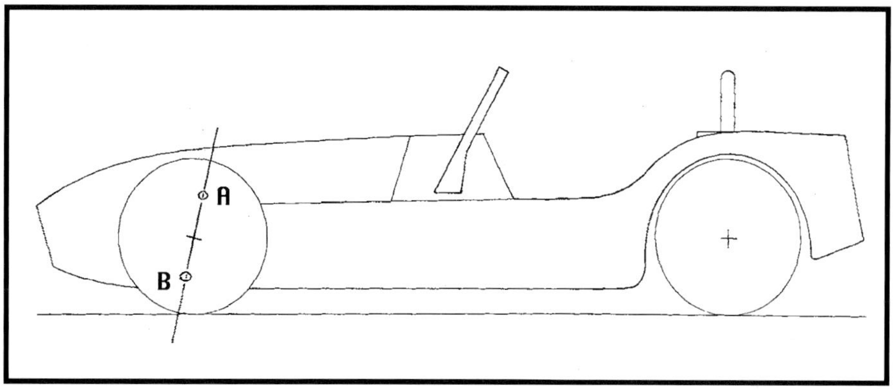

Front wheel of a sportscar viewed from the side and showing castor angle (AB). "A" is the centre of the stub axle's top balljoint and "B" is the centre of the bottom balljoint. "B" is in front of the centre of the wheel and "A" is behind the centre of the wheel.

CASTOR

This is the inclination in the vertical plane of the turning axis of the front wheels. Castor causes camber to change as the front wheels are turned left or right from the straight ahead position. For example, if the right hand front wheel is turned to the left, it should gain more negative camber while the left hand front wheel should lose negative camber (head towards positive camber). Both front wheels should be set with equal amounts of static castor.

The greater the castor built into the geometry the more negative camber or positive camber each wheel gets as it is turned.

The amount of castor can be increased or decreased to improve the attitude of the wheels when the car is cornering. If a car has a lot of static negative camber (2-3 degrees, or more) it does not take much castor to induce even more negative camber, and the wheel can end up with quite a lean on it (gross negative camber) during cornering. This, of course, only applies to the right hand front wheel of a car turning left or the left hand front wheel of a car turning right. The opposite front wheel, in each case, will lose negative camber, but seldom will it ever approach zero camber or go into positive camber. Basically, the wheel on the inside of the turn is not doing a lot, or certainly not as much as it could be doing. Lots of static negative camber is normally only used when it is difficult to increase castor to obtain sufficient dynamic negative camber during hard cornering.

When a car has too much negative camber for cornering purposes, the outer edge of the tyre tread seldom exhibits wear, or certainly nothing like the wear and tear that the inner side of the tyre tread suffers. The tyres wear out quickly, and nearly all of the wear is found on the inner side of both tyre's treads: tyre wear isn't evenly spread.

Suspension settings which induce excessive dynamic negative camber can lead to understeer on tight corners, but can have a lesser affect on long sweeping bends. Every car is different, of course, and minor adjustments need to be made to suit each car to ensure that the best possible handling characteristics are obtained from the suspension design.

Consider between 3 and 8 degrees to be the optimal range of castor settings. The initial setting should be 3 or 4 degrees, but be prepared to increase the amount of castor in 1 degree increments up to a maximum of 8 degrees, if during hard cornering, gross positive camber is present (positive camber on the right front wheel of a car turning left, that is). It's unlikely that more than 7 degrees of castor will be needed on a low slung sportscar or kit car. Consider 2 degrees of castor as the minimum, though this will rarely ever be enough.

KINGPIN INCLINATION (KPI)

'Kingpin' is a misnomer these days as

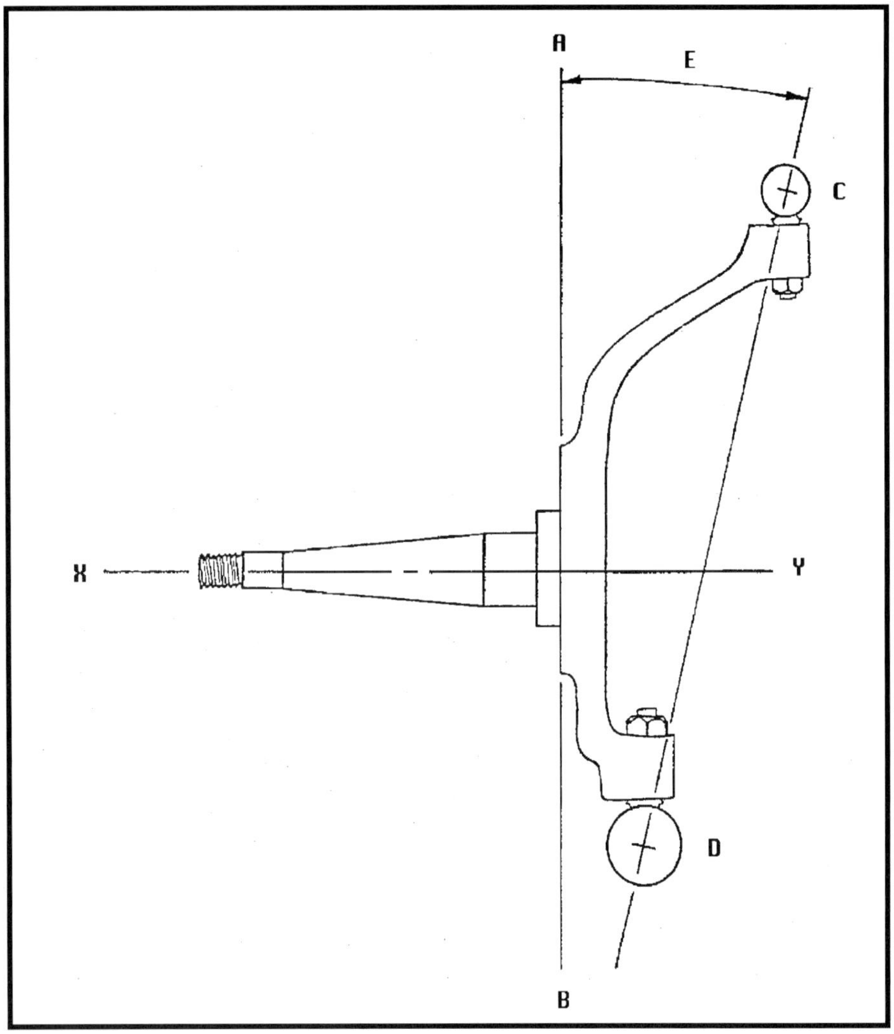

The stub axle (X-Y) and the machined face of the upright (A-B) are at 90 degrees. The axis line of the top and bottom balljoint centres (C-D) is also shown. Kpi is the angle (E) between the line A-B and line C-D.

most cars do not have kingpins anymore. However, the principle of the kingpin in steering geometry remains. Kingpin inclination represents the axis of a line through top and bottom ball joint centres of the stub axle carrying the wheel. The line through the top and bottom ball joints (or Rose-type joints for that matter) is projected to the ground, and it's the relationship between this point and the tread of the tyre that is important. The point of kpi contact with the road is normally somewhere within the tyre tread area, but when wheels with different offset (outside of wheel rim moved outward in relation to the hub) to the originals and/or spacers are fitted, the situation can become quite different with less than satisfactory results.

Consider the optimum range of kpi to be between 9 and 12 degrees, with 10 degrees being usual. It is not normally possible to alter the kpi of the stub axle although its effective angle can be altered by adjusting the negative camber of the wheel slightly but there is a definite limit to this. Stub axles are made with these angles set by design.

The majority of production saloon cars have wheels that feature a lot of inset. Having inset wheels with the kpi line ground contact being within the tyre tread contact patch is a well founded principle. Sportscars and kit cars often feature wheels with a lot of offset for no other reason than to make them look better, but this is often to the detriment of handling. Having a wide track is all very well within the confines of a good design, but not at the expense of good suspension geometry.

For instance, cars which originally had wheel rims that were inset and now have wheels that have a lot of offset and, perhaps, use spacers, could have wheels that are now 3in/75mm further away from the hub than originally. Track will have increased by 6in/152mm but the steering will tend to kick back a lot, especially over undulations and bumps. This is not a good situation at all and results in a loss of control. What happens is that when the wheel comes into contact with a bump in the road, it tends to want to turn towards the bump (the front left hand wheel on contacting a bump wants to turn left and, conversely, the right hand front wheel wants to turn right). This is caused by the leverage factor of the relative position of the wheel and its turning axis.

The closer the axis (kpi) is to the centre of the tyre tread contact patch, the less the adverse effect and, conversely, the further the patch centre is away from the axis, the more pronounced the instability will be.

Another scenario with a vehicle which has a lot of wheel offset is that if

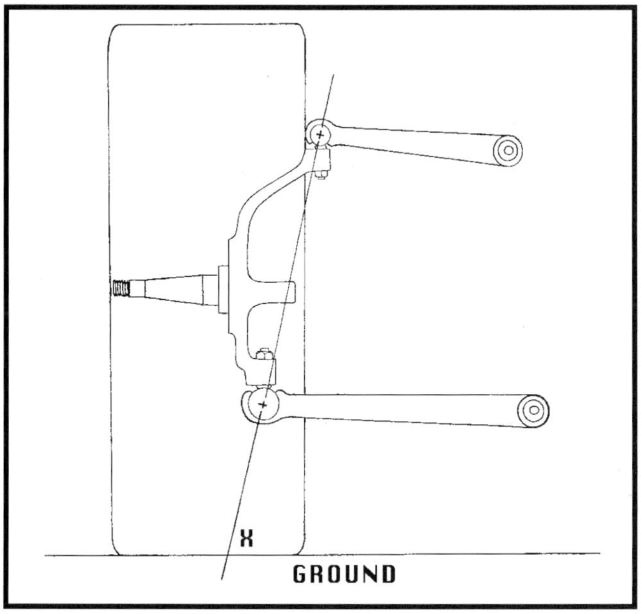

Kpi angle of the ball joints projected to the ground to show the relationship (X) with the tyre contact patch.

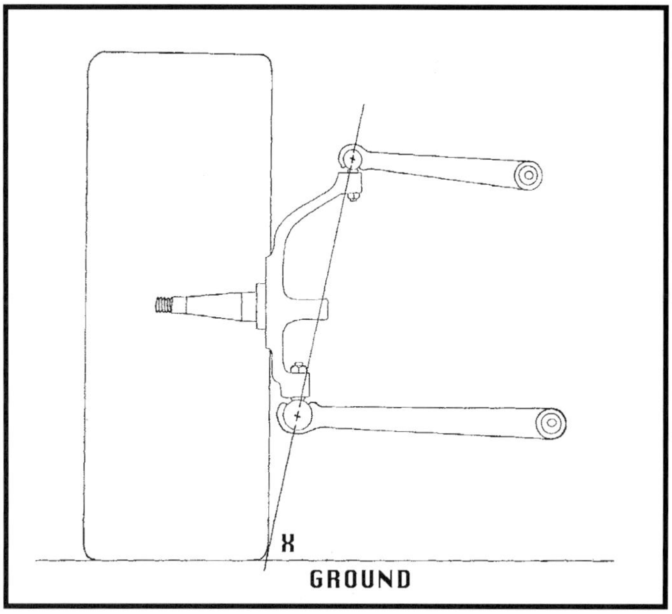

A different kpi axis line and its point of contact with the ground, and the relationship of that point to the wheel rim and tyre. If the line through the kpi axis contacts the ground at the edge of the tyre it is acceptable.

one front wheel is on a rough surface (left front) while the other (right front) is still on a smooth surface, the car will tend to turn to the left.

There is also geometric suspension alteration (go-kart style, but to a much lesser degree) when the wheels are heavily offset. What happens when a car has a lot of offset is that, as the wheels are turned left or right from the straight ahead position, the chassis is raised on one side and lowered on the other. That is, on a vehicle turning left, the left hand front wheel tends to lift that side of the car and the right hand front wheel tends to lower its side of the car. The more the offset, the more pronounced the raising and lowering effect on the chassis (geometry induced body roll).

Many cars end up with offset wheels, but there are detrimental elements which need to be taken into account. Essentially, if the car's track is to be widened, it's better to make up new suspension arms and steering rack arms and move the wheels outward by this means than to use offset wheels/spacers. There is, of course, a lot of work involved, but it's a better way to obtain a better handling car.

Consider that, at the very least, the kpi axis line needs to intersect with the ground at the very edge of the

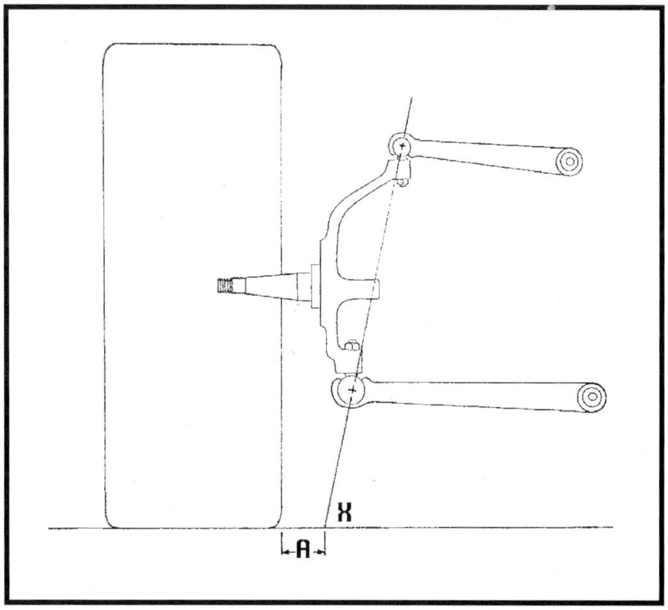

This wheel has too much offset in relation to the kpi line and the car will be unstable in certain conditions. Line contact point (X) is too far from the edge of the tyre. If dimension (A) is more than one inch/25.4mm, that's too much. Some cars have as much as 2 - 2.5inch/50 - 63mm and very wide tyres as well (8 - 10inch/ 200 - 205mm). Such cars are difficult to drive and are potentially dangerous.

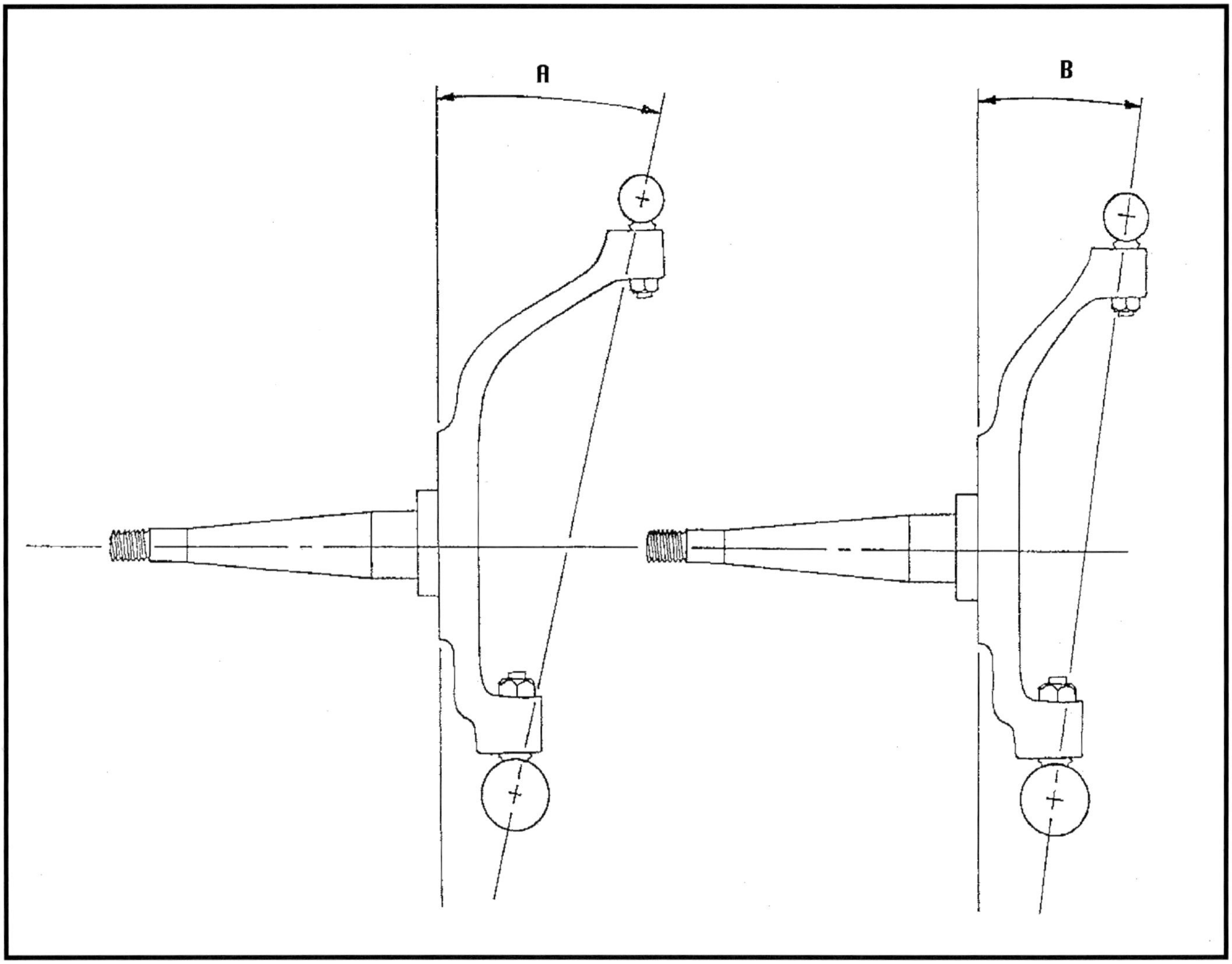

Stub axle on the left has more kpi (A) than the stub axle on the right (B).

inner tyre tread. Steering and handling are better when the kpi axis line passes through the centre of the contact patch of the tyre tread. **Avoid using too much offset**. Most modern sportscars feature wheels with a lot of inset.

Relationship between kpi & castor

These two steering geometry factors are closely related because, for a given amount of steering lock, the front wheels attain geometry-induced camber (increasing negative on one side, reducing negative on the other). For example, if the car is steered to the right the left hand front wheel gains negative camber while the right hand front wheel loses negative and moves towards positive camber. The opposite happens when the car is turned to the left. This feature of suspension geometry can be observed with a stationary car if you get someone to turn the steering from lock to lock while you watch the front wheels.

A combination of kpi angle and castor angle is what causes this desirable effect. The *lesser* the kpi angle built into the stub axle (upright if you prefer) the *larger* the amount of castor necessary to cause the required amount of camber change as the steering wheel is turned. So, for example, a stub axle which has 9 degrees of kpi combined with castor of 6 degrees is going to induce more wheel camber change for a given amount of steering lock than a stub

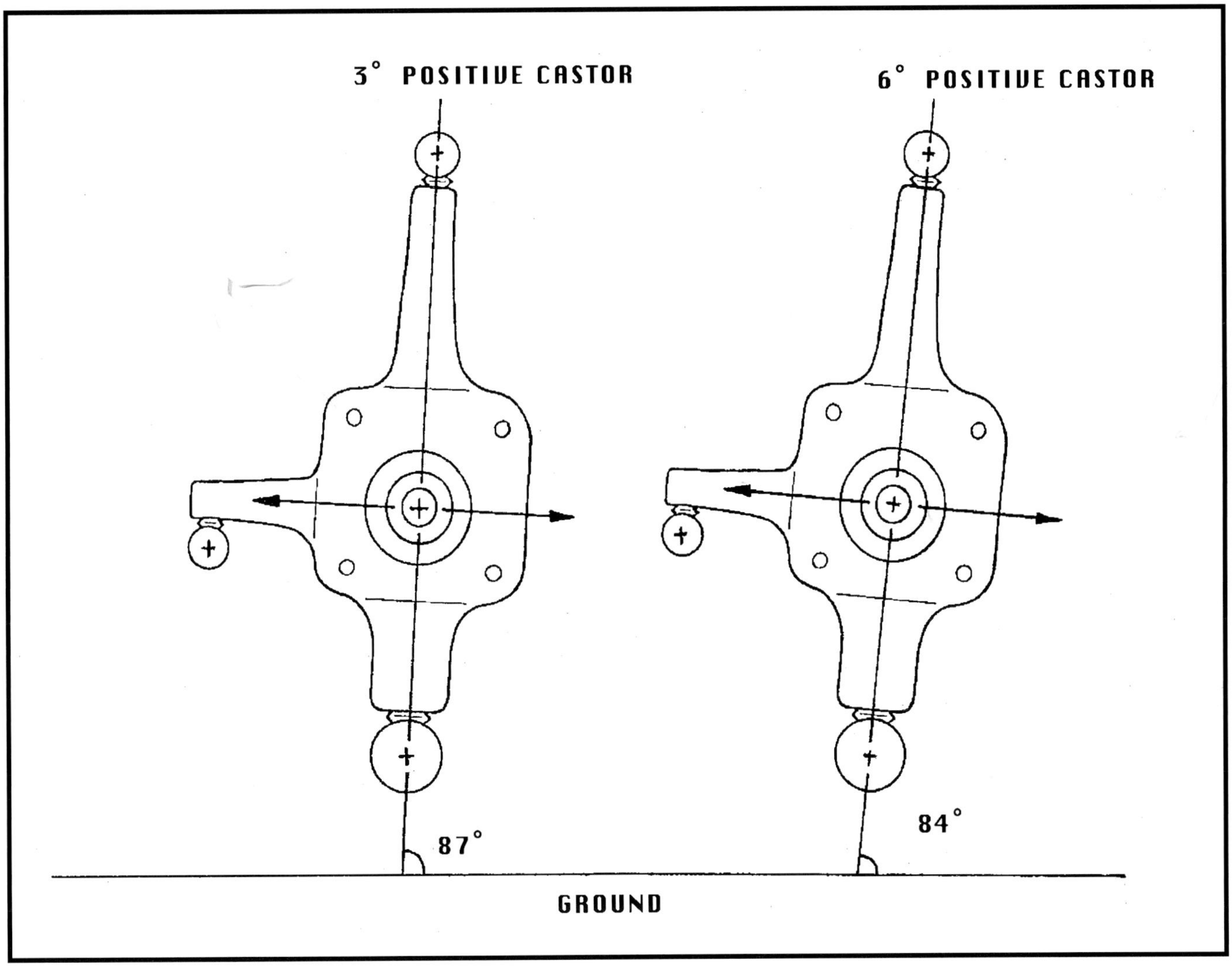

Comparison of stub axle positive castor of 3 and 6 degrees.

axle with 12 degrees kpi working with 3 degrees of castor. It is easier to adjust castor than kpi to get the geometric action required.

Given the relationship between kpi and castor, the required dynamic camber properties can be achieved by castor changes alone. Once this basic principle is clearly understood, your view of front suspension geometry will never be the same again - and you'll be studying front suspension designs with a renewed interest in how the suspension has been set up within the framework of its design.

A factor that comes into the relationship between kpi and castor is body roll. The greater the body roll the more the camber will change in the wrong direction for each front wheel. There is a balance here which has to be addressed: maybe by fitting stronger springs and, if necessary, anti-roll bars or stronger anti-roll bars.

Kpi, castor, wishbone angles, static negative camber and body roll angles all interact dynamically, making the front suspension a complex and difficult system to understand.

NOTES

Chapter 6

Ackerman angles, toe-in, toe-out, bump steer & anti-roll bars

ACKERMAN ANGLES

During a turn, the inside front wheel follows a tighter radius than the outside front wheel. To compensate for this, there are two basic ways that the inside wheel of a car in a turn can be made to have more lock (steering angle) on it than the wheel on the outside of the turn.

The first way is by having true Ackerman steering geometry built into the suspension/steering system. This, almost always, means that the steering system (whatever type it is) will be acting behind the centres of the front wheels (steering rack behind wheel centre). The main feature of Ackerman steering is that the steering arms will be angled inwards so, when the steering wheel is turned, this automatically ensures that the inside wheel, when turning into a corner, turns in more than the outside wheel. The steering arm of the inside wheel is already past the 90 degree point and is therefore, effectively, shorter than the steering arm on the outer wheel.

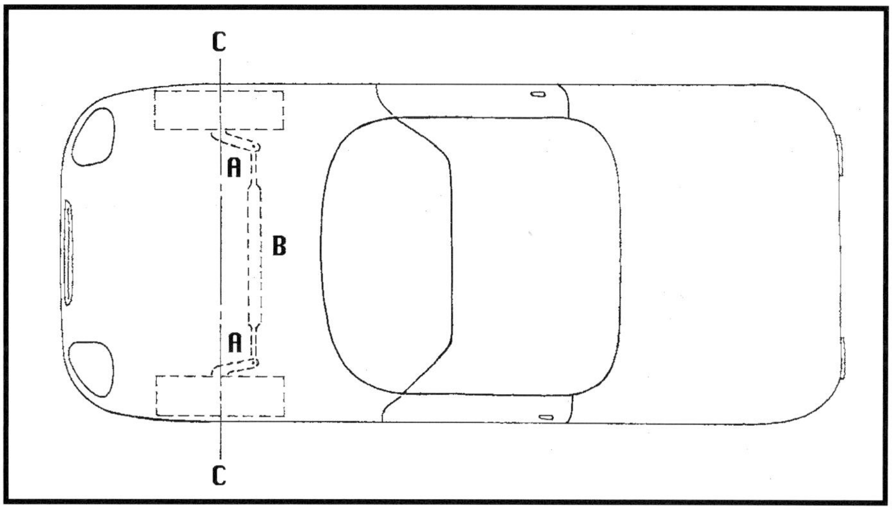

Ackerman steering requires the steering arms (A) to be angled inwards. The steering rack (B) is behind the centre of the front wheels (C-C).

The steering arms do not have to be behind the centre of the front wheels, they can be in front (in which case the steering arms are angled toward the tyre). The actual Ackerman geometry is the same in practice. The only limitation of forward mounted steering arms is that they can be angled toward the wheel/tyre only so much before coming into contact with the wheel rim (usually). The majority of stub axles are forged as one-piece items. Older cars had removable steering arms, but this now is uncommon. If the arms are removable, new arms, which reposition the pick-up points of the steering system and alter the Ackerman angle, can be made up out of high tensile steel. Such arms can usually be government certified as fit

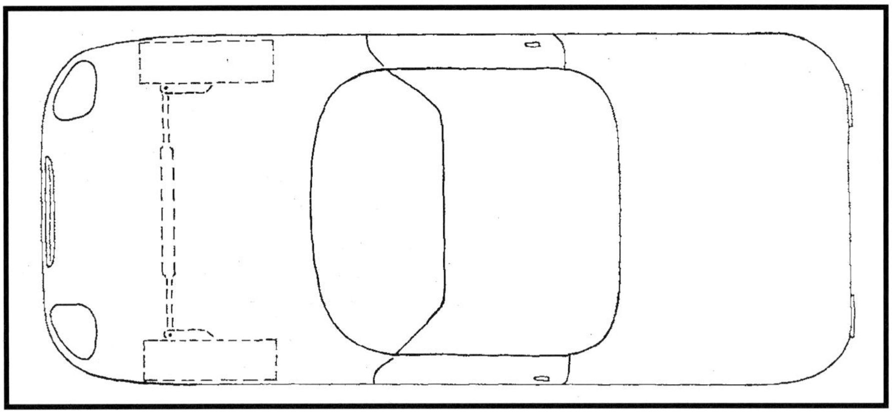

Here, the steering arms are in front of the centreline of the front wheels. The arms are often therefore angled slightly outwards. Geometrically, there is no major difference in this design to the one shown in the previous picture. If this is the case, geometrically there can be little difference in this design (effective Ackerman steering) compared to the one on the previous page although they seldom have as much effective Ackerman type steering as it is not possible to angle the arms all that much. Note that you can definitely have too much Ackerman action in the steering.

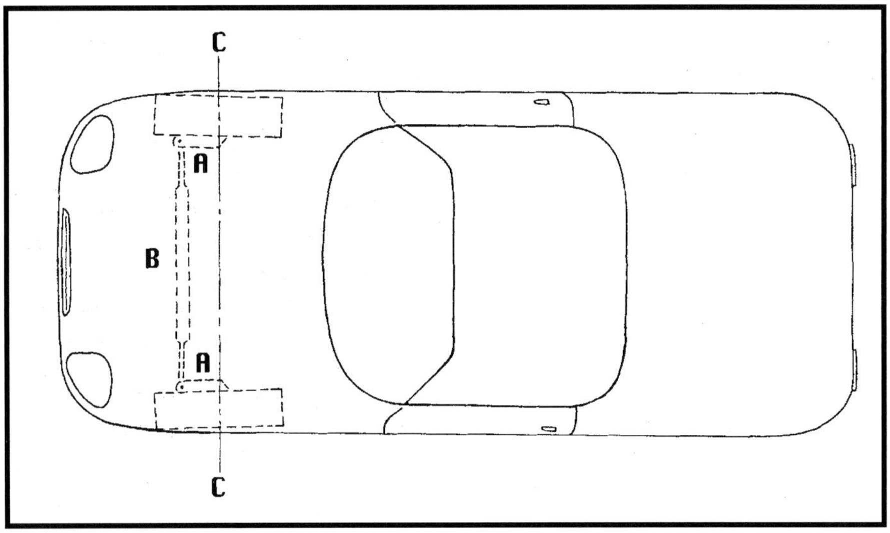

Front mounted steering rack and front wheels with toe-out.

for service, bolted onto the stub axle and legally used, but check local legislation before making this modification. **Warning!** - In the past, steering arms have been cut and welded or simply heated up and bent. However, this is a dangerous practice and, as a consequence, is **not** recommended and may well be illegal.

The second way to build in more effective Ackerman geometry is by setting the suspension with toe-out, but not more than 0.100in/2.5mm. The inside wheel (that's the left hand wheel of a car turning left) as a consequence will be turned into the turn more than the wheel on the outside of the turn. The wheel on the outside of the turn (that's the right hand front on a car turning left) is always the heavily loaded wheel and is the controlling wheel in this situation. Irrespective of the amount of lock the outer wheel has on it, the inside wheel will always have more by virtue of its toe-out. This toe-out method is used mainly when the steering arms are positioned in front of the centres of the front wheels. It's quick and easy and, usually, has no downside.

If, for example, the left hand front wheel turns in a lesser than ideal amount, the front wheels are effectively 'fighting' each other, which can cause understeer. When a car understeers, it wants to go straight ahead rather than turn into the corner, and gives the driver the distinct feeling that the car is not responding to the steering. More lock has to be applied in order to get the car to turn as required. Ultimately, speed is lost through this fault and, if no changes are made to the car's suspension to improve handling, corners have to be taken slower than should be possible.

Sportscars and kit cars often need to have an amount of Ackerman-type steering in the geometry to prevent understeer and ensure that the car has immediate turning response to the steering wheel. In the normal course of events, the front wheels do not turn (angularly) all that much from the straight ahead position (often not more than 20 degrees).

TOE-IN

This is the result of having a pair of wheels on the same axle angled towards the front (pigeon-toed). This feature is essential on any independent rear suspension system and always used to be a requirement for the front wheels of any car. This is not so today and many cars feature toe-out (front wheel drive cars, for instance). The common amount of toe-in on non-

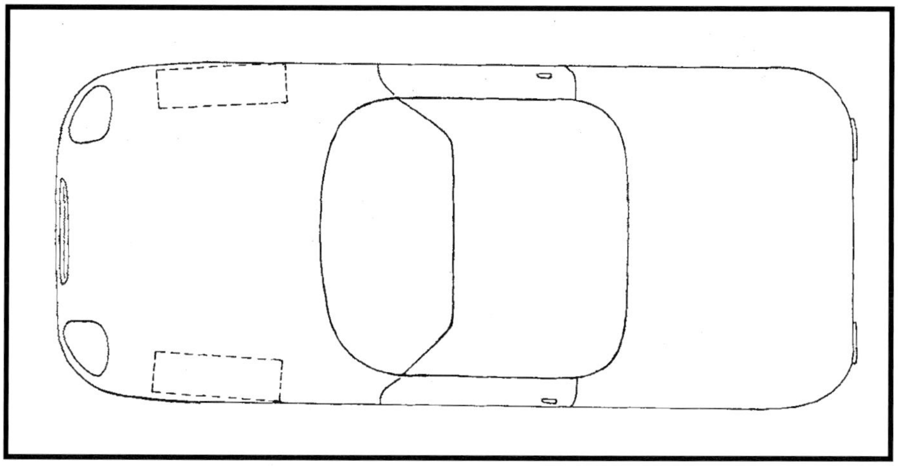

Front wheel toe-in.

front wheel drive cars used to be between 0.062-0.125in/1.5-3.2mm.

Take it that there should not be any toe-in with a forward (of wheel centre) mounted steering rack steering arms (use between zero and 2mm toe-out) and, if the steering arms are behind the front wheels (and there is true Ackerman geometry in the suspension) set between zero and 0.040in/1mm toe-in, or, if such a car understeers, set to 0.080in/2mm toe-out as a maximum.

One reason for using toe-in on a conventional rear wheel drive car is that toe-in causes the steering to self-centralize. If a car is designed to be set up with toe-in, this beneficial effect will be present and the Ackerman steering geometry will, by design, cause the front wheel on the inside of a turn to turn in slightly more than the outer wheel. This shows that a rear mounted steering arm system is better overall (improved cornering geometry). It is, however, not generally easy to accommodate rear mounted arms in many sportscars and kit cars.

Toe-in can be the cause of understeer as the wheels can, essentially, 'fight' each other in a high speed turn. This does not matter at low speed and will be totally unnoticeable until the car is driven fast. Toe-in (front wheels) can be used for a rear wheel drive car used as daily transport. Setting up a car - other than a front wheel drive car - with toe-out is a common method of gaining better cornering efficiency, but it can be overdone: too much toe-out makes a car unstable, especially under heavy braking.

TOE-OUT

Running front wheel toe-out on a car is a method frequently used to gain good Ackerman type steering angles. If the wheel on the inside of the corner does not turn in more than, or at least equally with, the outside wheel, understeer can be induced. There is a limit to the amount of toe-out that should ever be considered, and that amount is 0.140in/3.5mm.

The problem with toe-out, or too much toe-out, is that under extremely hard braking the front wheels tend to toe-out even more because of compliance in steering system joints and so on: in this situation straight line braking can be seriously affected, with the car becoming quite unstable and slewing from side to side in the worst examples. This point is often only reached after the front wheels have been set with more than 0.125in/3.2mm toe-out (up to that amount there is usually no hint of braking instability).

If instability under hard braking is experienced, remove the toe-out completely and try the car under hard braking with the wheels set with 0.062in/1.5mm toe-in. If the instability disappears, the fact that the front wheels had toe-out was definitely the cause of the problem. Next, reset the toe to straight ahead (no toe-in/out) and test for braking instability once

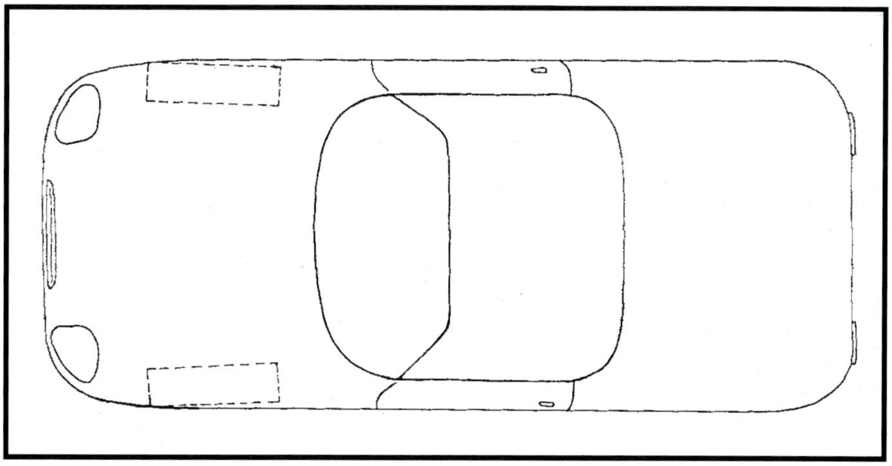

Front wheel toe-out.

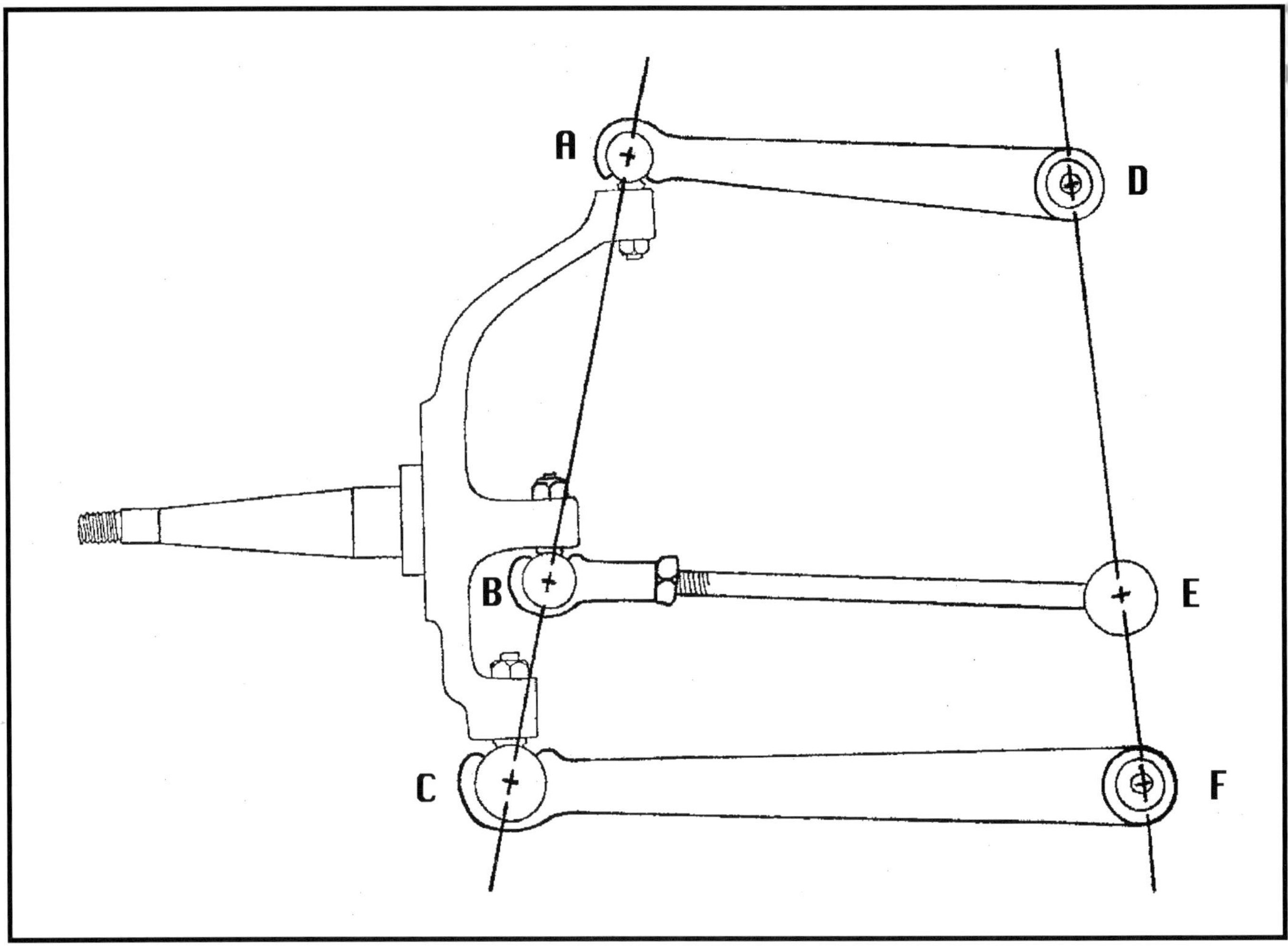

The steering rod arm balljoint centre of the stub axle (B) dictates the steering rack position on the chassis. The upper stub axle balljoint centre (A), the tie rod balljoint centre (B), and the lower stub axle balljoint centre must all be in line when viewed as shown in this diagram. The top chassis pick-up point (D), the rack's balljoint centre (E) and the bottom chassis pick-up point (F) must also be in alignment. The axes A-D, B-E and C-F must also be in similar planes to those shown in the diagram.

again. If there is still no instability set the toe to 0.062in/1.5mm toe-out, and test again.

Use the amount of toe-out that can be tolerated, but **not** at the expense of instability under hard braking. There are better ways of improving the steering geometry of a car, to make it turn into a corner better without understeer, than by resorting to a lot of toe-out (more than 0.125in/3.2mm. Running toe-out is just one way (but not the only way) of improving the 'turning in' response of a car. The ideal situation is to have zero toe (no-toe in or toe-out) but to gain better car handling (improve the turning into a corner aspect of cornering) the use of an amount of toe-out will be required. **Warning!** - Cars with too much toe-out tend to wander very easily, especially if the driver is not 100% attentive.

Toe-out can be used as a tuning method to achieve better turn in to corners, or better cornering power overall by providing Ackerman-type steering geometry.

BUMP STEER

This is the alteration of the attitude of the wheels (toe-in/toe-out) when they encounter a hump or hollow in the road. Ideally, there should be no bump steer.

The cause of bump steer is geometric and to do with the relationship of the steering rack

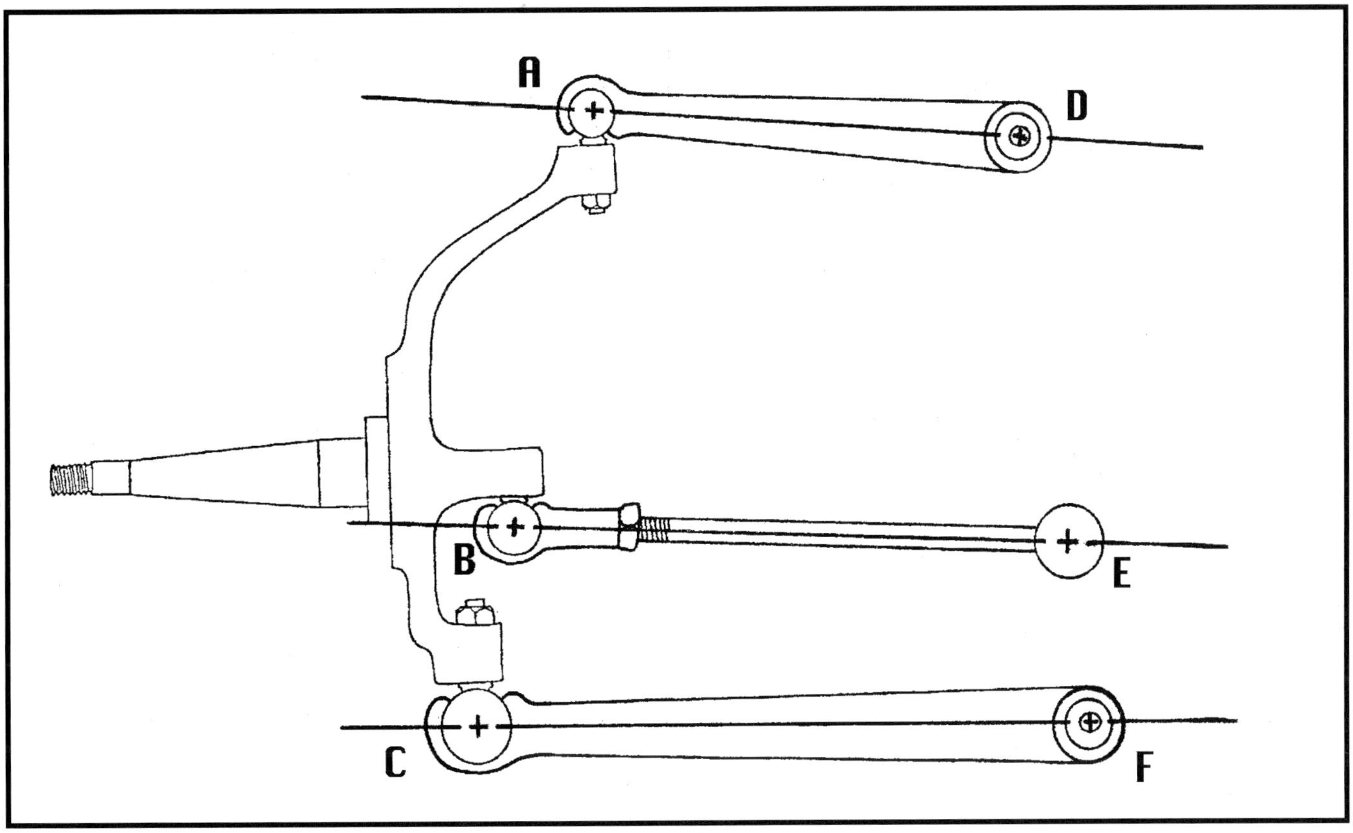

The steering rack height is dictated by the balljoint centre (B). What you must not have is balljoint centre (E) higher or lower (plus or minus approximately 0.0625in/1.5mm) than balljoint centre (B) which is on the rack centreline. Move outside this tolerance and bump steer will almost certainly result.

position and lengths of the steering rack (or other steering system) tie rods (or equivalents) in relation to the suspension system chassis pick-up points and ball joint centres, and lengths of the suspension wishbones.

With regard to bump steer, two considerations should to be taken into account. The first is the position of the tie rod (or equivalent) end ball joint centre when bolted onto the steering arm of the stub axle (which determines the basic height of the steering rack on the chassis). The second part is the position of the rack on the chassis (high or low in relation to the wishbone chassis pick-up points).

The position of the steering rod arm on the stub axle decides what the basic position of the steering rack on the chassis is going to be. Everything is worked back to the chassis. Provision must be made for slight adjustment of the rack's position on the chassis (up or down only) to accommodate the variation in length of the tie rods when the toe is set. For instance, if the car is set up with 1.5mm toe-in, the tie rods will be slightly shorter than when the car is set up with 2mm toe-out.

The steering rack has two ball joints, one at each end. The centre distance between the ball joints is a critical factor when setting the chassis pick-up points during design and manufacture of a chassis. The steering rack should be chosen before any major design work is carried out if bump steer is to be avoided.

Potential for bump steer is very easy to check, with each side of the front suspension being checked individually. The work involves removal of the coil-over shock absorber units or a spring to allow easy movement of the suspension arms. The front of the car is jacked up and the wheels set in the straight ahead position; the wheels are then removed, followed by the coil-over shock absorber units (or springs). The suspension arms, although not necessarily all that light, can now be moved through their full travel (lifted up and down by hand). Any significant amount of toeing-in/ toeing-out that occurs as the suspension is moved through the suspension's travel will be visable when viewed from above (or even felt). If the disc brake rotor is viewed front on as the suspension is raised and lowered, it will be seen to toe-in/out if any appreciable bump steer is present.

Minor adjustments, which will either reduce or remove bump steer, can be effected by raising or lowering the steering rack (this is why many steering rack mounting brackets have slotted holes). It actually does not take much movement of the rack to effect a correction if everything is basically in the right position by design, and the lengths of the steering system components are correct.

If it proves difficult to remove completely the toe-in/toe-out created by bump steer, make sure that the bias of toeing-in is when the suspension is under compression (rising) and toeing-out is when the suspension is in droop. The reason that this is an acceptable compromise is that, when a car is cornering, it exhibits body roll. So, for example, with a car turning left, the left front wheel will toe-out when in droop. The wheel on the outside of the turn does not tend to toe-in adversely because the springs do not allow much suspension compression. Bump steer (slight, of course) can work in your favour.

ANTI-ROLL BARS

Modern sportscars are always relatively low to the ground, and their centre of gravity is always very low; as a consequence, the amount of body roll that such cars exhibit is usually quite low. Even with low slung sportscars, body roll can still be a problem because their drivers like them to corner reasonably 'flat' at high speed, and be totally controllable. In the first instance, increase the spring rates to reduce body roll. The use of supplementary anti-roll bars is not really recommended for this purpose on the basis that these sportscars are usually already very low and very light and should not need an anti-roll bar at all if the correct spring rates are used. The loss of completely independent action of each front wheel is the main reason for not fitting an anti-roll bar; the stronger the ant-roll bar, the greater the loss of independent suspension action.

If the front suspension has an anti-roll bar as an integral part of the suspension (often the case when a donor vehicle's complete front suspension is fitted to a kit car, for instance), do not add another to increase roll stiffness or substitute a stiffer bar for the original. Instead, increase spring rates. On cars which have a high centre of gravity, there is often no alternative to fitting an anti-roll bar, or bars, to reduce body roll.

When anti-roll bars are fitted as original equipment to sportscars, it's to allow the use of relatively soft coil springs for all general ride situations but still provide good roll control when the car is driven in a spirited manner on a winding road. The anti-roll bars resist being twisted because they are made of spring steel and, the more the body rolls, the more the bars resist (up to the limit of the their strength). When the car is cornering hard its body rolls, but not more than 3-4 degrees because the anti-roll bars come into action at this point and prevent it doing so. This means that, if the car did not have the anti-roll bar/s fitted, it would roll more (up to 7 degrees or so). In this scenario the springs are of reasonable tension (soft to medium) and the anti-roll bars are used to increase roll stiffness of the suspension during cornering only.

Sportscars have a low centre of gravity by design; this plays a very significant part in allowing the fitting of reasonably soft coil springs and light anti-roll bars. Using relatively soft springs will allow a lot of nose dive under braking unless the suspension has anti-dive geometry designed in. Front springs **must** always be firm enough to prevent excessive nose dive under braking.

As a general rule, if an anti-roll bars (or bars) is going to be fitted, use anti-roll bars that are *just* strong enough to stop excessive body roll or reduce it to an acceptable level. There is a limit to how much roll stiffness an anti-roll bar can have for a given weight of car before it really starts to interfere with handling. This is because the anti-roll bar reduces the independence of the suspension.

Oversoft/worn anti-roll bar mountings can reduce the effectiveness of the anti-roll bar, though some compliance is often a good thing.

Veloce *SpeedPro* books -

ISBN 1 903706 76 9

ISBN 1 903706 91 2

ISBN 1 903706 77 7

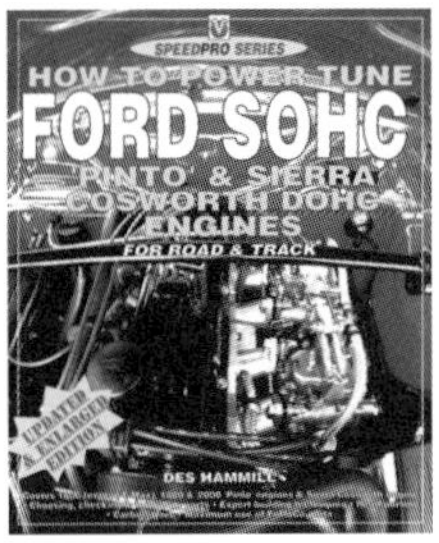

ISBN 1 903706 78 5

ISBN 1 901295 73 7

ISBN 1 903706 75 0

ISBN 1 901295 62 1

ISBN 1 874105 70 7

ISBN 1 903706 60 2

ISBN 1 903706 92 0

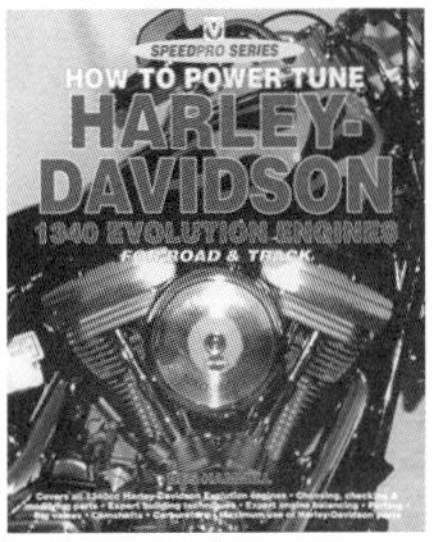

ISBN 1 903706 94 7

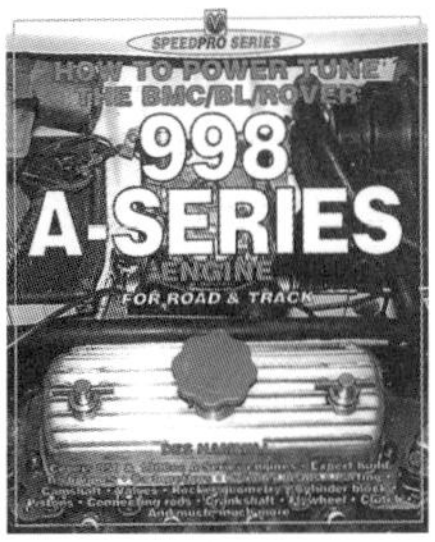

ISBN 1 901295 26 5

ISBN 1 901295 07 9

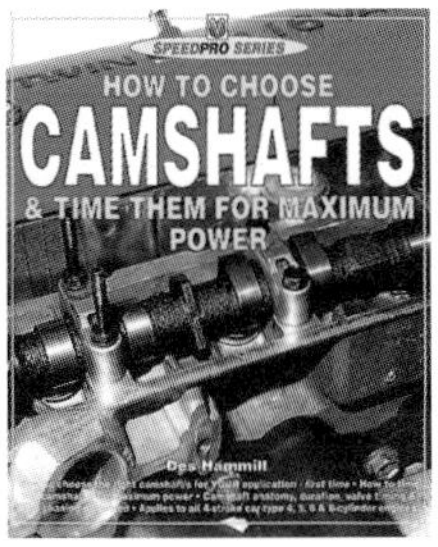

ISBN 1 903706 59 9

ISBN 1 903706 73 4

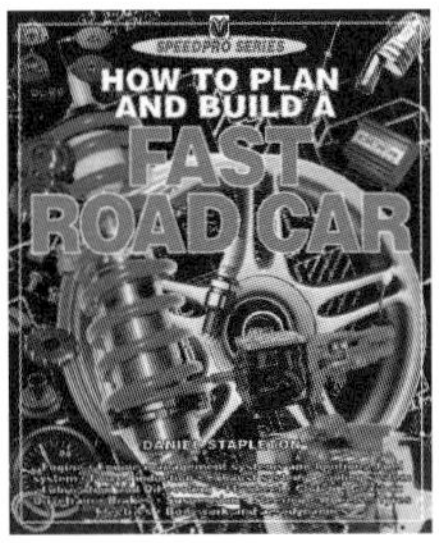

ISBN 1 874105 60 X

ISBN 1 901295 76 1

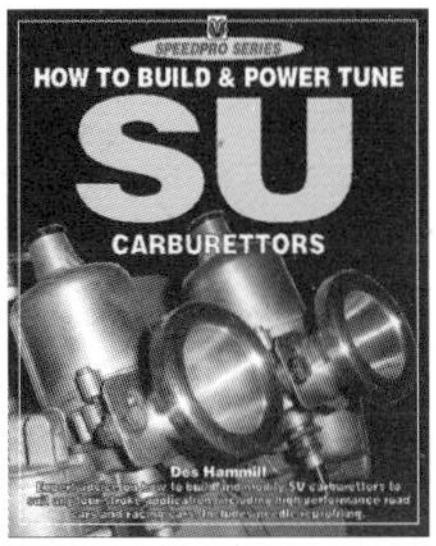

ISBN 1 903706 98 X

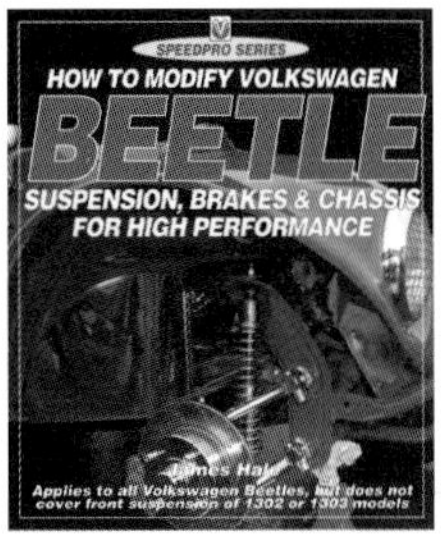

ISBN 1 903706 99 8

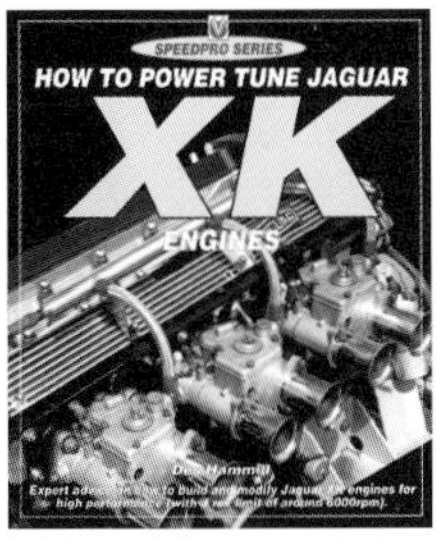

ISBN 1 901295 63 X

ISBN 1 903706 07 6

ISBN 1 903706 09 2

ISBN 1 903706 17 3

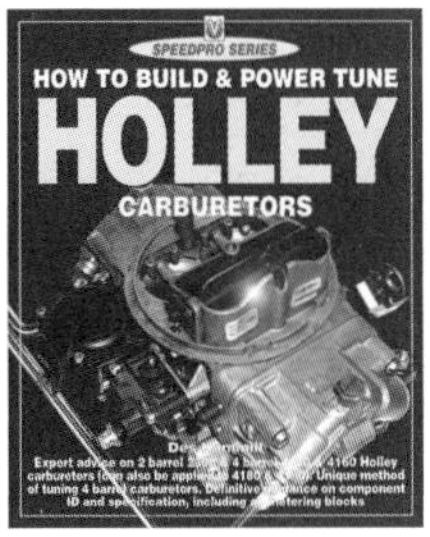

ISBN 1 903706 61 0

ISBN 1 903706 80 7

ISBN 1 903706 68 8

ISBN 1 903706 14 9

ISBN 1 903706 70 X

ISBN 1 903706 72 6

- more on the way!

Chapter 7
Rear suspension

LIVE AXLES

A 'live axle' (one through which the drive to the rear wheels is transmitted) is usually regarded as the cheapest arrangement and, although nothing can stop the 'axle tramp' problem (the type caused by loss of contact with the road over corrugations) associated with the live axle, they can be very effective compared to independent rear suspension systems and are quite light overall. The reason that live axles are used so much is because of their basic simplicity and adaptability. The live rear axle can give an excellent performance in a lightweight sportscar or kit car, provided it is set up correctly. Nothing can alter the fact that there is a lot of unsprung weight in a live axle, or that the rear wheels are not independent in operation. With knowledge of this limitation, the live axle can be made to work as well as possible and can be very effective.

Axle location

The most common method of live rear axle location has the axle constrained by four trailing links of equal or unequal length (longer bottom links) and a Panhard rod for lateral location. There are several variations on lateral location such as A-frames and Watts linkages. The Panhard rod is simple and effective. The up and down movement of the axle is never all that great on road cars, and even less on circuit racing cars (firm springs for a smooth surface), so a Panhard rod is a very acceptable method of lateral axle location.

The trailing arms can be of unequal length, with the two bottom arms longer than the top two. There is no problem with this arrangement if there is only a small amount of suspension travel. The need for unequal length arms often arises through chassis design requirements; the fact that the arms are of different lengths has little affect other than causing the front of the differential to rise slightly on acceleration and dip slightly on braking.

The length of the arms is not really too critical (8-12in/20-30cm is usual) and, as long as they are not ridiculously short (3-4in/75-100mm), there will not be any problems for a car that is used in normal road situations or for track work. When a lot of up and down suspension travel is required (6in/15cm, or more) the arms would need to be longer, but most road or track situations require a total suspension travel from full droop to full compression of only about 4in/10cm.

The shortest length for a top trailing arm is about 8in/203mm, and the longest for a top or bottom arm about 12in/305mm. Consider the ideal length for top and bottom arms to be 8-12in/203-305mm (plus or minus 1in/25.4mm is quite acceptable).

With the trailing arms set parallel to the ground at normal ride height, their up and down arcs of movement will be equal and, because suspension movement is limited to around 4in/100mm, the trailing arms do not effectively shorten too much. The whole idea of having the trailing arms reasonably long and parallel to the ground is to ensure that the axle is not moved back and forth by effective shortening of the arms as they move through their arcs of travel. Shortening of the wheelbase on one side of the car due to body roll, or one wheel only going into a rut or over undulations in the road is to be avoided. Overly short arms will cause the wheelbase to reduce on one side of the car (not by much, but enough to move the car off line) when the suspension on that side is in compression or droop. When the car is in body roll the wheelbase alters on both sides of the car, getting longer on one side and shorter on the other: this leads to rear wheel steering. There are cars, such as dirt track speedway racers, which can use this effect to advantage.

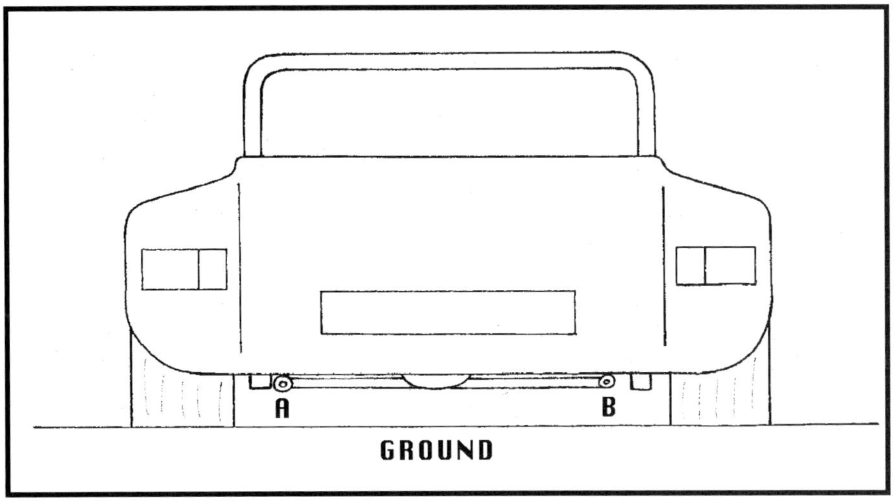

Looking at the back of the car, the Panhard rod will be parallel to the ground and connected to the axle at "A" and the chassis at "B" (can be the other way around).

Another aspect of trailing arms is the method of pivoting; this is usually via Rose joints or compliant bushings. There is nothing wrong with firm rubber (or other compliant material) bushings: they are reliable, last for a long time, are easy to replace and inexpensive. The Rose joint, on the other hand, offers adjustment of the length of the arm (at both ends of the trailing arm when there are the usual two Rose joints) and a constant length - until they are worn. The drawbacks of Rose joints are their rate of wear, possible transmission of noise/ vibration and, lastly, the high cost of replacing them fairly frequently, especially on a road vehicle that covers a much greater mileage than a track car.

Consider rubber bushings ideal for road cars and Rose joints ideal for track cars.

The Panhard rod used for lateral

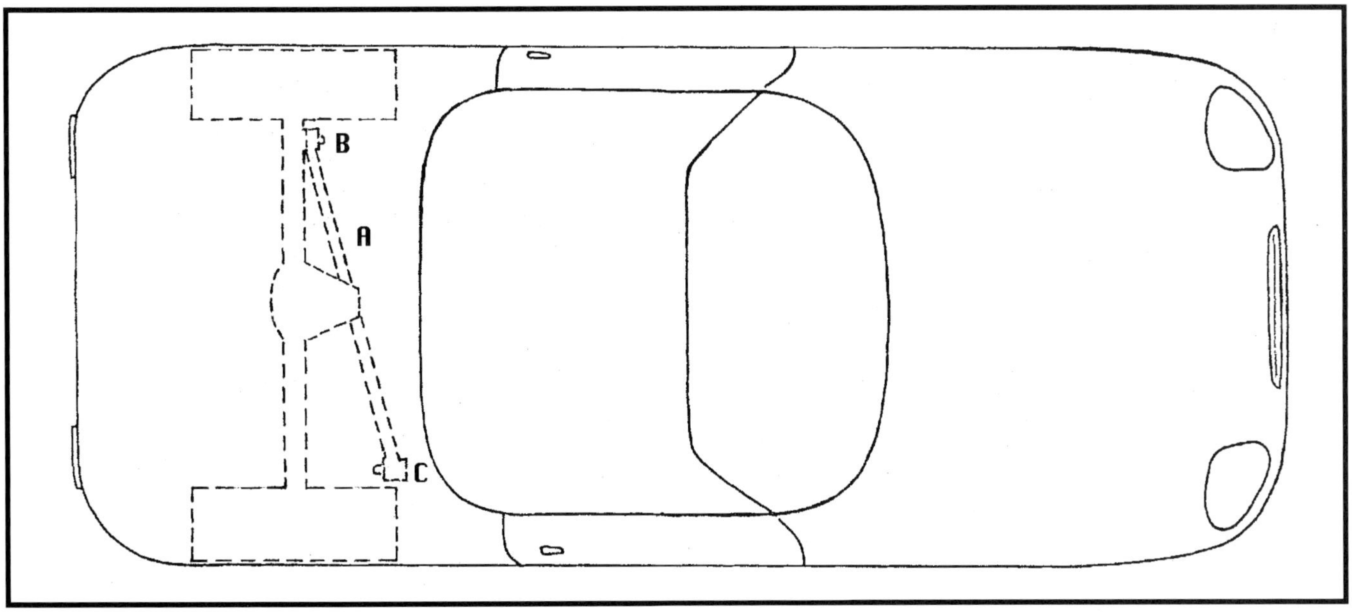

Panhard rod A is connected to the axle at B and to the chassis at C. The angle of the Panhard rod can be up to 15 degrees across the car.

location should be as long as is possible, so that the axle moves up and down with as large a swinging radius for the rod as possible. The longer the Panhard rod is the less side to side movement of the axle during suspension comression and droop. The Panhard rod should, ideally, be parallel with the ground with the car at its normal ride height, and should be as parallel to the axle as possible.

Limited slip differential (LSD)

In many instances LSDs are just not necessary. Most road going cars do not normally need an LSD, while cars used for competition do. With good rubber (meaning top quality tyres which offer the best possible grip) the grip of the right rear tyre, plus the forces acting down on the tyre (unsprung weight of the car), will frequently prevent this wheel from spinning. Wheelspin causes a loss of acceleration and is to be avoided at all costs. While wheelspin may look spectacular to some, it is completely counter-productive (car is slower getting away). In the first instance, irrespective of the type of car, fit the best tyres available. Top of the range tyres (meaning the most expensive usually) from each major tyre company offer the best of everything: you get what you pay for. Tyres can really make a difference to a car, and some of the latest designs have quite remarkable qualities. Consider the range of low profile road going tyres suitable for all-round maximum grip to be ones like the Michelin Pilot SX-GT, Yokohama A510 or Bridgestone RE 71, to name but a few, and there are plenty of others.

Note that the Michelin Pilot SX-GTs, for example, has very firm sidewalls (as in rigid) and if the use of this tyre is coupled with a suspension that has good geometry suitable for the tyre, the car will feel as if it's on rails. These tyres are very good.

If a car has excessive wheelspin from a standing start, the first solution usually considered is to fit an LSD and, in the normal course of events, this fixes the problem to the satisfaction of most people. However, the geometry of the live axle's rear suspension can play a significant part in preventing one wheel spinning more than the other during standing start acceleration using full power. In many instances, the full power of the engine cannot be used off the mark because the right rear tyre simply spins (and the left rear wheel does nothing). In such cases the best method of getting away requires knowing what rpm to use and slipping the clutch. The car gets away okay, but not in the same manner as it would by revving the engine to maximum rpm and dropping the clutch with both wheels gripping equally. It may seem impossible that an unlocked differential can be set up to provide equal rear wheel traction, but it isn't.

If a car is tested without a locked differential and full power put through the driveline, the right rear wheel will normally spin uncontrollably, leaving a very black line on the road surface for the full distance of first gear, and acceleration will be slow, which is just hopeless. What happens here is that all the power goes through to the right rear wheel as the torque reaction of the differential effectively lifts the right rear wheel off the ground. With less car weight acting on the right rear wheel, the tyre breaks traction. Once the rear wheel is spinning it is difficult to stop it.

The next step is often to buy and install an LSD. When full power is put through the driveline the left hand rear wheel receives a portion of the power and both wheels may spin/grip more equally and, certainly, the problem appears to be solved. However, there is a bit more to it than this. With the LSD installed, there will now be two black lines on the road but, if you look carefully, one line will be darker than the other. This is because the LSD does nothing to load each rear wheel equally with sprung weight; alternative suspension geometry can achieve this. The LSD prevents excessive wheelspin of the right rear wheel by transferring a portion of the power to the left rear wheel, but that is all the LSD does.

For straight line work, such as drag racing, with a little bit of

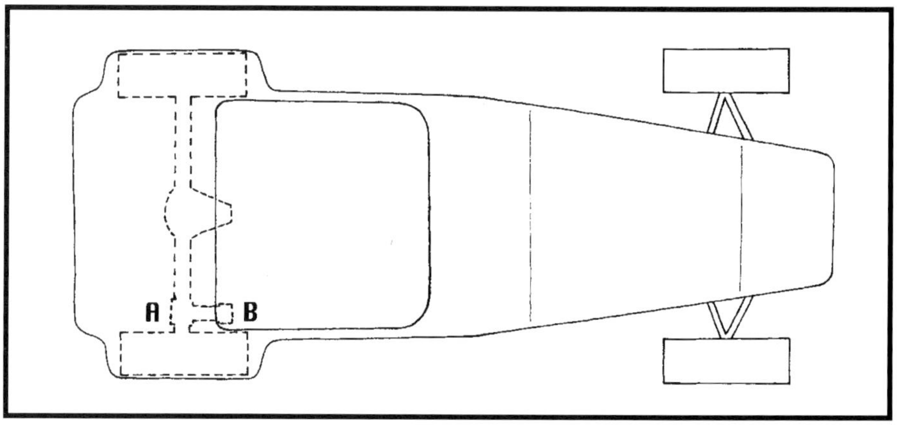

Top arm (A-B) is connected to the axle at "A" and to the chassis at "B." Arm is as near to the right rear wheel as possible and is usually quite short (6-8in/152-203mm long). There is no top arm on the left hand side of the chassis.

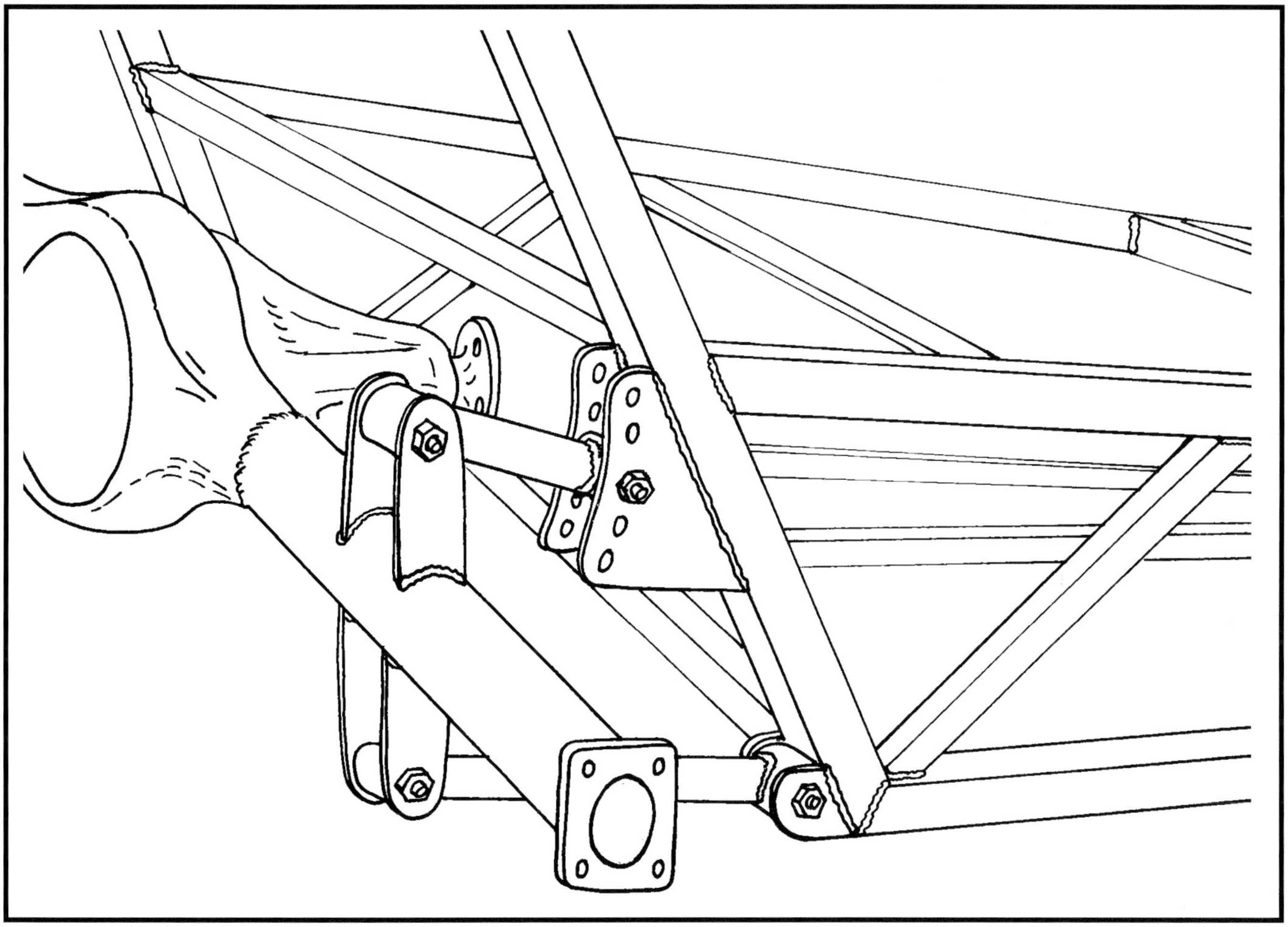

Bracket with adjustment holes fixed to the chassis, angled top link and bracket fixed to the differential casing. Increase the angle of the top link to increase weight transfer to the right rear wheel, reduce the angle to reduce the weight transfer to the same wheel.

fabrication a car with an unlocked differential can be made to leave two equal length, equally dense black lines on the road surface because each wheel has the same amount of unsprung weight acting on it. Both wheels may spin uncontrollably, but they'll be spinning equally as both have exactly the same amount of power (50/50) going through them - and you can't get better than that. It also takes a lot of power to make two top quality tyres spin in this situation.

Take, for example, a car fitted with a four link suspension and a Panhard rod for lateral location. The two original top arms are removed and an adjustable angle top arm fitted to the right hand side of the car. The new arm is adjustable for angle by way of a series of holes in the bracket.

The system works by virtue of the fact that, when the clutch is released and the power of the engine transmitted to the differential, the front of the differential lifts up or, to put it another way, the differential casing tries to turn in the opposite direction to the wheels. There is a considerable amount of turning force involved, and it is this force that is harnessed.

The fact that the single top link is on the right hand side of the car means that there is only one link connected to the chassis. As a consequence, the turning force of the differential pulls onto the chassis at this point and effectively puts weight onto the right hand rear wheel. This torque reaction weight is alterable by changing the angle of the top link, and it's quite possible to have the top link angled so steeply that the left hand rear wheel spins in much the same way as the right hand rear used to!

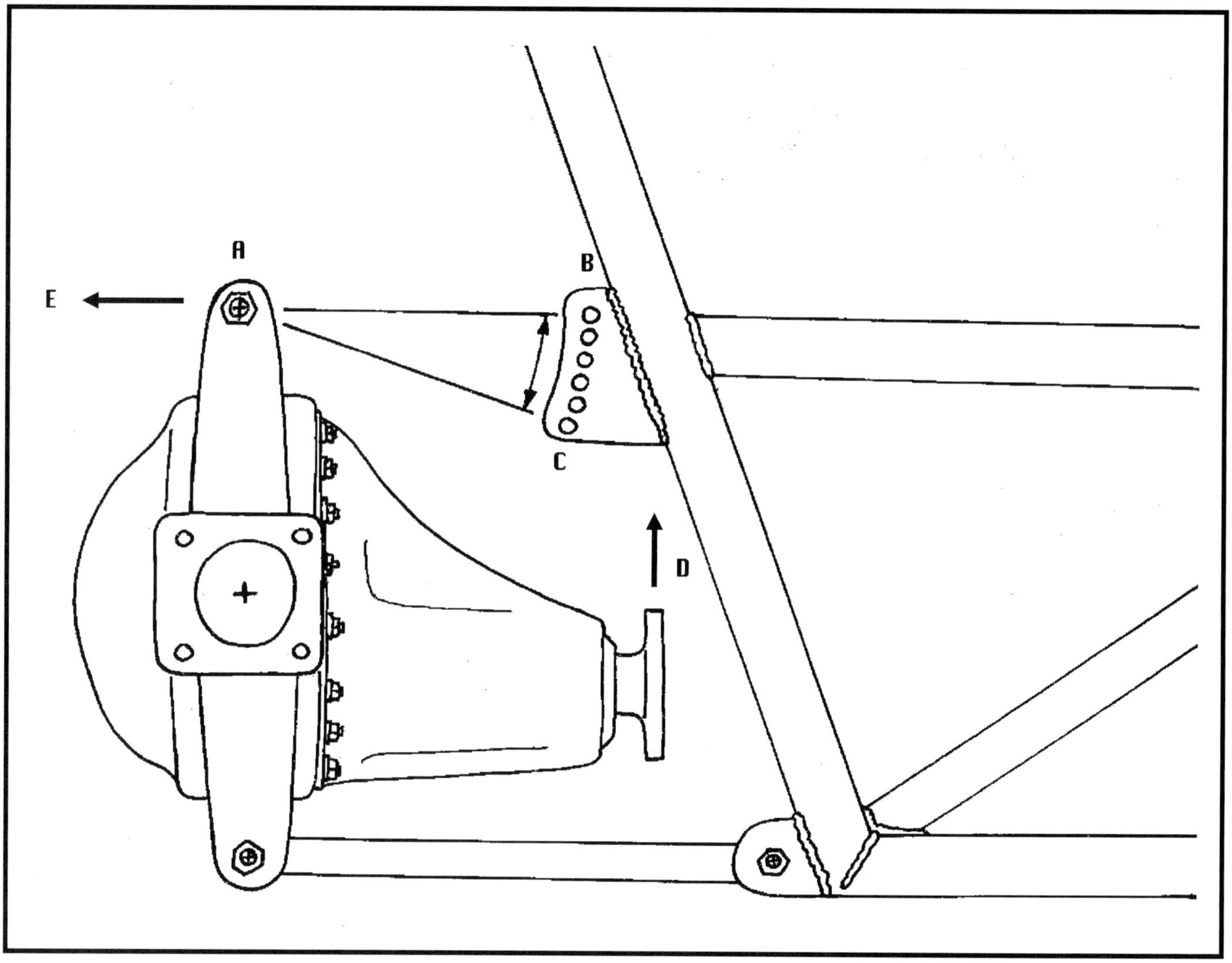

The single arm is permanently fixed at "A," but can be adjusted between holes (B-C). The adjustment holes (B-C) must be on the same radius from the pivot point (A). Arm is always the same length, but angle of arm can be changed very quickly. "B" is parallel to the ground, while the bottom hole (C) is angled down 15 degrees or so. Torque causes the differential to lift at front (D) and, as a consequence, causes the top arm pick-up point on the differential to go back as shown at "E" if the effect is not controlled.

The reason for this is that the right hand rear wheel can end up with more weight (transferred weight) on it. That is why the link is adjustable (anglewise). The angle of the arm should be reduced so that equal weight is present on both rear wheels under full power acceleration. A car that used this sort of system was the C-type Jaguar of the 1950s.

You'll know that the applied weights are equal when both wheels spin/smoke an equal amount when the clutch is released (not seen by the driver, but by others) and the two black lines left by the rear tyres are equal in length and depth of colour.

Unfortunately, such a suspension arrangement is not that good for circuit work and, more specifically, under hard braking (axle tramp), but for drag racing it's ideal. It's possible to stop braking induced axle tramp to a degree by adding a horizontally positioned shock absorber (weak). Effectively, the differential must be able to pivot in an unrestricted manner on the lower trailing arms. The front of the differential casing must be able to lift up. If there is no top link on the left hand side of the differential casing, and a small diameter shock absorber is fitted to this side of the differential, the

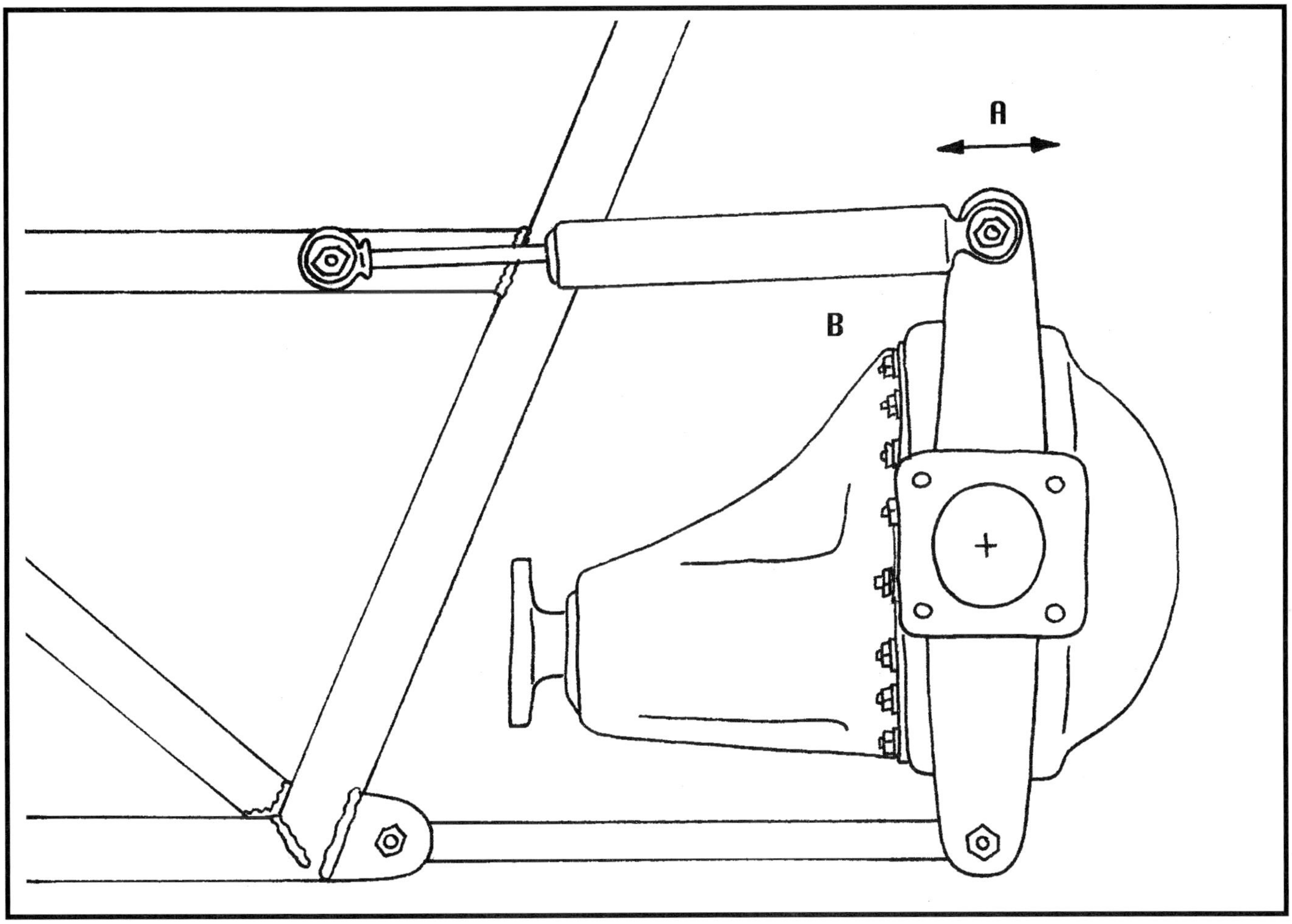

Shock absorber (B) allows movement back and forth at "A," but no sudden movement.

movement of the differential is unrestricted but it is still connected to the chassis via the shock absorber which prevents rapid movement and axle tramp. The other possibility is to limit the braking action to the rear wheel via a brake proportioning valve. This, however, can only be taken so far, since the rear brakes will not stop the car as effectively.

INDEPENDENT REAR SUSPENSION

There are a few types of independent rear suspension commonly found in sportscars and kit cars. The first type revolves around the use of a substantial single trailing arm either side of a centre section, and is either a complete suspension system (in a subframe) from another car which is then fitted to a kit car, or original equipment suspension as made and fitted by the particular sportscar manufacturer. Such cars are front engined and the fully assembled rear suspension is usually non-adjustable. The differential centre section unit is a housing that is often rigidly mounted into the subframe with swing axles coming off each side that have two constant velocity joints each. The whole set up is usually very heavy.

The second type of independent rear suspension revolves around the use of a transaxle arrangement and usually features two wishbones of one sort or another each side of the car. The wishbones may, or may not, be adjustable. This form of suspension is, for example, often found in kit cars which have used a transaxle from a production car and have the engine mid-mounted. The kit car manufacturer will have fabricated the rear suspension wishbones. The accuracy of all of the components, including the chassis, is critical to good handling: there can be no compromises (a possible problem is toe-out on one or both wheels, which results in an unstable car).

Note that many competition derivatives of kit cars and sportscars, and the most modern road going sportscars, often have fully adjustable front and rear suspension geometry (with regard to production sports cars it's all within the parameters of the geometry design, with definite limits on how much the suspension can actually be adjusted. Basically the suspension can't be adjusted too much and never out of reasonable adjustment). With such suspension systems, because of the complication of having so many adjustments, it's possible to get the handling wrong just as much as it is possible to get the handling completely right. Irrespective of how many adjustments are possible on a car, there is no reason why the right decisions cannot be made.

SUMMARY

The rear suspension must **not** have toe-out at any position in the suspension travel. This also means during body roll.

The rear suspension should be adjusted so that each side of the car has an equal amount of toe-in.

Consider 0.040in/1.0mm toe-in the minimum and 0.120in/3.00mm the maximum, equally dispersed about the centreline of the car. To clarify this, it's no use having a collective amount of toe-in of 0.120in/3.00mm all on one wheel whilst the other has zero toe-in. It must be divided equally between the wheels.

Large amounts of static negative camber seldom work, and while some people think it looks good, it very often does not result in an improvement in handling. Consider 0.5-1 degree of static negative camber to be almost always sufficient, and consider using stronger springs to reduce body roll, coupled with increased shock absorber damping if the rear of the car is unstable.

As a general rule **do not** lower the car without considering the rear suspension wishbone/trailing arm attitudes. For cars with dual wishbone rear suspension the lower wishbone chassis and upright pick-up points need to be an equal distance from the ground when the car is at its normal ride height. In many instances, handling will be better if the chassis pick-up point centre is higher than the upright's pick-up point by about 0.50in/12.5mm. The trade-off here is that the car will not be as low as it could be but, generally speaking, keeping the geometry correct and having the car a bit higher than you would like is better than having the car as low as possible but with bad geometry.

Some modern mass production sportscars feature what seem to be fully adjustable suspension systems. In reality, the suspension geometry of cars like this is only adjustable up to a point, with there being very definite limits to the amount of adjustment possible. What the manufacturers have done is build in an amount of adjustment which will allow some alteration to compensate for production tolerances, and to correct the effects of normal wear and tear. Within the range of adjustment possible in such systems, improvements can be made for some applications; certainly, the possible suspension adjustments, in conjunction with increased spring rates and shock absorber damping, can greatly improve handling characteristics. The price, of course, is a very firm ride.

Chapter 8
Brakes

It is not really possible to over-brake a vehicle. In nearly all cases, however, the complaint is that the brakes are not good enough and fitting uprated brakes (usually meaning larger disc rotors and calipers) will improve the situation to the point that the problem is solved. This does not always prove to be so; the fitting of larger disc rotors and calipers with more pad area and piston area can have quite disappointing results. Frequently, the problem is one of insufficient line pressure, but this is reasonably easy to check and, if necessary, rectify. There is no doubt that fitting the largest disc rotors and calipers (large pads with plenty of piston area but not massively heavy calipers) possible at the front of a car is a sound idea. However, it cannot be stressed enough that all of the components which make up the braking system must be in perfect condition if maximum efficiency is to be obtained.

There is something very satisfying, and confidence boosting, in knowing that the brakes on a car are so good that, even under the most arduous conditions, they'll pull up the car to the point of locking the wheels at any speed. Conversely, there is nothing satisfying, or confidence boosting, about driving a car which you, the driver, know has sub-standard brakes. The difference between having excellent brakes and sub-standard brakes can be the result of a minor thing such as incorrect brake pedal ratio.

BRAKE PEDAL RATIO

In the overall scheme of things, sportscars and kit cars are generally compact affairs and, frequently, there is a height restriction in the pedal area which means that the pedal assembly can only be so big. This may mean that the pedal ratio may not be all that great. Sometimes it may only be 3:1. You can take it that 5:1 is the minimum amount of pedal ratio you should really have and that 7:1 is the likely maximum to be found on any car of this sort, but pedal ratios of up to 10:1 are sometimes possible.

Some cars have brake pedal ratios that offer little mechanical advantage (3:1). However, the driver of the car can only comfortably push the brake pedal just so hard: it's not feasible to drive a car that requires so much pedal pressure that the driver has to brace him/herself just to pull up the car from speed. If everything else related to the brakes is correct, but braking performance is still poor, the problem is the brake pedal ratio.

Use the most pedal ratio you can to give as much mechanical advantage as possible, without excessive pedal movement being required to activate the brakes. The smaller the brake pedal ratio (3:1) the quicker the brakes will come into action, but the harder the brake pedal will be to push. Conversely, the larger the brake pedal ratio (5-7:1) the slower the brakes will be bought into action (a lot of pedal travel by comparison), but the easier the pedal will be to push to achieve effective line pressure and proper braking action. In this example just given, the master cylinder diameter is unchanged. The ratios recommended are a minimum of 5:1 and a maximum of 7:1, but 10:1 is possible and is the

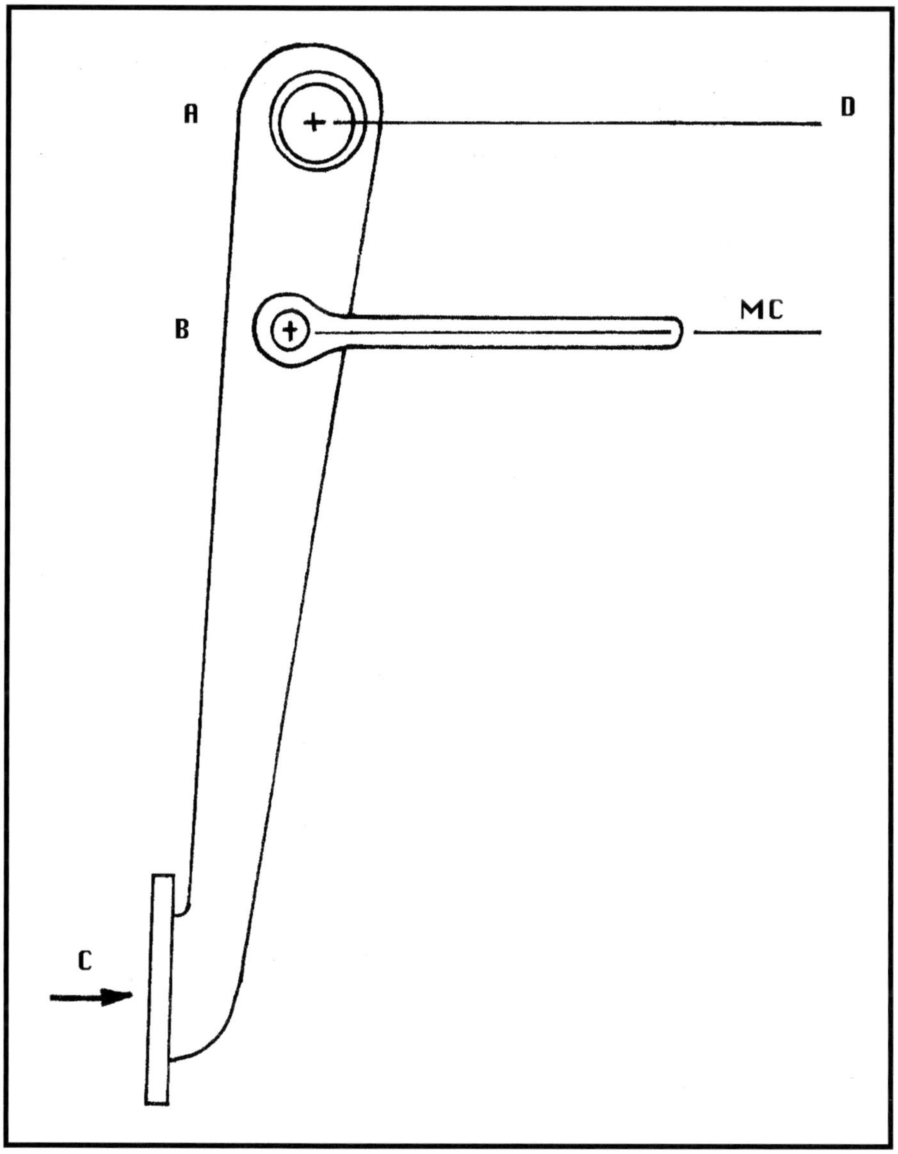

Ratios of mechanical advantage are worked out by measuring dimensions "A" to "B" and "A" to "C" and dividing the A-C dimension by the A-B dimension.

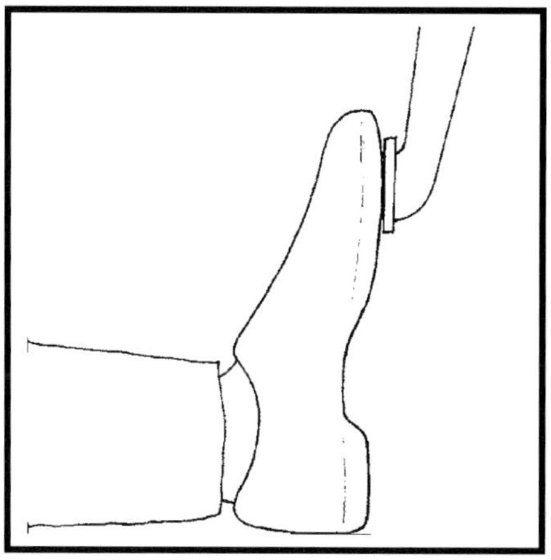

Ideal position of the foot on the brake pedal for most efficient action.

absolute maximum.

In the first instance, the driver should sit in the car and rest his/her foot on the pedal to see where the ball of the foot is in relation to the brake pedal pad. The heel of the driver's foot is the fulcrum point and the ball of the foot is the contact point with the pedal pad. The ball of the foot must be in the middle of the pad. If the pad of the brake pedal is higher than this, it can be lowered by altering the existing pedal or making up a new pedal to increase the ratio and to make it more comfortable for the driver. The driver can always exert more pressure on the pedal if it is in the right place, as it is naturally easier to push the pedal.

Warning! - Bear in mind that the brake pedal takes a lot of pressure: it has to be strong to avoid bending or, worse, breakage. After checking with local authorities on legality and quality /inspection requirements, get the brake pedal altered, or a new pedal made, by an experienced engineering firm to ensure that the welding is right and the pedal strong enough. An experienced engineer will know by looking at the pedal and checking with relevant construction requirements if it is strong enough, and what to do about it if it isn't. **If a brake pedal breaks the consequences could be disastrous.**

Feet come in different sizes and really all that is being done here is to make the car suit the driver for maximum efficiency. The fact that the brake pedal may no longer suit everyone is of no real consequence, and when every possible advantage is being sought, this is a small price to pay.

Measure the distance from the centre of the brake pedal pad to the pivot point or fulcrum of the pedal and make a note of the dimension. The next distance to measure is from the master cylinder clevis pin point to the brake pedal pivot point. This dimension affects the other component of the brake pedal ratio.

Reduction of this distance increases the mechanical advantage ratio of the pedal. Normally, there are distinct limits to how much this distance can be reduced, but what can be done should be done. There are all manner of adjustments that can be made to effect a reduction in this distance, it just depends on the design of the mechanism, but the principles remain the same for all mechanisms.

Very often the master cylinder can be brought closer to the fulcrum of the brake pedal (0.062-0.125in/1.5-3mm), a new hole drilled in the original brake pedal and, instead of the pushrod that operates the master cylinder piston being dead straight, it will be angled slightly (up to 5 degrees) without detriment. The difference between a 3:1 and a 5:1 pedal ratio means a considerable reduction in the effort required to push the pedal for the same amount of line pressure, and being able to generate an acceptable amount of brake line pressure (to specification), meaning the brake pads are forced against the disc rotor harder for the same amount of effort. Everything is improved as a consequence. There will seldom be excessive brake pedal movement before braking action takes place with a 5:1 pedal ratio system.

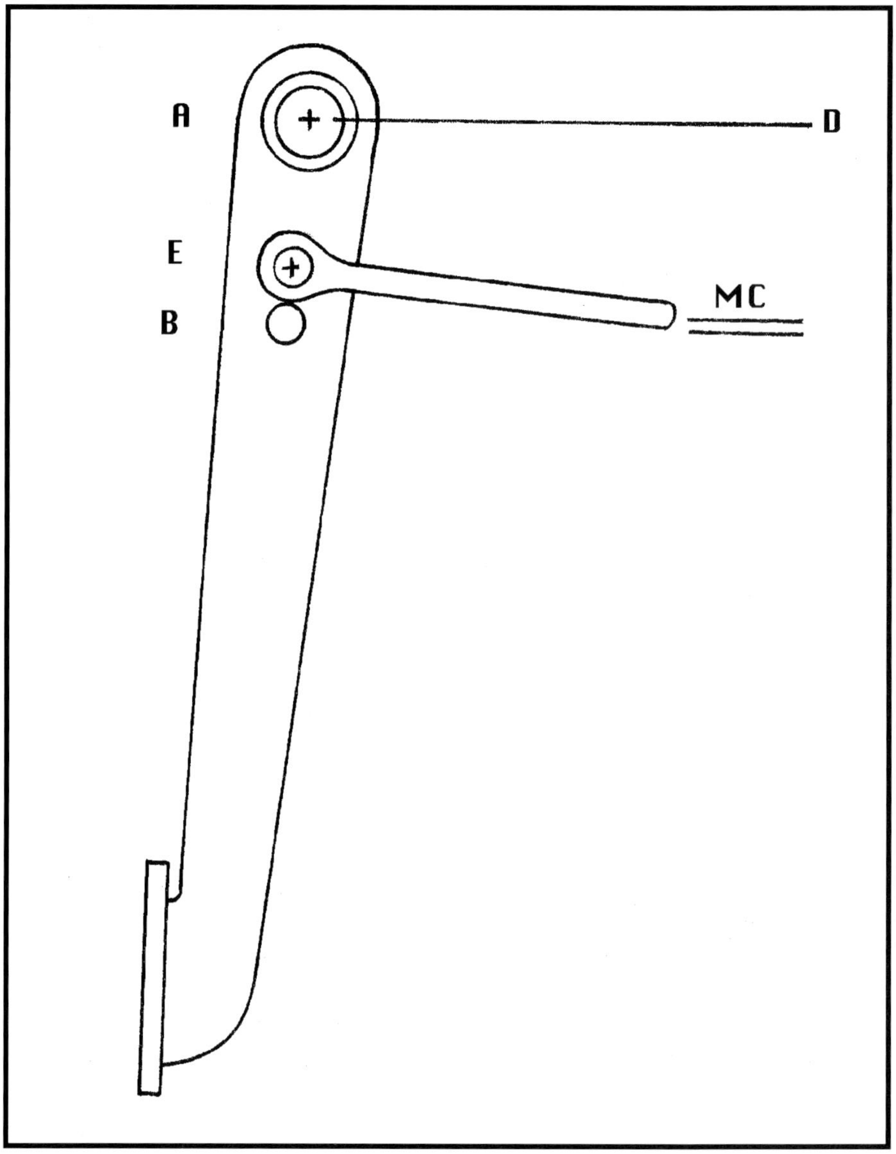

Here, the master cylinder (MC) has been repositioned closer to the brake pedal pivot point and axis line (AD). A new hole for the master cylinder actuating rod was drilled in the brake pedal at "E." Original actuating rod hole (B) is not used.

MASTER CYLINDER BORE SIZE

In the first instance the new size of the master cylinder bore has to be decided on. It's not just a simple matter of using any cylinder that looks like it will fit. There is the requirement of mechanical advantage to be considered. The smaller the master cylinder bore diameter is, and the higher the pedal ratio, the greater the line pressure: it is this generated line pressure that pushes the disc pads against the disc rotors and the drum shoes against the drums.

The problem here is that a certain volume of brake fluid must be moved before the brakes are on, and the more worn the parts, the more movement required. This is the reason why fitting new brake parts is recommended.

If the master cylinder capacity is not large enough, the pedal has to be moved too much, or a lot, before braking action starts and, by the time the brakes are applied, the cylinder may be nearly out of travel. Even though the pedal is pressed very hard, the line pressure is limited because the piston bottoms out (this is not an impossibility). Also, the higher the brake pedal ratio is, the greater the pedal movement required before braking action starts. If parts are worn, more movement is required to get the brakes to actually start to work. If all components are in as-new condition, there is a minimum of movement before line pressure is generated and the brakes applied (disc pads/shoes in full contact) instead of pedal movement taking up slack in the system.

Note, also, that the reservoir capacity of the master cylinder needs to be enough to allow for pad wear. Caliper piston bores can, collectively, account for quite a lot of fluid as the pads wear and the pistons move further outward: the result can be no brakes if master cylinder capacity is too small. This is why brake master cylinders often have larger capacity reservoirs than clutch master cylinders.

Use the smallest bore master cylinder that provides a hard pedal with no more than 1.25-1.5in/32-38mm of pedal travel. The better the condition of the components (things like brake drums and rubber hoses, for example) the smaller this amount of movement will be. Start with a 0.75in/19.0mm bore master cylinder (a very common size), although there may well be an advantage in fitting a 0.625in/16.0mm cylinder - but only if pedal travel is not too great. The 0.75in/19.0mm master cylinder will usually be about right and the mechanical advantage can always be altered by relocating the pivot point of the pedal itself and/or the master cylinder pushrod pick-up point on the pedal.

Consider that a 0.625in/16.0mm diameter bore master cylinder is the smallest size to use on a single bore braking system (or a tandem for that matter), but the more common size of 0.750in/19.0mm is more readily available. The 0.625in/16mm bore diameter master cylinder will produce more line pressure, all other things being equal, but can only be used if the resulting pedal travel is not too great.

If the brakes still prove unsatisfactory once this element of the braking system is sorted out, the calipers and disc rotors will need to be uprated to increase the size of the brake friction areas.

BRAKE SERVOS

Brake servos (vacuum operated power brakes) reduce the amount of effort required to apply the brakes. Most kit cars, for instance, do not have power brakes, although most production sportscars do. Brakes which are not power-assisted have more 'feel' to them, which is why they are still used in many applications. Pedal pressure will always be higher on a non-power-assisted braking system, but this is not normally a problem, especially if the brake pedal ratios are correct and excellent line pressure can be generated.

A lightweight sportscar prepared for racing should not need power-assisted brakes. If the brakes on a racing Caterham, for instance, are large enough, say, 11.5in/30cm diameter disc rotors on the front with four pot calipers and long pads, and the rear brakes are suitably large at, say, 10in/26cm in diameter (drums or discs), there will be enough braking power to pull up such a car very quickly from 130mph/210kph.

For this sort of speed the master cylinder can be anything from 0.625in/16.8mm to 0.750in/19.0mm with a pedal ratio of between 5:1 and 7:1. A 0.625in/16.8mm diameter bore master cylinder, using a 7:1 pedal ratio, is able to generate more line pressure than a 0.750in/19.0mm diameter bore master cylinder using a 5:1 pedal ratio with equal foot pressure being applied. Either combination may slow the car equally well; it depends on the driver's strength and how much foot pressure he or she can apply to the pedal.

The 7:1 ratio pedal is going to require more movement than the 5:1 pedal. We are all different in our preferences here, which is why it is not possible to give absolutely hard and fast rules. Generally, small-framed people will require a high pedal ratio (7:1) and will use the smallest possible master cylinder (0.625in/16.8mm diameter). The point is that the master cylinder must be able to move sufficient brake fluid to operate the brakes effectively. The large amount of pedal movement is the price of generating sufficient line pressure to operate the calipers to maximum effect. A 0.750in/19.0mm diameter bore master cylinder, coupled with a 2.5 to 1 ratio brake pedal, is going to be hard work for anyone. There's always a limit to how much pedal travel you can have, a limit to how much brake pedal ratio you can have, and a limit to how small the master cylinder diameter can be.

The ideal situation is to have pedal travel as short as possible, brake pedal ratio as high as possible and master cylinder bore diameter as small as is practically possible.

All braking system componentry has to be in as-new condition: any wear will have a cost (usually in brake pedal travel), and the hoses must not move when the brake pedal is depressed as this indicates hose deformation of some sort which, in turn, means more pedal travel before effective braking occurs. Metal braided hoses are readily available from high performance parts suppliers. While more expensive than standard hoses, metal braided hoses do not baloon under pressure and, as a consequence, give a firmer pedal and more efficient braking action.

Warning! - Take no chances with brakes, use only new components.

BRAKING PERFORMANCE

Essentially what is required from the brakes of a road car is to slow the car (even from maximum speed) to a dead stop in the shortest possible time. Further to this, the car must be controllable and stable whilst being stopped, and the brakes should not fade with repeated hard use.

A car used exclusively for racing has different criteria. A racing car seldom has to be slowed to a dead stop although, obviously, it must have the capability to do so. A car used on a circuit should be able to be slowed from the speed being used (including maximum) to the speed required for all manner of corners, in the fastest possible time (which also means in the shortest possible distance) while remaining controllable. Also, the brakes must be able to do this repeatedly with the same efficiency.

If a road car is taken to a race track for a test day, the brakes are adequate if, when applied heavily at maximum speed, the car reduces speed **the instant** the brakes are applied. Reduction in speed from the maximum **must be immediate** and the decceleration felt immediately. There must be no vagueness (as in waiting for decceleration to be felt). **Warning!** If there is vagueness, it means only one thing - **the brakes are not efficient enough for the car's performance. In short, the car is *not* safe**.

If a car has adequate braking performance, expect to have to reduce the actual braking pressure being applied to the brake pedal as the car slows to prevent locking the front wheels. This scenario is most usually seen with lightweight sportscars which have very large diameter front disc rotors and large multi-piston callipers. The driver of such a car (without abs) will certainly get used to the brakes being so good and will seldom lock the wheels.

Warning! - Get the brakes right in the first place, irrespective of the cost. Brakes *must* be uprated to match the performance of your car.

FRONT DISC BRAKES

The front brakes do the most work and really need to be good. As a general rule, fit the largest diameter disc rotor and largest area disc pads with multi-piston calipers (four piston) that you can within the constraints of wheel size. The bigger the diameter of the disc rotor and, correspondingly, the further the caliper is away from the centre of the wheel, the more mechanical advantage the brakes will have. The usual limiting factor of what rotor size can be used is the diameter of the wheels. The disc rotor and the caliper have to fit inside the wheel rim and have at least 0.187in/4.5mm of clearance between the caliper and the rim itself. The problem here is the possibility of small stones getting caught between the caliper and the rotating wheel rim.

The solution to the rotor size situation is to fit larger diameter wheels (15 inch, or larger) and low profile tyres so that overall tyre diameter remains unchanged, yet there is maximum room available for a bigger disc rotor. The trade-off here (for the better) is that the low profile tyres available offer the very best in roadholding. There are no losses (except a harder ride and, possibly, heavier wheels) in using 15in diameter (or larger) low profile tyres and wheels on sportscars as low profile tyres offer superior handling to high profile tyres.

If small disc rotors are used along with small diameter wheels, braking efficiency will always be less than with a large disc rotor set up, but this does not mean that the smaller brakes will be inadequate. There are plenty of things to check before the brake rotor size has to be increased: very often vital basics are neglected. Before the rotor size is increased, check that everything is working to maximum efficiency. Check to see what the brake pedal leverage factor is, that the calipers are in correct alignment with the rotor, that the brakes lines are fully bled (and that it is possible to bleed the brakes 100%), what the master cylinder bore diameter is, what the condition of the master cylinder is, the condition of the brake hoses and that the disc rotors are as-new.

Front disc brake check list

Disc pad contact

The disc brake pads must be in full contact with the disc rotor. Frequently, alternative/uprated calipers are fitted to a car in such a way that the pads are not in full contact with the disc. This usually happens when the caliper from a different car is used and the mounting holes are not in the same position as those of the original calipers. Rectification may take some work, but there is just no point whatsoever in having pads which are not 100% in contact with the disc rotor. Every situation is different but, one way or another, any caliper can be realigned so that the pads are in full contact with the disc rotor.

Brake line bleeding

Warning! - All air **must** be expelled

from the system as air is compressible. The whole idea of a braking system relies on the principle that it is not possible to compress a liquid. Once all of the air has been removed from the system, when the brake pedal is pressed *all* the fluid is moved whereas, if there is air in the system, the air bubbles compress as pedal pressure increases, absorbing valuable pedal movement.

Braking systems which have air in them often work well enough, up to a point, but never as well as they could. The problem of insufficient braking power is usually encountered just when the brakes are needed the most, such as when approaching a corner, realising you are going too fast and needing extra braking. More foot pressure is applied to the brake pedal, but there is no more line pressure to be had. If there wasn't air in the system, line pressure would increase and, as a result, the pads would exert more pressure on the disc rotors.

The other part of this is, of course, that there are limits to how much pressure is required to operate the brakes. There comes a point when increasing brake line pressure does not significantly increase the effectiveness of the brakes (the caliper and disc pads are at maximum efficiency). In this case, the only solution to innadequate braking is to increase the diameter of the disc rotor and/or increase the pad and caliper piston area. Fitting the largest diameter disc rotors, together with the largest pads and calipers (piston area), are well-founded principles as, even if the brakes are never used to maximum potential, they will generally be more reliable.

Brake lines must be able to be bled effectively

Warning! - It **must** be possible to bleed the brake lines so that there is **no** air in the system. The bleed nipples of calipers are not always in the correct position (above the caliper oil level). This happens when calipers from another vehicle are used for a different application. The bleed nipple ends up in a slightly different position, air is trapped in the system and, as a result, the brakes cannot be fully bled - irrespective of the method used. Often, the only solution is to remove the caliper from the stub axle, place a close fitting piece of wood between the pistons (to stop them coming out too far) and hold the caliper so that the bleed nipple is definitely in the highest position. Once the caliper has been bled in this manner it can be refitted to the vehicle but, every time the brakes need to be bled, the caliper/s will have to be removed.

There are various ways of bleeding the brakes, but a pressure brake bleeding system is the preferred method. There are several inexpensive systems available which work very well. One of these is Gunson's Eezi-bleed which uses tyre pressure (20psi maximum) to provide air pressure. This kit is easy to use, and is one of many d-i-y products made by this American-owned British company. The use of any device which makes it easier to bleed the brakes correctly is a good move, and will help to ensure that your car is correctly prepared.

Brake lines and hoses

Warning! - If the brake lines or fittings are leaking, then they **must** be replaced. All brake lines should be new to ensure reliability and safety. Consumable brake parts like this are not expensive.

Brake hoses in poor condition can lead to a loss in brake line pressure (they 'balloon' under pressure). This fault is very easy to check visually because, when the brake pedal is depressed, the brake line moves in a pulsing motion. Replace any brake line like this. The braking system on any car is of such importance that all parts should be new and renewed at regular intervals to ensure absolute reliability and consistency of action. An alternative to standard-type hoses are braided Aeroquip-type hoses and fittings. These remove all possibility of ballooning hoses.

Master cylinder

In the first instance the master cylinder(s) is checked for leaks. If a problem is found, the solution may be as simple as fitting a repair kit but, more often than not, the master cylinder will need to be replaced as the bore is no longer on size (the original as-bored and honed size, that is). Master cylinders can be remanufactured, which entails having the bore machined oversize and having a sleeve pressed into the bore which restores it to original size. Many types of master cylinder can be bought brand new for a very reasonable price. The latter is recommended as new parts are almost always dead right and offer new component reliability and long life. Buying new brake parts is usually cost-effective.

What you don't want is a reconditioned master cylinder that has had the bore of the unit honed to clean it up (the bore may not be parallel and may not be on size). Buy new if in any doubt about the quality of reconditioned parts.

The bores of cast iron master cylinders tend to become pitted, causing the piston to seize or destroy the edges of the neoprene cup/s and allow leakage. Aluminium master cylinders wear oval and can become scored. Master cylinders in poor condition can bypass brake fluid; this causes a reduction in efficiency (line pressure). Sometimes, the amount of leakage is so much that the fluid level in the reservoir can be seen to increase as the brake pedal is depressed. When an insufficient amount of fluid is available to be pressurized, pedal travel is always excessive before resistance is felt. Another factor is that the piston can also bottom out before any real brake line pressure is generated. The only solution to this sort of problem is replacement of the master cylinder or to have a proper corrective repair made to it.

The bore of a master cylinder can be measured using a telescopic gauge. The wear, even when measurable, is often not visible, so visual inspection is a waste of time other than to detect obvious pitting, scoring or galling. Consider any master cylinder that is not near-new (visual appearance, receipt of purchase available or known use since being purchased) to be unsuitable for further service. Buying a brand new master cylinder is the best option.

Solid rotors (discs)

These were the most common rotors and are normally quite adequate for the majority of applications, such as road going vehicles. At the very least, fit the largest diameter disc rotor that was fitted as original equipment to the stub axle in question. Many production cars were, at some stage, fitted with uprated brakes (rotors and calipers) and, frequently, these parts are still available from suppliers and will retro-fit.

Many disc rotors feature drillings to increase the cooling surface area. Other discs have grooves machined in the surface for the same purpose and to facilitate self-cleaning/water dispersion; this is a better option.

Vented rotors

Most production cars now come fitted with vented disc brake rotors. Vented rotors run cooler and are essential for any competition car, or any other application in which the brakes are going to get really hot and where reliable repeat performance is vital. Aftermarket vented rotors (available as direct replacements for solid rotors) are not usually larger in diameter than the originals, so braking efficiency is not improved by fitting vented rotors (or not until the brakes get hot, that is). Repeat braking efficiency certainly improves when vented rotors are fitted but, by and large, solid disc rotors never get all that hot on road cars (disc rotors have been hot when they are permanently blue in colour).

Large diameter ventilated rotors are often seen on cars which are not used for competition. The reason for this is that such rotors are readily available as direct replacements, and are very reasonably priced. The ventilation factor is not always needed, but the larger diameter is, and buying large ventilated rotors is often the least expensive way to get large discs and calipers that are, basically, bolt-on replacements for original equipment.

Calipers

Disc brake calipers come in two common types. The first is the single action caliper, which uses one piston to apply pressure to both pads. These calipers are on pins or slides that allow the caliper to move so that equal pressure is applied to the disc pads on both sides of the disc. There is nothing really wrong with these calipers, but they are less suitable for swapping from one stub axle type to another.

Other caliper types are fixed and have two or four pistons. The four piston caliper is the standard by which all other readily available production calipers are measured, and with good reason; they are simply better.

Two pot calipers

These are the normal cast iron type of caliper, as found on the majority of production cars, regardless of whether the disc rotor is vented or solid. Although efficient, the amount of pad area is often not all that great. For any road going sportscar they will prove adequate but, for any form of competition, fitting four pot calipers is pretty well mandatory and will, almost always, give better results. There are not many production type six pot calipers available, but there are plenty of four pot calipers around.

Four pot calipers

A cast iron mass production-type four pot disc caliper is generally more efficient because it allows the use of a larger disc pad (to give more friction area). The four pistons exert even pressure on the long pad while the caliper remains relatively light and compact. Four pot calipers are, by their very construction, slightly heavier than single pot calipers, but their advantages far outweigh their disadvantages. There are several reasonably light, compact cast iron four pot calipers available at very reasonable cost, such as those from the Austin Metro (non-vented disc), MG Metro Turbo (vented disc) and the Austin Princess (non-vented disc), to name but three. These calipers can be made to fit many other applications if suitable brackets are fabricated. The Austin Princess caliper, particularly, is a good example of an inexpensive four pot caliper that is reasonably easy to find. Also, kits are available to space the caliper halves so that they can accommodate a vented disc rotor.

Consider mass production four

pot calipers together with vented disc rotors the minimum requirement for circuit racing. Further to this, for maximum braking efficiency in competition applications, use six pot calipers as made by one of the various specialist manufacturers, together with the largest vented disc rotors that can be accommodated.

REAR BRAKES

These can be either disc or drum. There is nothing really wrong with drum brakes at the rear of a lightweight car; they do not do anything like the work of the front brakes. Disc or drum brakes can actually be too effective at the rear of a car and may require some form of limiting valve to prevent rear wheel lock-up. Brake proportioning valves are available that do just this.

Adjustable brake proportioning valves should be placed close to hand so that the brake bias can be altered while driving. Having a brake bias valve is ideal for racing as the bias can be altered to suit prevailing conditions (wet or dry). It will seldom ever be necessary to alter the brake bias on a road car, but at least the bias can be adjusted to the optimum setting very easily. Brake bias valves that are infinitely adjustable and ideal for fitting on any sportscar or kit car are not that expensive. Brake bias valves have been used on some road going cars for years, and these can often be adapted to new applications. The Austin Rover Mini and Metro cars are examples of production cars which have brake bias valves fitted as standard. There are two types: the Mini valve is not adjustable (except by dismantling the valve and changing the spring, but they can be made externally adjustable with some work); the brake proportioning valve of a Metro van, for example, is of a different type and can be adjusted simply by altering the angle of fixing on the chassis.

Brake bias valves are always readily available from aftermarket suppliers.

Rear drum brakes

Drum brakes are most commonly found on live rear axles. While disc brake conversions are now offered for most of the common live rear axles, they are seldom really necessary unless the car is used exclusively for racing purposes. Many people fit rear disc brake conversions just because they prefer discs to drums, or because the cost of refurbishing the original drum brake system is not so different to the cost of an all new disc brake kit.

Cars which are going to retain the original drum brakes should have all parts renewed to ensure that everything is to original specification. The drums must be virtually unworn to be of any real use on a high performance car. New wheel cylinders and shoes are not expensive.

Rear disc brakes

Rear disc brakes are very common now, and are very effective. A hand-brake mechanism is universally incorporated into these rear units. For kit cars using adapted production car parts, fitting an adjustable brake bias valve will almost always prove necessary as the rear disc brakes will usually be too effective. The rear disc brake rotors will usually be solid and not vented.

CHECKING BRAKES

Warning! - Take appropriate precautions to ensure your own complete safety and that of others during the following tests. Brakes must be checked for efficiency by thoroughly testing them (off road) under maximum braking conditions. This involves approaching a set point at a reasonable speed (50mph), applying the brakes fully and seeing how the car pulls up. Does the car pull up square? Does any individual wheel lock up (as opposed to all four or, perhaps, two wheels lock-up)? The brake bias valve can be used to alter the front to rear apportionment of braking force. The distance it took to pull the car up should be measured (approximately). Provided the car pulled up square without any problems the speed can be increased to 70mph and the test repeated. The wheels should not lock, but should be on the point of locking throughout the stopping process. This will mean that the amount of pedal pressure will have to be reduced as the car slows to avoid locking the wheels. Once again the car must pull up square and without any individual wheel locking up. If the front or rear wheels both lock up, adjust the bias mechanism until the bias is correct. Measure the distance (approximately) it takes to pull up the car to a standstill. Increase the speed at which the brakes are applied, checking for stability on each occasion. In this way the braking capability of the car will be known and there will be no surprises when the brakes are used to the full.

Cars used for competition only do not often need the brakes to stop; they are really only used to slow the car as quickly as possible, to negotiate a corner or avoid other cars. The front to rear bias of such cars may well be set for high speed braking rather than low speed braking. **Warning!** - Always check the brakes of a circuit car before the start of a race to check their efficiency. This can be done in the warm-up lap at as high a speed as possible.

BLEEDING BRAKING SYSTEMS WHICH ARE DIFFICULT TO BLEED

In most instances the bleeding of brakes is quite straightforward, and a 'hard' pedal is more or less obtained immediately once all of the air has been expelled from the system. The braking systems that are easy to bleed generally have the master cylinder at the highest point in the system and the bleed nipples on the actual brakes are at the highest point on each brake. Bleeding problems usually crop up when these criteria cannot be met. If you are having trouble bleeding the brakes properly on your car this information is for you.

Sometimes, bleeding the brakes isn't so easy to do, irrespective of which one of the common methods of bleeding brakes is used. After all of the usual methods have been tried the brakes can still have air in them. A 'spongy' pedal due to air in the system is potentially dangerous; don't leave home with the brakes in this condition!

The following method will test any conventional hydraulic brake system, isolate the problem area, or areas, and allow the brakes to be bled 100%. Two people are needed for the job, and you'll also need at least two brake clamps. The hydraulic fluid is drained away from the bleed nipple, via a tight fitting clear plastic tube, into a clear container (glass or plastic, with plastic being more ideal because of the risk of breakage with glass). The end of the clear plastic tube must always be immersed in brake fluid, which means that you should put some brake fluid into the container before starting to bleed the brakes.

The first thing to do is check the master cylinder(s) to make sure that they hold pressure when the brake pedal is depressed. Brake systems usually have one of the following three master cylinder configurations. The first is a single master cylinder with one piston and one outlet line supplying brake pressure to all four wheels. The second system uses a tandem master cylinder which has two pistons, one inlet line in a common bore, with two separate outlet lines supplying brake pressure to two wheels. The third system is a tandem system which has two completely separate master cylinders side by side, with both cylinders coupled by a linkage to the brake pedal. There is almost always a method of apportioning the effort put into the brake pedal into the two master cylinders so that one can receive more pressure than the other through alterable mechanical advantage.

Irrespective of what type of master cylinder is being used, they can and should all be checked for the ability to produce and hold brake line pressure. Even brand new cylinders should be checked just to make sure that they are right. This involves removing the brake line from the master cylinder, or in the case of a tandem master cylinder the two outlet pipes, and fitting a bleed nipple, or nipples, into the outlet hole or holes. Bleed nipples with the right thread are available from most motor parts suppliers. There is some variation in the threads used in braking systems so nipples with the right threads must be used. Scrapyards or breakers' yards are also a good source of bleed nipples.

With the brake pipes removed from the master cylinder(s) and bleed nipples fitted in their place, the master cylinder(s) can be bled in much the same way as if it was a disc brake caliper or a drum brake wheel cylinder. The reservoir is filled up with brake fluid, the nipple is undone and the brake pedal is pushed to the floor. With the brake pedal held down on the floor the bleed nipple is done up and the brake pedal released. This is done two or three times to expel any air from each bleed nipple. The brake fluid that is bled out of the master cylinder goes into a container via a clear plastic tube with the end of the tube immersed in the brake fluid. This prevents any possibility of air being drawn back into the line.

After the master cylinder(s) has been thoroughly bled, with no air coming out, tighten up the bleed nipple(s) and firmly depress the pedal (with maximum effort). Ideally the brake pedal will be 'rock hard', with virtually no pedal movement needed to achieve this. If the pedal doesn't feel absolutely 'rock hard' there is some fault in the cylinder. The master cylinder(s) will either pass or fail this test.

The next part of the master cylinder testing is to keep light foot pressure on the brake pedal and release the bleed nipple slightly so that the pedal goes down about 1/8in/3.5mm. The bleed nipple is locked up and maximum effort applied to the brake pedal again. The cylinder must hold position and the pedal must not move towards the floor. Repeat this process every 1/8 of an inch of brake pedal travel until the pedal is near the floor (near maximum travel). On a tandem cylinder, release each bleed nipple in turn until the pedal is almost at the floor (it's not necessary, or desirable in some instances, to go right down to the floor). The reason for making this check is to ascertain the cylinder's ability to seal for the length of the pedal travel. If a master cylinder bore has wear or damage at some point, the seals may not be in full contact with the bore and the cylinder pressure won't be held. This test will find the problem and the master cylinder will have to be replaced if it fails.

In all situations it's recommended that only brand new master cylinders and brake parts be used. Brake failure on a sports car through faulty componentry can have fatal consequences. It's not worth taking the risk. All new components should be checked in the manner described since even these can be at fault.

With this test done the integrity of the master cylinder(s) is beyond doubt. Whatever the problems that remain with the braking system, they do not rest with the master cylinder.

Reconnect the pipework to the master cylinder and fill the system with brake fluid and pump it through.

BLEEDING A SINGLE PISTON MASTER CYLINDER BRAKING SYSTEM

If the car has a single master cylinder, as many older cars have, the next step involves bleeding the brake at each wheel in the following manner. All brake hoses, except for the brake being bled, must be clamped so that no brake fluid can move past that point and activate the other brakes (a minimum of two clamps per hose will be required). Proper brake hose clamps are available from car part suppliers. There is usually one flexible hose going to each front wheel and one flexible hose going to the rear axle (three in total). The brake clamps should be positioned as close to the chassis or body of the car as possible.

Before proceeding with brake bleeding, check that none of the metal brake lines have any abrupt humps or loops in them (where such action has been taken to avoid under body obstacles, etc.). These are potential air traps, and it can be virtually impossible to shift the air from such a pocket. Re-route the brake line if at all possible.

With the clamps in place, and the brake pedal depressed to bleed the brakes, the master cylinder's full capacity will be routed through only one flexible pipe to the brake that is being bled. In this situation there is no possibility of air trapped elsewhere in the piping or brakes taking up any of the master cylinder's displacement. The full shot of master cylinder displacement going through one brake is almost always enough to shift all the air in that part of the brake system.

Some disc brake calipers are difficult to bleed because of the position of the bleed nipples. In such cases the brake caliper will have to be removed from the stub axle and held with the bleed nipple axis in the vertical plane. Bleed each brake in turn by depressing the brake pedal with the bleed nipple open, and then closing the nipple when the pedal is pressed to the floor. The fluid is drained away from the bleed nipple via a clear plastic pipe and into a partially filled bottle of brake fluid. Any air will be seen through the clear plastic pipe. Repeat the procedure until the fluid coming through is completely clear and has no air bubbles in it.

Note that before bleeding the brakes with the caliper removed from the stub axle, a piece of wood or steel should be wedged between the disc pads so that there is no possibility of any piston movement.

Use new fluid only and make sure that it has been allowed to stand undisturbed for at least 24 hours before being poured into the master cylinder. **Never** use brake fluid that has been shaken.

On some live axle vehicles, the two rear drums are linked side to side via metal pipes, and there is only one bleed nipple. This is not normally a problem if both front hoses are clamped and the full master cylinder displacement goes to the rear of the car only. Make sure that the metal pipes that go side to side of the rear axle are straight (and level with the ground), and have no humps or hollows in them which could be potential air traps. Make new pipes if those on your car aren't straight.

Since the very first test used the master cylinder on its own, the 'ideal' brake pedal feel is now a known quantity. Nothing less than this rock hard feel will do when the whole system is operational. A small amount of extra downward pedal movement, due to brake fluid displacement, is permissible though. Excessive displacement means that there are worn or poorly adjusted components in the system.

If the pedal still feels spongy after bleeding the brakes in this manner, there is still air in the system. Isolate the front brakes from the rear to find out where the problem actually is. The problem is most likely to be due to one of the bleed nipples not being at the very top of the braking system or, alternatively, that one of the internal holes in a caliper has not been drilled correctly so that there is an area where air can get trapped above the level of the bleed nipple take-off point.

The next step involves clamping off the rear brake hose so that no fluid is displaced to the rear brake circuit at all. With the clamp in place, firmly press the brake pedal and note the 'feel' of the brake pedal. If the brake pedal suddenly becomes firm, for example, (in much the same way as when the master cylinder was isolated) the problem is in the rear part of the braking system. If the spongy feeling in the pedal remains, however, the problem is at the front of the car. Using another brake clamp isolate each front brake in turn to see whether the problem is in one front brake or both.

With the offending brake or brakes known, one or both are bled in turn once again but this time the brake pedal is depressed as quickly as possible. This is usually enough to shift any remaining air.

If there is still a 'spongy' feel to the brakes there is still air in the system somewhere. A part of the problem of bleeding some braking systems is the amount of fluid that can be moved in one pedal stroke of the master cylinder. Fluid can move past the trapped air in the brake line instead of shifting it. The problem at this stage is really one of poor brake line fitting, with one or more abrupt 'humps' in the metal lines, and an insufficient surge of fluid to move the trapped air.

Apart from fitting new brake lines, a possible solution is 'pressure bleeding'. The simplest way of doing this, is to fit a tubless tyre valve assembly into the cap of the master cylinder and, using a car tyre pump which has a gauge, put about 20-30psi into the space between the cap and the top of the brake fluid. The reason for the 20-30psi and not more is the fact that most caps are plastic and will only stand so much of this sort of treatment. 20-30psi will usually be sufficient anyway but, if necessary, 40psi can be considered to be the limit.

The advantage of having air pressure above the brake fluid is the fact that when the brake nipple is opened there is going to be a large and constant stream of brake fluid passing quickly through it. This is almost always enough to shift any trapped air. No amount of pedal pumping can equal this system.

Summary

After this sort of treatment there is unlikely to be any air in the braking system. The master cylinder has been checked on its own, each front brake has been individually bled, with the bleed nipple known to be at the highest point in the system (the back brakes were isolated during this procedure), and the rear brakes were bled with the two front brakes isolated. Proper brake clamps must be used to ensure that the brake hoses are firmly clamped but are not damaged.

Note that some front disc calipers have two hoses going to them (BMC/BLMC/Austin Rover products, for example), and in many instances kits are available that convert these twin brake hose calipers to single hose calipers, reducing the pipework of the front braking system. It does, of course, remove the 'fail safe' aspect of the original design and this may not be legal in some countries.

BLEEDING DUAL MASTER CYLINDERS

On these systems one master cylinder activates the front brakes and the other master cylinder activates the rear brakes. The master cylinders are checked by removing the pipework, fitting bleed nipples, and then bleeding both cylinders as described above.

With the master cylinders bled, the brake pedal is firmly depressed (maximum effort) and, ideally, the brake pedal will be rock hard with virtually no pedal movement required to achieve this. Keeping a constant light pressure on the brake pedal, release fluid from each master cylinder in turn every 1/8 of an inch of pedal movement and check for a rock hard pedal each time until the pedal is near the floor. A successful test proves the integrity of the master cylinders.

Re-fit the pipework to the master cylinder that activates the front brakes, fill the front brake system with fluid and then clamp off one brake hose as near to the chassis as possible. Bleed the front brake until the fluid coming out of it is clear. Repeat this procedure on the other front brake. Both front brakes should now be successfully bled.

The next step is to connect the pipework to the other master cylinder and fill that part of the system. With both master cylinders now in operation the two front flexible brake hoses are clamped as near to the chassis as possible.

There is some variation in rear braking system designs. If the car is equipped with a live rear axle there will probably only be one bleed nipple, but there may be two. If there are two bleed nipples in the line, bleed the one closest to the master cylinder first and then do the second one.

The car could also have two flexible hoses in the rear brake system. If so, clamp one as close to the chassis as possible while the other brake is bled and then swap the clamp and bleed the other brake. Throughout this process the two front flexible hoses are firmly clamped so that all of the pedal action and the master cylinder's displacement is going to just one brake. Each brake is bled individually and checked for a rock hard pedal. If the pedal remains spongy even after an individual brake has been bled there is a fault in this brake. No progress can be made until the fault is found and rectified.

BLEEDING A TANDEM MASTER CYLINDER

In the first instance the master cylinder is checked with both brake lines removed from the master cylinder and the pipework replaced with correctly fitting bleed nipples. One bleed nipple is undone and bled and then the other bleed nipple is undone and bled in the normal manner. When the brake pedal is firmly depressed the pedal should be rock hard, with virtually no movement whatsoever. If the pedal is spongy, however, or if fluid goes back into the reservoir, the master cylinder is faulty and must be repaired or replaced. Release fluid from each bleed nipple in turn every 1/8 of an inch of pedal travel and check for a rock hard pedal each time until the pedal is nearly to the floor.

With the master cylinder checked in the prescribed manner for its ability to hold pressure and the feel of the pedal now a known quantity, the next step is to isolate each brake in turn and bleed it. It's not all that uncommon for some late model cars to have as many as six flexible brake hoses in the system, but even so only three proper brake hose clamps are normally required.

With the master cylinder known to be working exactly as it should, the next step is to remove the bleed nipple from the master cylinder that would normally feed the front brakes and re-connect the front brake pipe. Leave the bleed nipple that is being used to blank off the rear brake line connection in place at this point. Proceed to bleed the two front brakes.

Note that there is sometimes a complication on some cars due to the fact that one section of the tandem master cylinder will feed one front brake and one rear brake. In such cases the first flexible rear brake hose gets clamped as close to the chassis of the car as possible when the front brake is to be bled and then the front flexible brake hose gets clamped when the rear brake is to be bled.

Each front brake is bled in turn after blanking off the brake hose that is not being bled with a proper hose clamp. The fluid that is bled out of the brake is taken from the nipple via a clear plastic tube to a container partially filled with brake fluid. The end of the clear plastic pipe is immersed in the brake fluid so that there is no possibility of air going back into the brake.

When both front brakes have been bled and the brake pedal proven to be 'rock hard', the second section of the tandem master cylinder has its pipe work connected and the rear brakes bled. If the front brakes do not offer a rock hard pedal there is a problem which will have to be found and rectified.

Each rear brake is bled individually, in the usual way, with the flexible hose that leads to the opposing brake clamped as close as possible to the chassis. The two front brake flexible hoses are also clamped. Push the pedal to the floor quickly on these systems.

If bleeding the rear brakes fails to produce a rock hard pedal, check that the steel brake lines are parallel with the ground and do not have potential air pockets in them.

The system of bleeding brakes outlined here obviously involves more work than would normally be required, but it does work in 'problem cases' and was devised out of sheer frustration of not being able to bleed a braking system.

Chapter 9
Setting up the car

Setting up **must** be done on a flat level floor. The two front tyres of the car **must** be inflated to the same pressures, as **must** the two rear tyres. The two front tyres should be from the same manufacturer and of identical type, as should the two rear tyres. The two front tyres **must** be of the same circumference (measure it), as **must** the two rear tyres.

CHECKING TYRES

The circumference of the tyres must be checked with the tyres inflated to the correct pressure as generally recommended by the tyre manufacturer. Find out what the usual recommended tyre pressure is for the particular tyres you have on your car from the company you bought the tyres from. Expect the pressure to be anything from 22 psi to 28 psi. The tyres must be off the road as in jacked up so that the wheel can be rotated or when all of the tyres are off the car when the circumference is to be measured.

Tyres are often not the same size front to rear, but this is not a

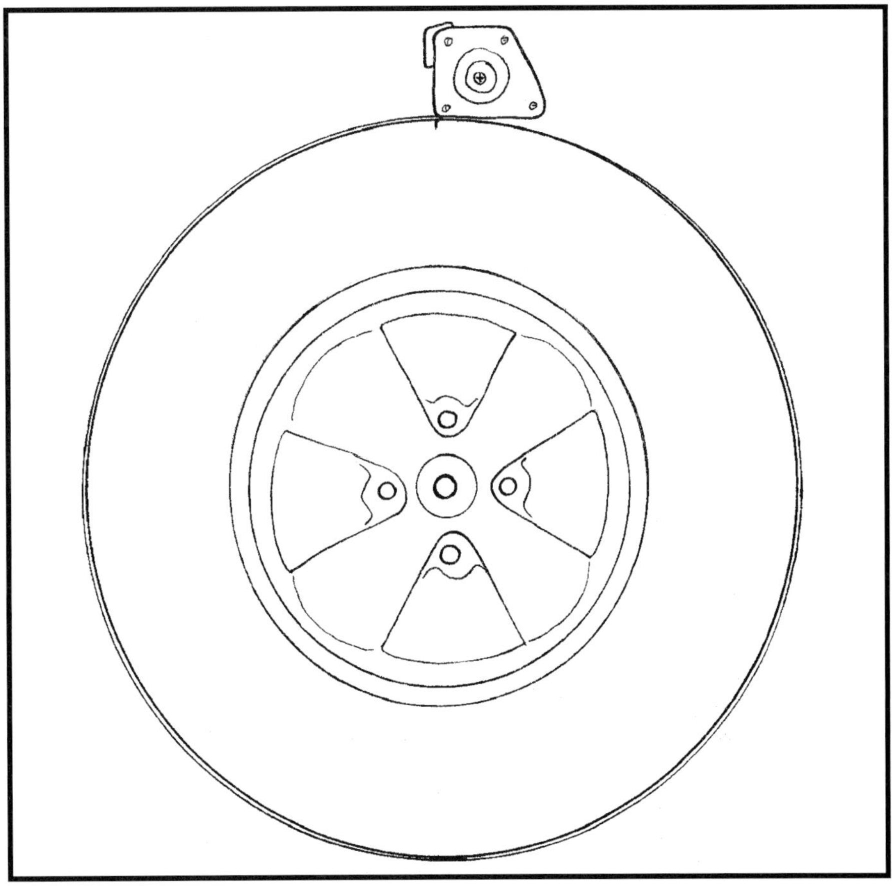

Tyre circumference being measured using a tape measure.

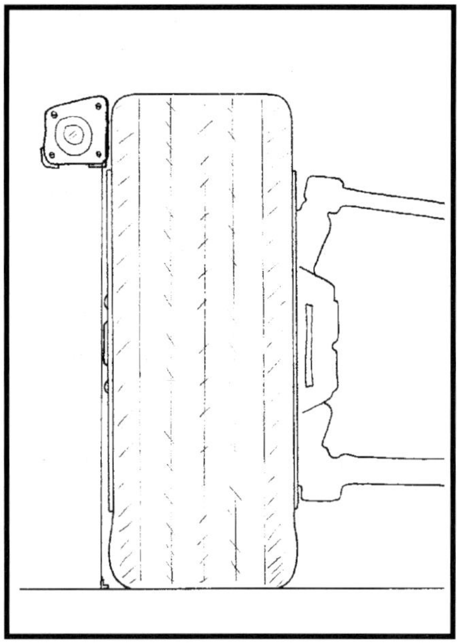

This wheel is being measured from the ground to the top of the wheel rim.

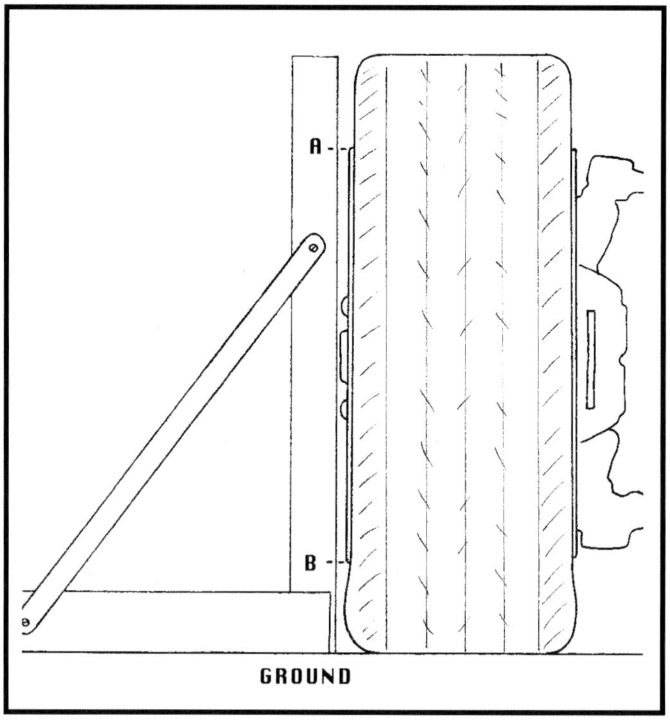

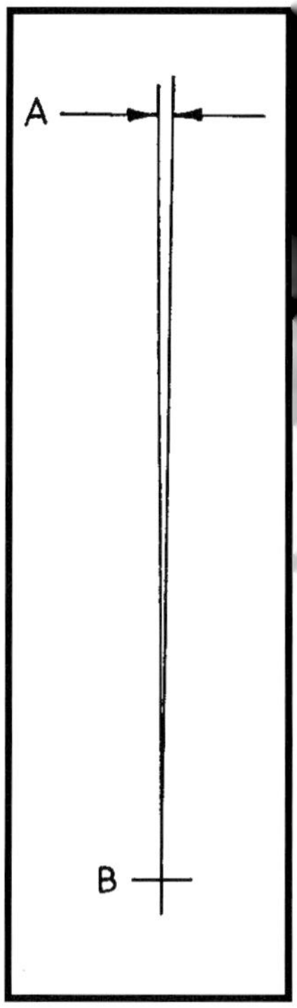

A set square is positioned next to the tyre. Measurements are taken between the edge of the set square and the top of the wheel rim (A), and the bottom of the wheel rim (B). The angle can then be calculated using the difference between the two measurements and a simple line drawing, as shown on the right.

significant factor when setting up a car. The two tyres on the front must be equal in circumference, as must the two tyres on the rear of the vehicle.

Measuring the circumference of a tyre is much more accurate than measuring the diameter of a tyre. This generally means that the tyres must be the same type and of the same size, although it is possible to have tyres from different manufacturers measuring exactly the same. It is not usual, or recommended, to mix tyres on the same axle or axis as tyre grip varies, even if they measure up as being identical in all other respects.

Check the diameter of each rim with a tape measure just to be sure that all rims are of the same diameter; they are usually very accurate, but a rim could have been remachined at some stage and this will lead to inaccuracies in the checking procedure. If a rim has been remachined, the difference between the two rims (divided by two) must be taken into account.

This checking system takes into account the deflection of the tyre with the weight of the car on it. The measurement is valid, and accurate to within 0.040in/1.0mm. With equal pressures in the two tyres on the same axle and the car's weight acting on the (front or rear) wheels, the rim heights should always be the same. With the suspension/steering geometry set correctly, the two tyres inflated to the same pressure, the chassis measuring points the same distance off the ground and the opposite end of the car completely raised off the ground (using a single central point), the rim heights should measure the same.

If the wheels on opposite sides of the car are of different diameters, the car and its suspension will not be square to the road and the wishbones will have different attitudes. The wheels on a 'live rear axle', or on a car with a limited slip differential, must **always** be of the same diameter. If they are not the same diameter the car will have what is called 'stagger'. In this instance (a sportscar) this can lead to some pretty undesirable handling characteristics with the greater the diameter difference leading to greater handling problems.

TYRE PRESSURES

Sportscars and kitcars are much lighter than saloon cars and, although they use the same tyres, the pressures are often going to be much less than what everyone is used to using in tyres. Having tyres that are over inflated for the weight of the car is not going to result in good handling characteristics.

Many lightweight sportscars which have very wide tyres will often respond very well to having tyre pressures of 15, 16, 17, 18, 19 or 20psi. The way to find out what your particular car requires is to test it with a range of tyre pressures and see which works best. Start with high pressures, such as 28psi, and drop the pressures by 2psi after each test down to 20psi, and then go down in 1 pound steps to a minimum of 15 pounds.

In many instances there will be a difference in the pressure requirements front to rear. A kitcar which has a heavy engine in the front, for example, will require slightly more pressure in the front tyres, perhaps 2 or 3psi more, than in the rear tyres. Always be prepared to increase or decrease the tyre pressures and find the right pressure for the car by experimentation.

If the whole car feels to be floating, and generally unstable in turns, the tyre pressures are likely to be too high. Conversely, lots of tyre noise in a turn is a definite indication of insufficient tyre pressure.

Run the tyres with the highest pressure in them that gives the best overall handling characteristics.

CHECKING NEGATIVE CAMBER

The static negative camber is checked when the car is on a dead level flat floor with the steering wheel locked in the straight ahead position (taped up, if necessary). The equipment needed to do this is a large set square and a metal rule. The set square needs to be 20x20in/50x50mm, and can be made up out of pieces of wood glued together if getting an appropriately-sized set square proves difficult: all that matters is that it be dead square, and long enough on one side to go from the floor to the top of the tyre.

Before proceeding, all of the tyres must be lifted off the ground and each wheel rotated to ensure that the rim is not buckled, which would give a faulty measurement. Wheels do get damaged, so it's a good idea to check them in this manner on a regular basis.

The chassis bottom suspension pick-up points must be measured to make sure they are the same height from the ground. If they are not, the chassis must be jacked up on the low side until they are. If the chassis pick-up points are not parallel with the floor, the suspension geometry will not be the same on each side of the car and the camber will not be the same on each side either.

With the car's chassis pick-up points in the right position, the camber can be measured by setting the square against the tyre. There is a problem when doing this as tyres bulge out at the bottom because of the car's weight; this means that the square cannot be positioned right up against the tyre top and bottom. To get around this, the set square is positioned against the sidewall bulge and a rule used to measure from the edge of the set square to the rim at the top and bottom. The difference between the two measurements is the figure, in conjunction with the diameter of the wheel rim, that is used.

With the diameter of the rim actually measured, and the two measurements taken from the set square, the figures can be used to calculate the angle of the wheel's camber or, simply, to construct a scale drawing and the angle formed in the drawing read off directly with a large protractor. Admittedly, this system is not dead accurate, but it is certainly accurate enough if due care is taken obtaining the measurements.

The wheels should ideally be checked at 10 degrees and 20 degrees of steering lock in both directions. Draw accurate 10 and 20 degree lines on the floor and line the wheels up with the lines and then use a set square to take reasonably accurate measurements as shown in the centre diagram on page 85. Put the measurements into a diagram/calculation as shown on the right of that page. You can actually do a remarkable amount of checking and setting up of a cars suspension yourself with just a few simple tools. The wheel camber changes as the steering wheel is turned. If a car is turning left, for instance, the left hand front wheel loses camber while the right-hand front wheel gains it. How much camber each wheel gains, or loses, when turned depends on how much the steering wheel is turned and how much castor and kingpin inclination there is built into the geometry.

As an alternative to the foregoing procedure, the car can be taken to a workshop that specialises in car wheel alignment (tyre shops almost always have the right equipment) - though it will still be necessary to ensure suspension pick-up points are at equal heights. There, the car can be checked using modern equipment and dead accurate measurements obtained, but, overall, the results from either method will be about the same. A possible advantage of having the camber checked on specialized equipment is that the wheel can be swivelled and the camber angles known throughout the arc of wheel turn.

In the first instance, the object of the exercise is to see whether the camber is the same on both front wheels, if not it should be adjusted to be so. Avoid camber angles (when both wheels are in the straight ahead position) of more than 1.5 degrees,

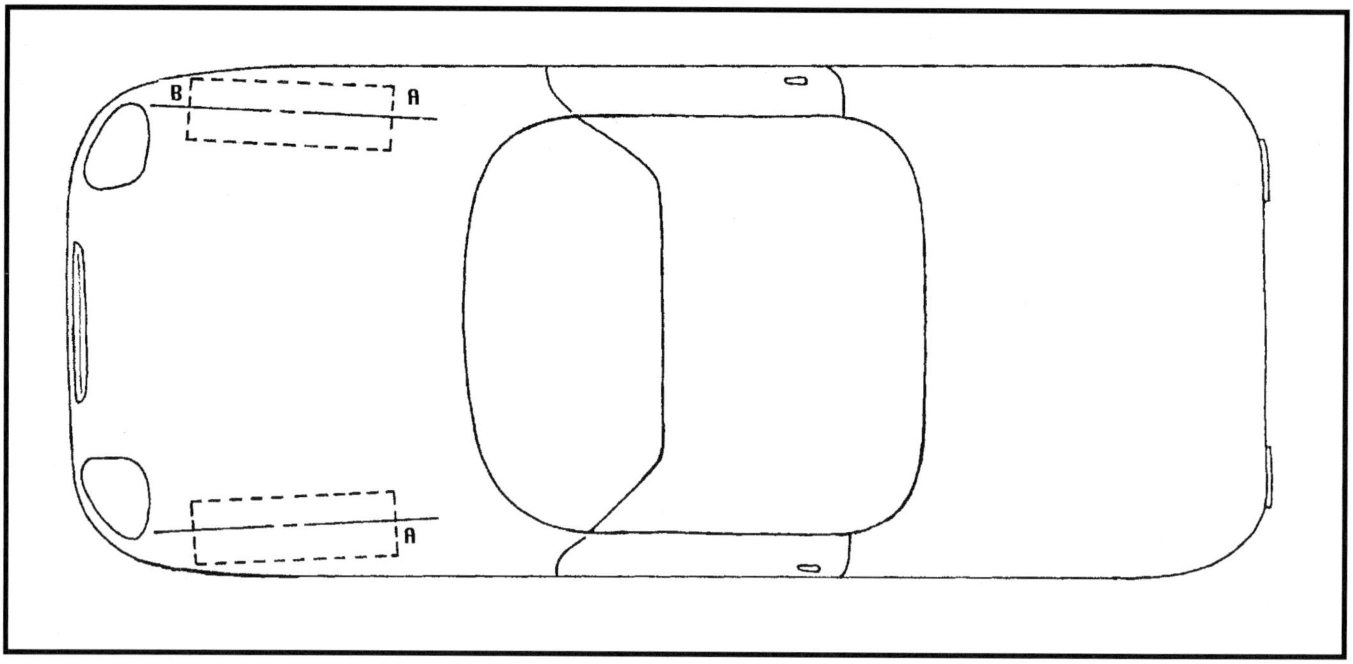

In this instance front wheels have toe-out. The lines (A-B & A-B) represent the centreline of each tyre's width. As the wheel rotates it remains on the same axis; consequently, the distance between A-A is smaller than B-B. This method of measuring toe-in or toe-out revolves around the principle of projecting lines down from "A" & "B" to the ground. The ground is marked and, once the car is removed, a tape measure is used to measure the distance between A-A & B-B.

and consider settings of between 0.5 and 1.5 degrees negative camber to be usual and ideal.

The checking of the camber changes by a wheel alignment shop or drawing degree lines on the floor and checking them roughly yourself is ideal for making sure that both wheels have the same amount of camber (positive or negative) on them at the same amount of steering lock. What this checking does not tell you is how much camber is right for your application. This can only be done by testing the car with however much camber is in the suspension and finding out whether it is right, too much or too little and then making alterations from the known settings.

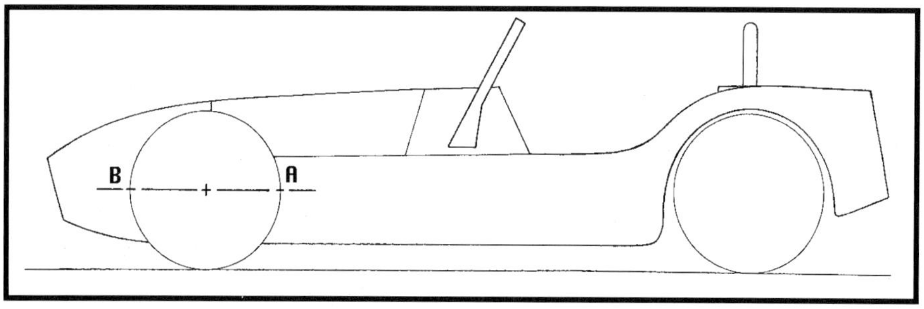

Each front tyre is marked at "A" which is approximately on the centre of the wheel (line A-B) in the middle of the tread (anywhere across the tread, it is not critical)). A white tipped pen is used for this purpose. A set square is used to project the two marks to the ground.

MEASURING AND CHECKING TOE-IN/TOE-OUT

An easy way of doing this, without sophisticated equipment, is on a flat and level floor. The only things needed are a white out correction pen which has a 1.0mm ball, a tape measure and an accurate, reasonably large, set square.

In the first instance check, using a tape measure, whether, or not, the two tie rod arms are the same length. These two arms **must** be adjusted to the same length, and any subsequent major adjustments (more than a quarter turn of a tie rod end) must not be made on one arm only. These two arms need to be within 0.040in/ 1.0mm of each other's length. Also check that the steering wheel is firmly locked in the straight ahead position (taped up, if necessary).

The car is then rolled back not

Tyre marked at A with a white pointed marking pen.

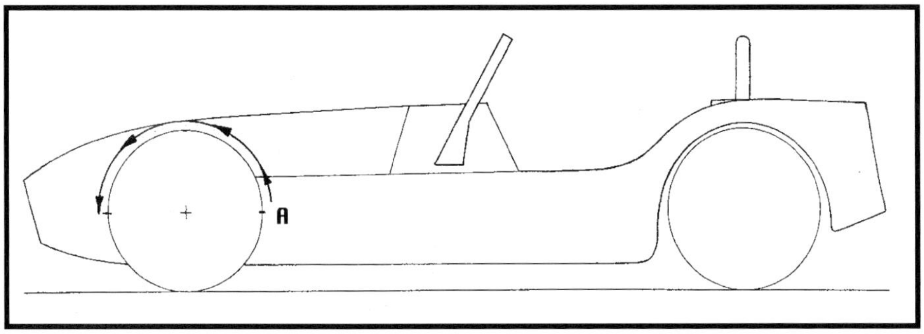

With both front tyres marked at the back at "A," the car is rolled forward so that the mark is now at the front of the tyre. A set square is then used to project the position of the marks to the ground. The difference between the two front marks as measured (effectively across the car) and the two rearmost marks is the toe-out.

less than 3 feet/1 metre, and then rolled forward to settle the tyres. The two tyres (front or rear, whichever are being checked) are marked at the back on the tread area at exactly half tyre height. The marks need only be 0.5in/ 12mm long. Using a large set square, the marks on the tyres are then transferred to the floor and the floor marked. Next, the car is rolled forwards until the white lines on the tyres are again at half tyre height, but now at the front (*i.e.* half a wheel revolution). The set square is again lined up with the white lines drawn on the tyres and the floor marked.

The car is then rolled back out of the way and a tape measure used to measure the distance between the front pair of lines and then the back pair of lines. If the distance between the front pair of lines is greater than the distance between the back pair of lines, the car has toe-out. If the distance between the back pair of lines is greater than the distance between the front pair of lines, the car has toe-in. The difference between the two measurements is the amount of toe-in/ toe-out. If an adjustment is needed, make the alteration and check the toe again. Remove all previous marks from the tyres and the floor before doing this. This is quite an accurate way of checking the toe-in/toe-out of any pair of wheels (front or back), if done carefully.

Another way of checking the toe of a car is, for example, to use a Gunson's 'Trakrite' drive-over wheel alignment gauge, which is reasonably inexpensive and very easy to use. The gauge is used to check each wheel (front or rear) of the car in turn. With this gauge the car is wheeled over the gauge and the degrees of toe read directly off a scale. An important point is that this gauge can be used to check the rear wheels of a car and, more specifically, identify which wheels show incorrect toe if the suspension has been set up incorrectly. The scale on the Trackrite reads degrees, but if toe-out is required, the pointer needs to be at the edge of the "OK" portion of the scale on the toe-out side; if toe-in is required, the pointer needs to be at the edge of the toe-in side of the "OK" portion of the scale.

It's possible to have slight toe-out on one wheel and excessive toe-in on the other. The gauge will pick up this problem straight away. These gauges are available from Gunson's head office in Britain or America, as well as retail outlets.

WHEEL WEIGHTS

"Wheel weight" (the amount of the car's total weight apportioned to each individual wheel - not the weight of the wheel itself) is important if a car is to handle correctly. Many cars are never checked to see how weight is apportioned to individual wheels. This procedure is often regarded as being applicable only to sophisticated racing cars, but this is just not true. It does not take too much wheel weight imbalance to cause handling problems.

If the wheel weights are not equal side to side of the car, the car will definitely not handle well. However, a wheel weight imbalance is often used to advantage on cars that only turn in one direction, such as oval track racing cars.

In many instances, people are put off even thinking about weighing the wheels of their car because they've seen racing cars being weighed using sophisticated weighing systems (which comprise four specially-designed sets of scales, all linked to a control panel). A near equally good result is possible for anyone who has a flat and level floor, a small trolley jack and a tape measure.

The next issue to consider is the relationship between the suspension geometry and the wheel weights of a loaded car (the driver's weight comes into the equation). The geometry of a two-seater sportscar is always set up without the driver in the car (or at least initially). The suspension geometry needs to be identical side to side of the car, irrespective of what each wheel's loaded weight is and, unless the driver is sitting in the centre of the car, there is almost always going to be an element of compromise. On any single seater car, where the driver is centrally situated, his or her weight is equally dispersed side to side and front to rear and there is no compromise. With two-seater sportscars, if the driver and a passenger are of roughly equal weight then, again, there is no real compromise.

If a two-seater car is mainly going to carry only one person, the effect on suspension geometry is not as great as you might think because the driver's weight is actually carried by all four wheels, though possibly slightly disproportionately. The driver is not usually all that heavy, relative to the rest of the car, and the driver's seat is usually closer to the centre of the car than its side, this means that the difference in wheel weights side to side is usually not great and, for convenience, is often disregarded.

The way to check whether or not your car is going to be affected by the driver sitting slightly off the centre line of the car is to actually sit the driver in the car (or substitute the weight of the driver in the seat position) when the car is in the setting up position as described in this chapter.

In the first instance the car should be wheel weighted without the driver's weight being taken into account. Good handling - as in being felt through the seat of the pants, or measured in lap times and how easy the car is to handle over the course - are the real guide to how 'good' the car is.

Keep in mind that in many instances things like the battery and fuel tank can be relocated to balance wheel weights and/or offset the driver's weight. Placing the battery low down in the chassis and on the opposite side of the car to the driver is almost always a good idea.

Even after all this work has been done, there is still the problem of the forces which act on the car in a cornering situation. G-forces are often considerable: it's possible to have the two inner wheels of the car virtually off the road surface in a very fast tight turn because, in this situation, those two wheels are very lightly loaded, with nearly all of the car's weight acting on the two outer wheels. This, believe it or not, is seldom a serious problem if the car's suspension geometry is correct: if the wheels are positioned by the geometry to support the tyre and not roll the tyre off the wheels rim, the car will still be reasonably stable even though it has become, in essence, a two wheel vehicle.

Clearly, stationary wheel weights are not the same as those which apply when the car is moving. However, if a car is set up statically, the data can be used as a base setting in relation to which wheel weights can be adjusted. If, after testing and experimenting with wheel weights, you decide that the car's handling is deteriorating, or you're getting a bit lost, you know exactly what to go back to.

The wheel weights of any car can be checked without using scales. Admittedly, the actual amount of weight acting on each wheel will not be known, but the weight acting on each wheel will be the same and that is all that matters for good handling. The one thing that is vital when using the method of setting the wheel weights suggested in this book, is that the floor **must** be **absolutely level**. If the floor is not dead level, the wheel weights will not be set right. The weight of the driver, or driver and passenger, is not taken into account in this instance.

For competition purposes, where the car is only going to have the driver in it, the weight of the driver *can* be added to the equation. In such cases, the driver sits in the car but must remain still. Alternatively, deadweight, equivalent to the weight of the driver, is placed on the driver's seat. Always test the car after setting the wheel weights to take into account the driver's weight: there is not always an improvement in handling because, depending on spring stiffness, the driver's weight may have little affect on individual wheel weights. On the basis of consistency, it can be easier to set the wheel weights of the car without the driver.

With every other aspect of the geometry checked on a car and correctly set up, the wheel weights can be checked and, if necessary, adjusted. The following check list must be completed before continuing -

1) The wheel circumferences must be identical (front to front/rear to rear).

2) The tyre pressures must be identical (front to front/rear to rear).

Car with independent front suspension & live rear axle

Warning! - before going beneath the car to take measurements, ensure that axle stands (jack stands) are in place to 'catch' the car if the jack gives way. **Do not** rely on a jack alone.

In the first instance, measure to the centre of the differential casing and mark it with a white correction pen or with a dab of white paint. Better still, get an expert to weld a short leg - that a trolley jack can contact as the jack lifts the back of the car - onto the

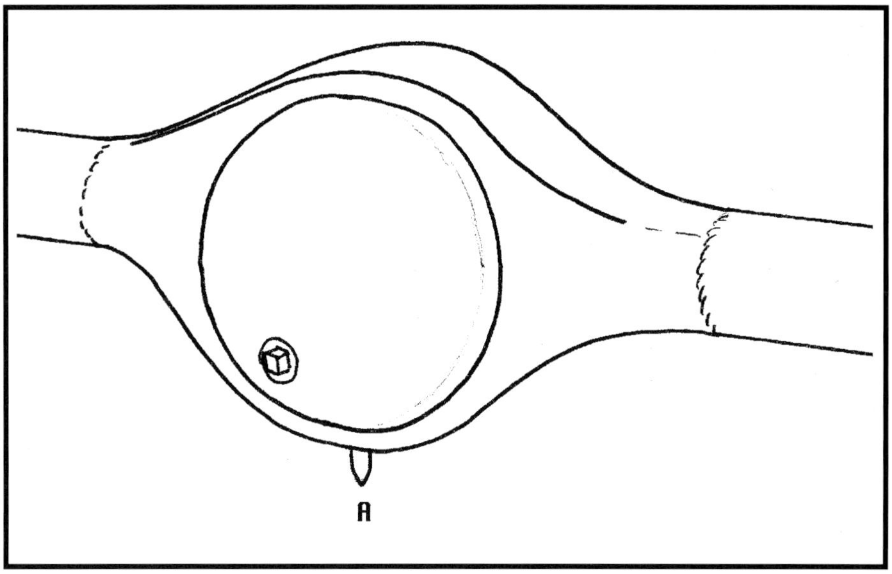

Short leg (A) welded to the bottom of differential casing.

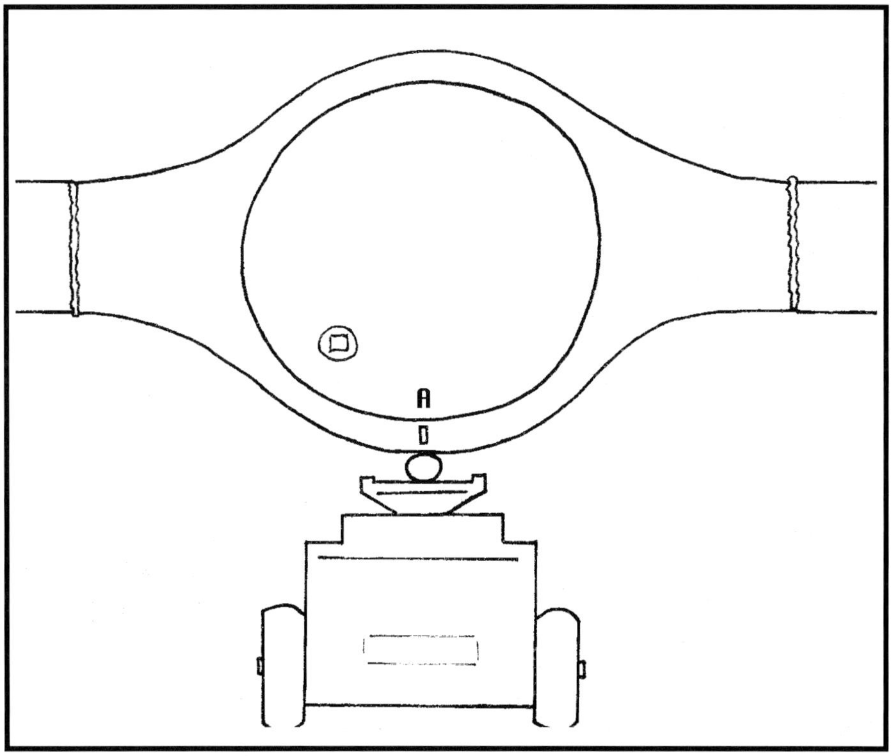

Trolley jack with a round metal bar placed between its pad and the centre of the differential casing.

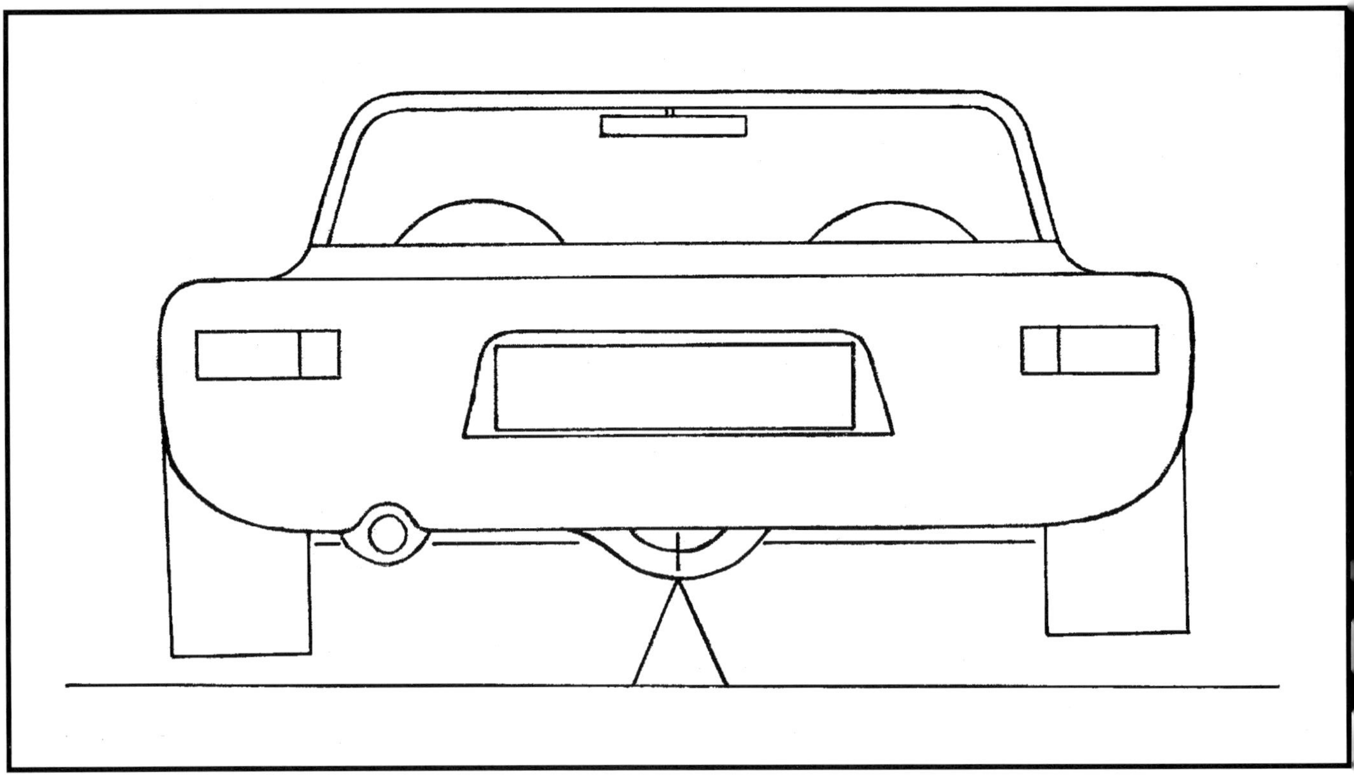

Rear of car is raised until both rear wheels are off the ground.

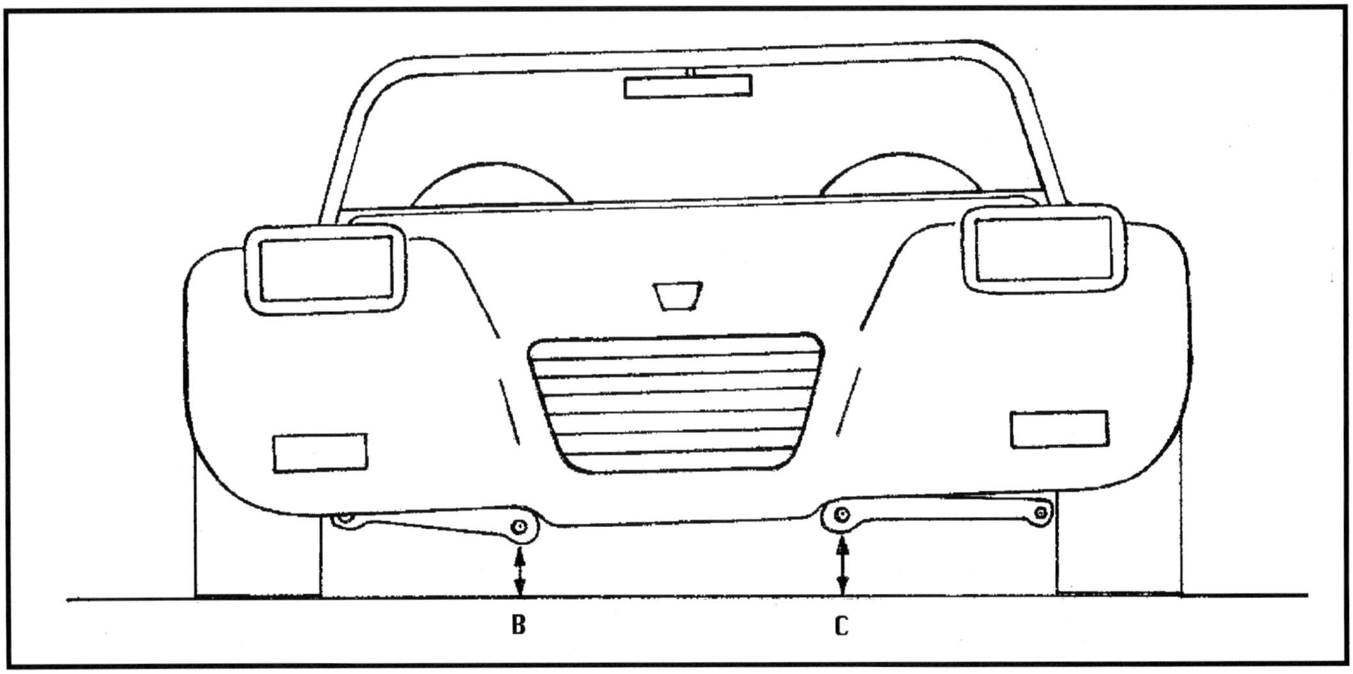

If the car leans to one side, as here, adjust the front spring platforms or reduce tension in one spring until the car is level. Measure from the ground up to the two lower chassis pick-up points (B & C).

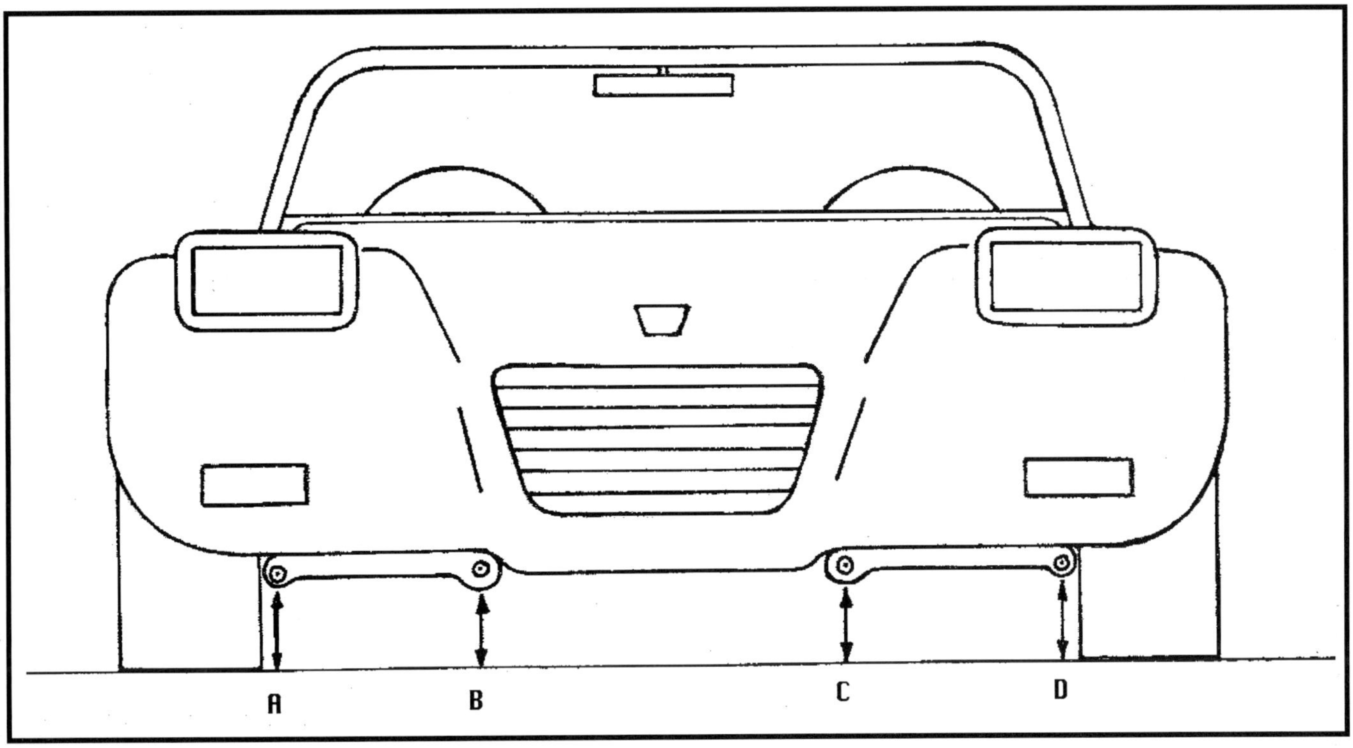

"B" & "C" must be the same height from the ground (within 0.040in/1mm or 0.080in/2.0mm absolute maximum). "A" & "D" should also be the same height from the ground within the same tolerance. Tyres must be of the same circumfrence and at the same pressure.

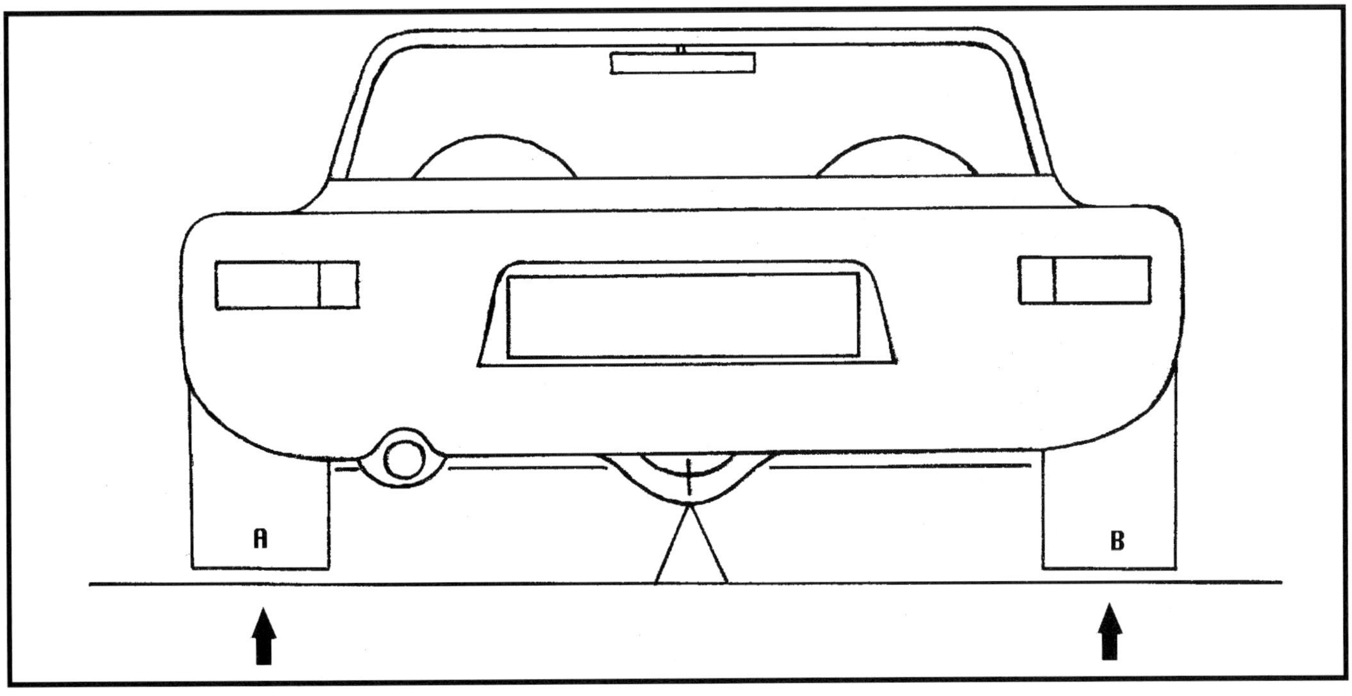

With the wheel weighting at the front of the car known to be correct, the rear of the car is also correctly weighted if there is an equal gap under both rear wheels (A & B).

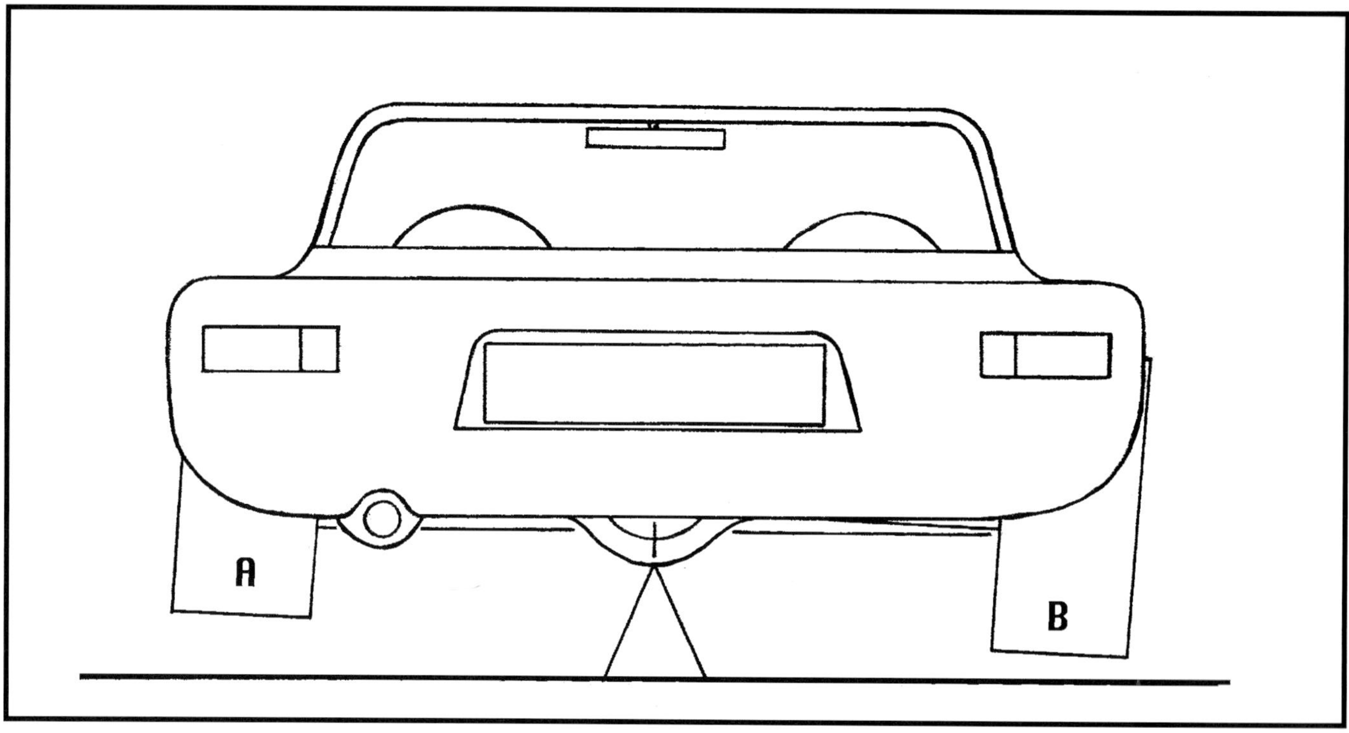

Rear wheel weights are well out at as shown by unequal gap (A & B) between tyre and ground side to side. Increase the spring tension for wheel "A" and reduce spring tension for wheel "B."

differential casing. This way it is positively known that every time the wheel weights are checked, this point is in the centre of the rear axle.

A small trolley jack is positioned under the differential casing and the car is lifted up. There is room for error here as the lifting pad of most trolley jacks is at least 3in/75mm in diameter so, to improve this situation, place a socket set extension bar across the top of the trolley jack lifting pad and, with the extension bar positioned directly inline with the centre mark on the axle, lift the car up until both rear wheels are off the ground.

Go to the front of the car and, using a tape measure, check the distance from the floor to the bottom suspension arm pick-up points. These two measurements must be identical. If they are not the front suspension spring platforms must be adjusted until they are. Bear in mind that when a spring base platform is altered, the car will be raised or lowered on that side. Alter one spring platform to lower one side of the car and then alter the other to raise the other side of the car. This way, the overall central ride height will not be altered, but the chassis pick-up points on one side of the car will rise while the other will lower. The chassis pick-up points should be at equal heights from the ground to within 0.040in/1.0mm of each other (0.080/2.00mm absolute maximum). Setting up of the front of the car is now complete.

Caution! - Do not adjust the adjustment collars of a coil-over shock absorber while the weight of the car is acting on that particular wheel. Jack up the corner of the car sufficiently to allow easy movement of the collar. Use a pin spanner to turn the collar and two pin spanners to lock the collars. Spanners like this are readily available or can be made up. Burred-over collars look terrible.

With the spring platforms adjusted so that the chassis bottom pick-up points are exactly the same distance from the ground, release the trolley jack, push the car back 20 feet/7 metres, or so, and then bring the car back on to the level floor area again. The idea of moving the car back is to settle the springs and shock absorbers so that the car is at its correct ride height.

Reposition the trolley jack under the differential casing and lift the car up sufficiently to raise the rear wheels off the ground about 0.5in/12.5mm. Go to the front of the car and re-measure the distance from the floor to the bottom pick-up points. When the distances are identical the task is

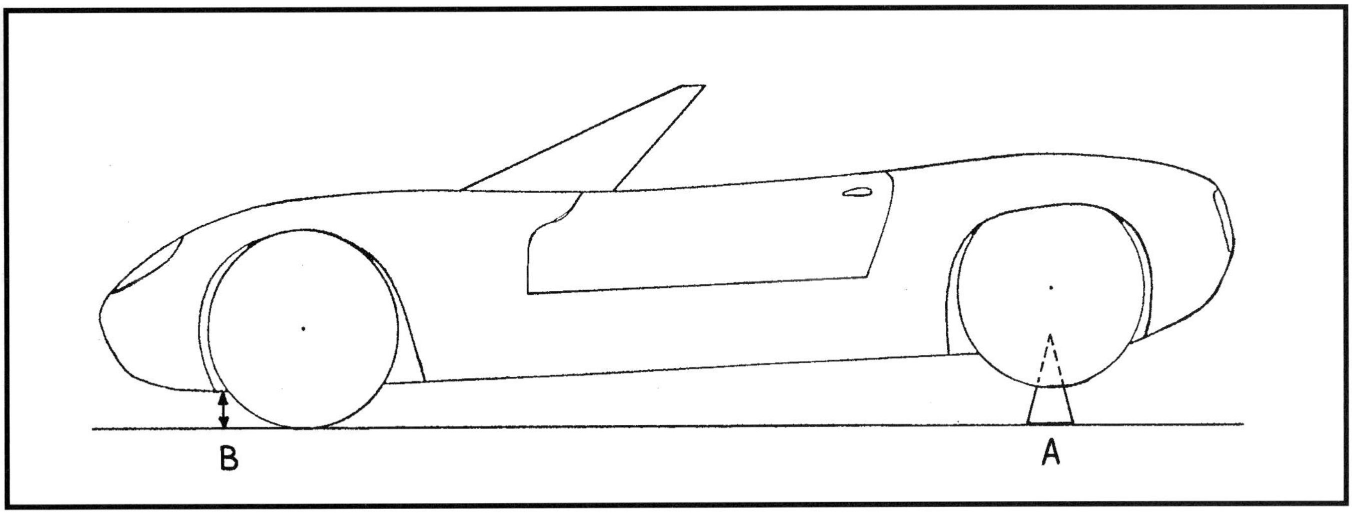

Support the rear of the car at the centre of the axle (A). Measure the height of the front suspension pick-up points (B) at the front of the car. Measurements must be equal side to side.

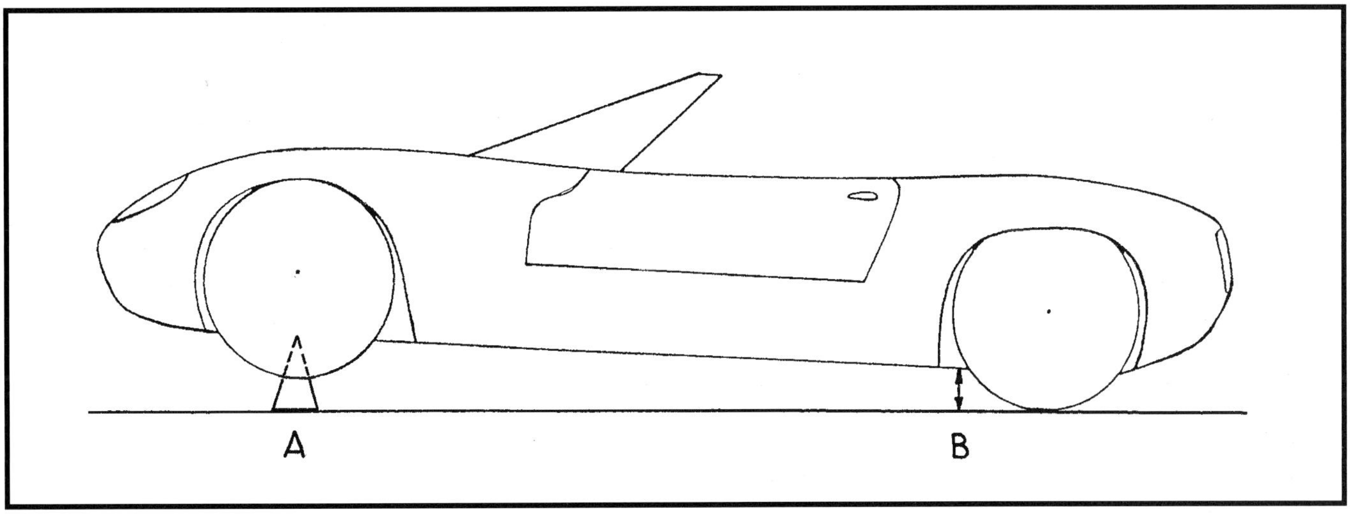

Support the front of the car at axle centre (A). Measure the distance from the ground to the rear suspension pick-up points (B). Distances must be equal side to side.

complete. Now go to the back of the car and check to see what size the gaps are between the rear wheels and the floor. If the gaps are identical the wheel weights are correct. If they are not, raise the spring platform of the coil-over shock absorber of the wheel which has the biggest gap and lower the spring platform of the wheel which is closest to the ground. The gaps **must** be equalized.

At this point the driver or another person who weighs the same as the driver must sit in the drivers seat of the car or weights the total weight of the driver must be placed where the driver sits (seat out) and the gaps under the rear wheels looked at again to see whether or not there is any change. No change in the gap size side to side of the car means that the weight of the driver has had no or little effect on the weigh acting on the wheels. Check the distance up from the ground to the lower front suspension arm pick up points on the chassis. No change means that there has been no measurable weight transfer apportioning.

If there is any loss of gap on one side of the car at the rear and an increase in the gap size on the other side of the car the coil over shocks can be adjusted to compensate by making the gaps equal again. The front suspension can be adjusted by altering the measurement heights so that they are equal side to side. It takes quite a heavy driver for this to have to happen. Having the drivers seat as close to the centre line of the car is important!

With the gaps equalized on the rear wheels, the two front wheels will have equal weight on them and so will the two rear wheels. Release the trolley jack and check the ride height of the car. This completes wheel weighting of this type of car. The crucial points are to jack the rear axle centrally, make sure that the front suspension arms are set to the right geometry and then adjust the rear suspension to suit.

Car with independent front & rear suspension

Warning! - before going beneath the car to take measurements, ensure that axle stands (jack stands) are in place to 'catch' the car if the jack gives way. **Do not** rely on a jack alone.

This is a little bit more complicated than checking a car with an independent front suspension and a live axle. In the first instance, the rear of the car is raised (using a trolley jack) off the ground until the rear tyres are just clear. The point of jacking **must** be **dead centre** of the car, and as close to the rear of the car as possible. **Caution!** - Any point used to jack the car must be substantial enough to take the weight without damage. Some suitable point must be found and measured and marked as being central. Point contact by the trolley jack lifting pad is essential so place a socket set extension bar between the trolley jack lifting pad and the car.

Go to the front of the car and measure from the ground to the front suspension bottom pick-up points on each side of the car. If they are exactly equal no further adjustment is required. If they are not equal (the most likely situation), the spring platforms must be adjusted until the measurements are exactly equal. Take the weight off the corner of the car being adjusted so that it is easy to turn the spring platform collars of the coil-over shock absorbers or, if the car doesn't have coil-over shock absorbers, pack up the spring on the low side of the car. After each adjustment settle the car back again by removing the trolley jack from the rear of the car, rolling the car back 20 feet/ 7 metres, or so, and then bringing the car forward again and carrying out the checking procedure again. Adjust until the measurements are exactly right.

Now go to the back of the car and measure from the ground to the rearmost bottom arm chassis pick-up points. These two points are used as reference points to link the front of the car to the rear of the car. The two measurements side to side of the car should be the same (front and rear can, of course, be different). Measure the distance from the ground to these points on each side of the car. If the chassis is square the measurements will be the same. An acceptable amount of error is 0.040in/1.0mm (0.080in/2.0mm absolute maximum) but, ideally, there should be none. This all comes down to how accurately the chassis has been made. A chassis which has the suspension pick-up points welded to it, must have them accurately positioned and, if they are not accurate to within 0.040in/1.0mm (0.080in/2.0mm absolute maximum), they should be removed and relocated. Not to do this is folly. Make a note of any slight error as this will have to be allowed for in the next part of the sequence.

The amount of chassis error can be split between the front or rear geometry or, if it is a very small amount (0.020in/0.5mm), compensated for in the rear suspension. The point being that correct front geometry is slightly more important because the directional stability of the car is vital, whereas slight rear instability is usually more easily accommodated.

If the rear suspension is attached to the car via a subframe, it needs to be moved so that the suspension points are equal distances from the ground. Usually, the subframe can be packed up with spacers to get it into alignment with the front of the car. If the chassis is slightly out it doesn't matter, provided the subframe can be moved and trued-up in relation to the front suspension pick-up points. It is almost always easier to move or adjust the rear suspension subframe than to start altering front suspension componentry.

Note that the distance from the ground to the chassis pick-up points is determined by the suspension geometry and attitude decided on earlier. The attitude of the car is altered to make the distances from the ground to the chassis pick-up points equal side to side of the car, but the ride height must be maintained.

Remove the trolley jack from the back of the car and take it to the front. Find a suitable jacking point as near to the very front of the car as possible and, after determining the exact central point, jack up the car until the two front tyres are just off the ground (0.25in/6mm). Point contact of the trolley jack lifting pad is essential, so place a socket set extension bar between the jack lifting pad and the car. **Caution!** - Any point used to jack the car must be substantial enough to take the weight without damage.

Go to the rear of the car and measure from the ground to the bottom chassis pick-up points. The distances from the ground need to be equal, or the springs adjusted until the measurments are equal (if the chassis is not straight, the springs are adjusted to compensate for any slight amount of error). That is, if one side was measured as being, say, 0.040in/ 1.0mm higher when the rear wheels were jacked up and off the ground, the amount of error is now allowed for. The point being that it is better to have any error in the rear suspension than in the front suspension, but only a small amount (0.040in/1.0mm). Ideally, there will be no error but 0.040in/1.0mm is not a lot in the overall scheme of things.

Assuming that there is error, the suspension must be adjusted by altering the spring platforms so that the chassis pick-up points are an equal distance from the ground. Jack up the corner of the car up to be adjusted, to remove the weight from the spring platform, before adjusting it. Re-settle the car after the adjustments have been made by removing the trolley jack, moving the car back 20 feet/7 metres, or so, and then bringing the car forward and setting it up again.

Once the rear suspension has been adjusted accurately, go to the front of the car and measure from the ground to the bottom pick-up points that were measured in the first instance. These points are now used as reference points to link the rear of the car to the front of the car, and to cross reference (with the previous reference measurements taken at the back of the car). The measurements should both be the same side to side of the car. With these two procedures completed, the end of the car which has its wheels on the ground has been individually set up, while the other end has had its chassis pick-up points measured to see that they too are an equal distance from the ground. If the chassis has been accurately made, the distances will all be equal.

The final check is made after the trolley jack has been removed and the car rolled back a suitable distance (20 feet/7 metres, or so) and then bought forward to settle the suspension/ chassis. The four individual pick-up points are then measured up to from the ground. This is done to ensure that the geometry and ride height is correct and to make sure that the pick-up points used also measure up against each other when all four wheels are on the ground. Any measured height error must be allowed for if the wheel weights are to be accurate, meaning that the side to side wheel weights are more important than slight geometry error. It is better to have a slight error in the suspension geometry than it is to have large error in the side to side wheel weights.

At this point the driver, or a person who weighs the same as the driver, should get into the driver's seat and the measurements from the ground up to the chassis pickup points (front and rear) all be taken again as a repeat procedure. If there is any difference they can be adjusted for by altering the coil over shocks so that the measurements are the same side to side of the car. It takes quite a heavy driver to make a difference, especially if the driver's seat is near the centre line of the car.

The ideal is, of course, to have the suspension geometry in perfect alignment, the pick-up point heights correct side to side and the wheel weights exactly the same side to side, with no error anywhere.

Chapter 10
Vehicle testing & adjustments

With the car set up to this book's recommended settings, it needs to be tested because all sorts of variables can affect stability. Even if the settings are right in theory, in practice things can be quite different. For example, if a sportscar has been set up with toe-out, expect it to need virtually constant steering attention, because it will wander to a small degree if the driver is inattentive. This is part of the price of having a car set up for optimal cornering performance: however, when cornering hard, directional stability will be excellent and the car will be able to negotiate curves with that 'on rails' feeling.

WHEEL ALIGNMENT

Before the car is taken to a track or other off road tarmacked venue for testing, the following procedure can be carried out to double-check all of the previously recommended setting up work. It is pretty pointless going to all of the trouble of taking a car to a track for a test day without double checking everything first.

With the car on a flat, level floor (checked as being so), turn the steering wheel so that the two front wheels are in the straight ahead position (visually).

Now check that the two tie rod arms are the same lengths when measured with a tape measure. This will involve a little guesswork because of the rack's rubber boots and the track rod ends' rubber boots. However, a very close approximation can be made: the object of the exercise being to make sure that the two tie rod arms are as near as possible the same lengths, centre to centre (that's the centre of the steering rack ball joint to the centre of the tie rod end ball joint). Adjust the tie rods ends if necessary so that the tie rod arms are the same length.

Roll the car backwards and forwards a few times, a distance of 10 yards/10 metres, or so, to 'settle' the suspension and to make sure that the car is steering straight and not turning. Then tape (duct tape) the steering wheel so that it can't move. Using a Gunson's Trackrite gauge or similar, roll the two front wheels over the Trackrite gauge and see if the two wheels have equal toe, whether it be toe-in or toe-out.

The likely scenario is that they will not have the same toe setting. Undo the tape holding the steering wheel in a fixed position and turn it a slight amount to make a correction. If the right hand front wheel has more toe-out (or less toe-in) than the left hand front, turn the steering wheel to the left, or vice versa. Re-secure the steering wheel and roll the car backwards and forwards a few times to settle the suspension again. Then roll the car over the Trackrite gauge as before.

When the two front wheels toe equally, if necessary, reposition the steering wheel on its splines so that it is in an easily recognisable central position. Most sports steering wheels are three spoked which means that they are generally designed to have one spoke at about 10 o'clock, one at 2 o'clock and the third downward pointing spoke in the 6 o'clock position. There is some variation in the designs of steering wheels but, essentially, all that has to be done is to have the steering wheel in an easily recognisable straight ahead position.

Once this adjustment has been made, the steering wheel need only be turned to the known straight ahead position and it will be positively known that this is the central steering position. When the car is driven straight on a level road or track, the steering wheel will always be in this position (extreme camber roads excepted). The steering wheel position is now a checked reference point for the straight ahead position.

With the two front wheels set equally, check that they have the correct toe setting. If it is necessary to adjust the toe it means adjusting each track rod arm equally. Take it that zero toe is the minimum setting for the majority of sportscars, as opposed to actually having toe-in. Check the vehicle's handbook and see what the factory recommended tolerance is on the toe setting. If you are going to run with toe-in, always set to the minimum. The factory will always list a minimum and a maximum. To prove once and for all what your particular car responds to best with regard to toe, test the car with 0.125in/3.2mm toe-in, then with zero toe and finally with o,125in/3.2mm of toe-out. You can do this during your test day.

The car now has a correctly set steering wheel, the two front wheels set with the required amount of toe and the two tie rods the same centre to centre length. Now roll the two rear wheels over the Trackrite gauge.

If the car has a live rear axle the gauge will give a zero reading if the axle is accurately positioned, meaning that the two rear wheels are in the straight ahead position. If the gauge does not show this and one wheel has toe-in and the other toe-out, the axle is not straight across the car and needs to be adjusted by whatever means is available. If the rear axle is left like this the car will oversteer when the rear wheel with the toe-out is on the outside of the turn and vice versa.

If the car has an independent rear suspension, the two rear wheels must have toe-in and an equal amount. This is where this sort of tracking gauge is an advantage because it gives an individual reading for each tyre. Toe-out is no good at all on an independent rear suspension assembly, and leads to oversteer and rear wheel steer (rear of the car instability over undulations). What happens with a independent rear suspension car that goes into toe-out over undulations is that, as the wheel attains toe-out, it steers the car slightly in that direction: this is very disconcerting. Adjust any independent rear suspension so that it has toe-in. Consider 0.125in/3.2mm to be the average setting that will be successful (that's 0.0625in/1.5mm per wheel).

WHEEL WEIGHTS

Most two-seater sportscars are checked for wheel weight (the weight acting on the wheel, not what the wheel weighs) with the weight of the car itself being all that is used to apportion weight to each wheel. Just because a car has four wheels it does not mean that each wheel has the same amount of weight acting on it. If a car weighs 1600 pounds and has a weight distribution factor, front to rear, of 55/45 (that's 55% of the car's total weight acting on the front wheels and 45% on the rear wheels), it means there will be 880 pounds at the front of the car and 720 pounds at the rear of the car.

Whether or not this front/rear weight is apportioned equally to each wheel on an axle is another matter. If the weight is apportioned equally it would mean 440 pounds acting on each front wheel and 360 pounds on each rear wheel. If the weight is apportioned equally the car will handle better.

Ideally, the weight at the front and rear will be apportioned equally side to side of the car but, in practice, this is not always possible. The weight side to side of the car can vary considerably, and this can be the cause of serious handling problems. What is often not understood is that weight is also apportioned diagonally across the car.

In our example 880 pounds act on the front two wheels and 720 pounds act on the rear two wheels; however, instead of 440 pounds acting

55% of the weight is apportioned to the front of this car and 45% to the rear.

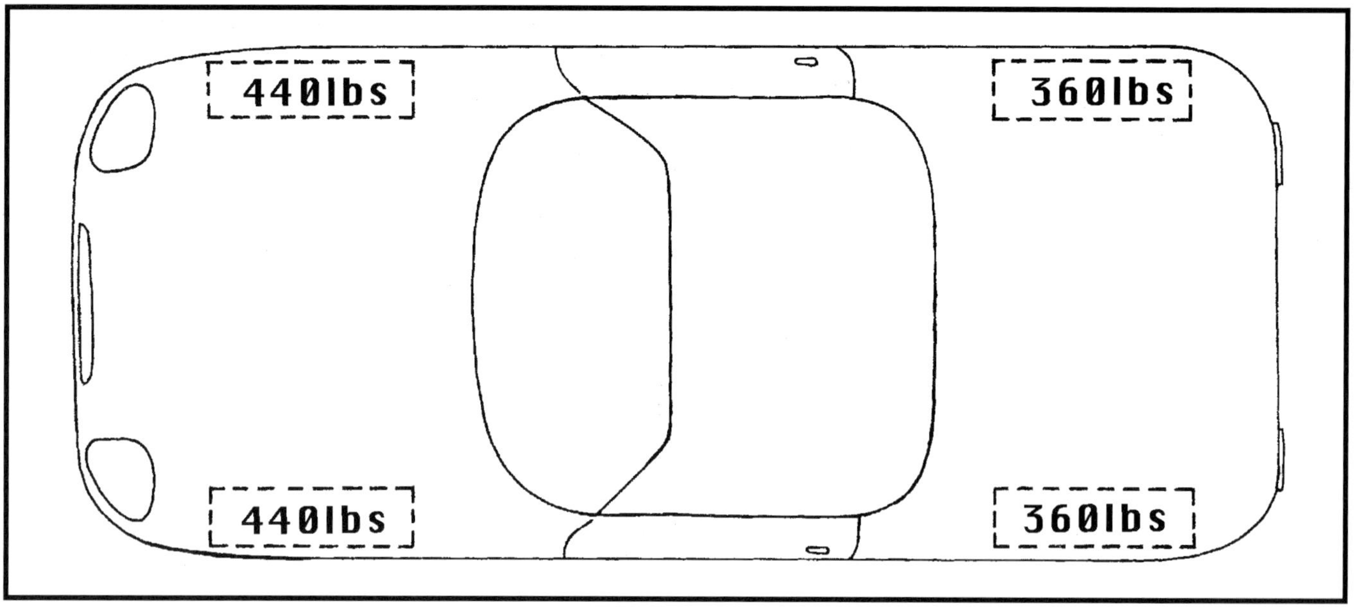

Weight acting on each wheel is equal side to side of this car, but not front to rear.

on each front wheel and 360 pounds on each rear wheel, things can, in fact, be quite different. If the spring heights are adjusted when wheel weights are far from equal (per axle) the car might well have a reasonable looking stance, with the suspension components having roughly the right attitude, but that might be all the car has going for it. For example, the discrepancy in wheel weights could well be 540 pounds in the left front, 450 pounds in the right rear, 340 pounds in the right front and 270 pounds in the left rear.

In most instances, sportscars are made with the heavy bits like engines, clutches, gearboxes, radiator and fuel tank, for example, placed on the centreline of the car so that the weight of these items can be equally displaced to the wheels side to side of the car.

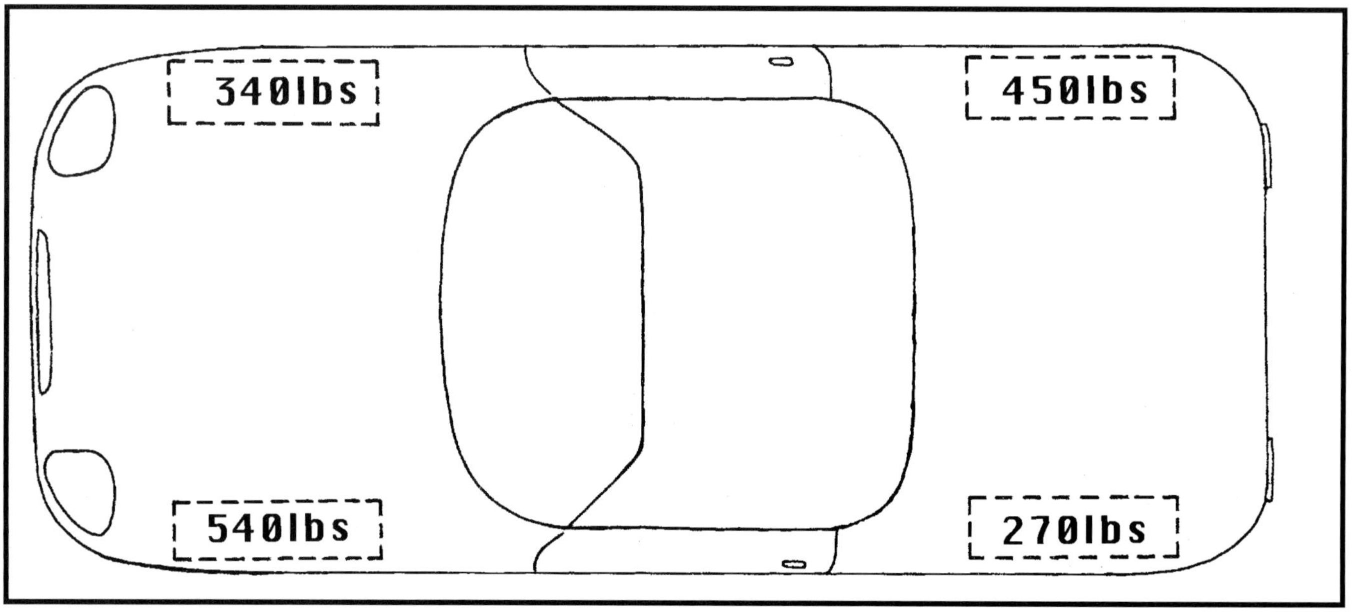

Wheel weights are quite different side to side of this car.

There is, however, a bit more to it than this because the apportioned weight of the front of the car, and the apportioned weight of the rear of the car is displaced to each wheel via the springs (of whatever type). This is a very significant point because, if the springs are not adjusted correctly, the fact that the bulk of the car's weight is centrally situated will not mean that it is equally apportioned.

This is why it is imperative as a criteria to have equally rated springs side to side of a car, and to set them for equal poundage displacement to each wheel. This is also why having adjustable spring platforms is an excellent idea as slight changes to spring tension can be made quite easily. Test all springs for poundage at the same compressed heights.

This situation of unequal wheel weights arises, for instance, when, say, the spring of the right rear wheel of a car is applying more pressure to the body/chassis than it should (damaged componentry, weak spring, incorrectly adjusted spring platform). The balance of the displaced weight will predominantly go diagonally across the car to the left front wheel and not to the right front wheel as you might think. The left hand front wheel spring tension could be increased until the attitude of the car improves, but the wheel weights will still be incorrect.

It is quite possible for a car to have reasonable-looking geometry but wildly different wheel weights. Essentially, what is happening, for example, is that the left hand front wheel and the right hand rear wheel are taking the majority of the weight of the car. The right hand front wheel and the left hand rear wheel, while still bearing plenty of weight, are not supporting the car (weight-wise) as they should, which will show up when the car is driven fast.

If a car with grossly uneven wheel weights is driven fast, when it is turned left, for example, it will tend to oversteer as it exits the corner. The car will (if the geometry is about right), turn into the corner very well because the left hand front wheel is heavily loaded (a lot of static weight on it). As the car goes into the corner more, the right rear wheel, which is also very highly loaded (a lot of static weight on it), goes into an oversteer situation. These are not the actions of a good handling sportscar but it's common enough. Cars set up like this are difficult to drive, to say the least.

These features can, of course, be used to advantage if the car is only turning left hand corners or right hand corners (oval racing, for instance). This, however, is not the usual environment of a sportscar which has to do all things well. Grossly mismatched wheel weights are the problem (not minor wheel weight mismatches). If the springs are soft, the effect of uneven wheel weights is almost always going to be worse than when the springs are quite firm.

The recommendation is to wheel weight the average two-seater sportscar which weighs 1500 pounds or more (and that is most of them) using only the weight of the car. Certainly, for general road use this is

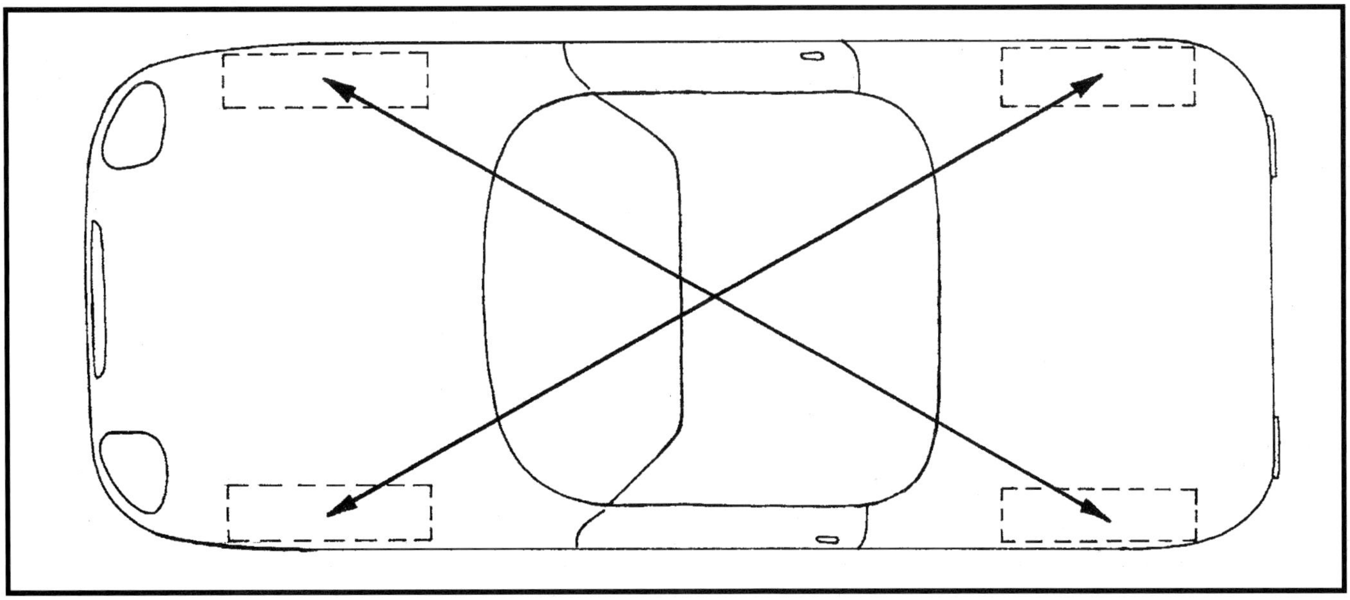

Weight predominantly goes diagonally across the car.

all that's required, whether there be one person in the car or two.

Most sportscars have the seats quite close together, as near to the centreline of the car as possible. This means that when only the driver is in the car, his or her weight, while upsetting a perfectly wheel weighted car, does not cause too much of a problem. It is a compromise, however, but how big a compromise depends on how heavy the driver is, how stiff the springs are and how far away from the centreline of the car the driver's seat is. Since sportscars are almost always better balanced when there are two people seated in them, despite the obvious weight penalty, the driver-only situation can be the cause of wheel weight problems, especially when optimum vehicle handling is required.

Note that some specialist front engined single-seater sports racing car designers go to the trouble of fitting the engine nearly alongside the driver's seat to get the engine and driver as close to the centreline of the car as possible to concentrate and equalise the weight distribution. Most sportscars are not, however, designed like this.

When a two-seater sportscar which has been set up using the car's own weight has two people seated in it, there will frequently be an extra 300 pounds or so of additional weight in the car. Because the two seats are side by side, the weight of the two people tends to be evenly apportioned into each wheel of the car. There are obviously possibly going to be differences in the weights of the two people, but if the two people were exactly the same weight the corner weights of the car would increase equally side to side of the car (no wheel weight compromise). With two people of vastly different weights in

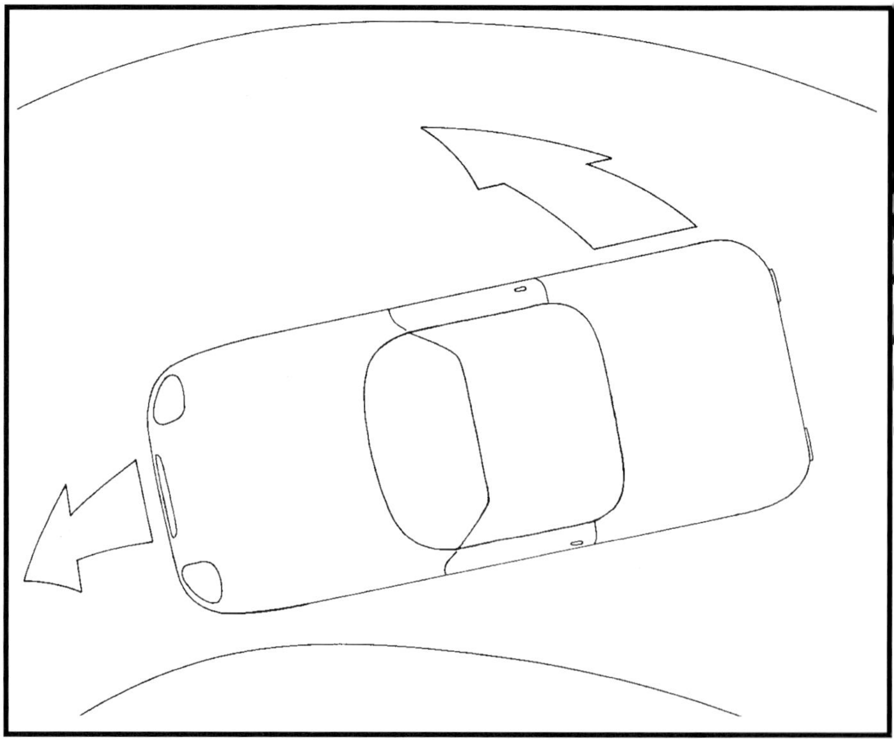

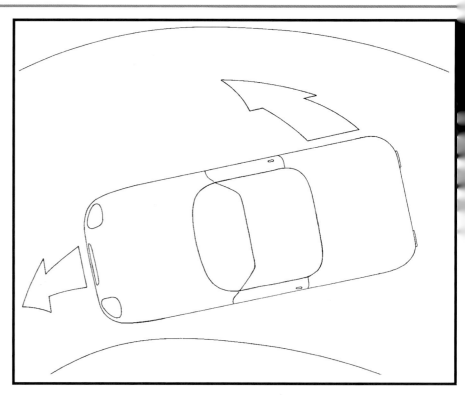

Car is turning left and in oversteer.

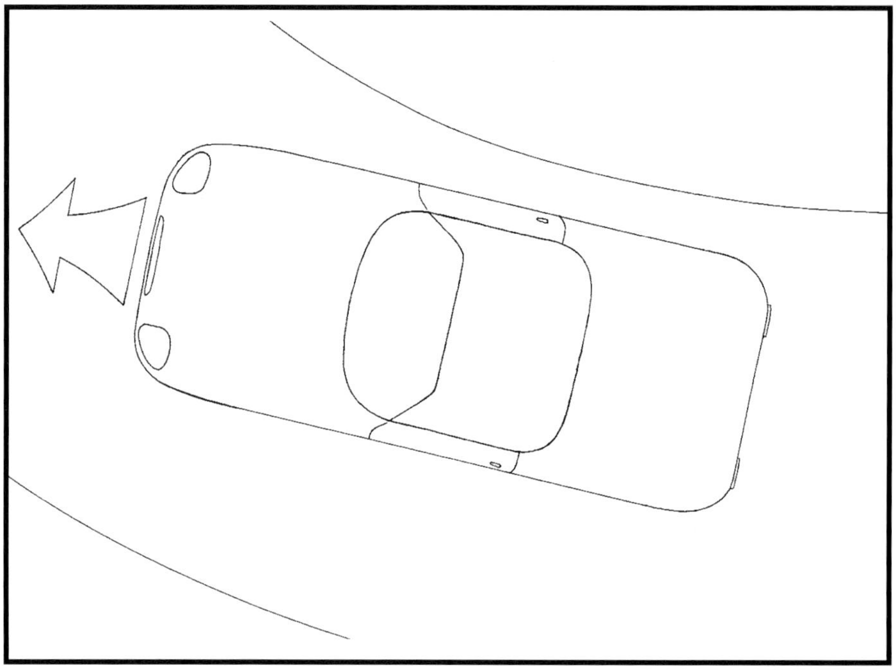

Car is turning right and is understeering.

the car the heavier person cancels out the weight of the lighter person with some weight left over. If the heavier person is sitting on the right, the extra weight will go to the right rear wheel and across the car to the left front wheel more than it will go to the left rear wheel and the right front wheel (slight wheel weight compromise).

Another factor here is spring rate. The stiffer the springs the less affect (geometry alteration) there is when the driver gets into the car. On some cars when the driver gets in the suspension hardly moves at all. In this situation the geometry remains basically as it was before the driver got into the car, but his or her weight does go to the wheels one way or another. This is quite a significant point as spring rating choice is part of the solution to the problem of driver-only situations and maintaining equal weighted wheels side to side of the car. Firm springs, but not too firm: a 1500-1600 pound car with a front engine, for example, is likely to need 250-350 pound front springs and 130-200 pound rear springs.

In the final analysis, either the weight of the driver (sole occupant) is going to be taken into consideration or it isn't: the decision revolves around the application. Racing is one application where the wheel weight situation needs to be dead right. There is not much doubt that wheel weights are exceedingly important for optimum all-round good handling characteristics, even if at the expense of very slight geometry inaccuracy. With a firmly sprung car, the geometry will never be very far out, and seldom ever enough to be the cause of handling problems.

As a guide to spring firmness requirements in this situation if, when the driver gets into the car, it sinks by more than 0.25in/6.35mm, the springs are probably too soft: they need to be firmer to prevent excessive geometry differences side to side of the car.

The other aspect of all this is, of course, the action of centrifugal forces acting on the car during hard cornering (body roll), which tend to accentuate differences in wheel weight if they are wildly out. If the driver's seat can be moved closer to the centreline of the car, even by an inch or two (25-50mm), do it. Very often racing seats are quite slimline and can be moved a considerable distance towards the centre of the car without making it awkward to use the foot pedals.

If the driver's weight is going to be taken into consideration, the actual driver must sit in the car (or equivalent weight placed on the driving seat). With the car on a flat level surface, it is jacked up at the dead centre point of the differential until both rear wheels are off the ground. Then, the front spring heights are adjusted (whether you lower the 'high' spring or heighten the 'low' spring is up to you) so that the suspension pick-up point centres on both sides of the car are an equal distance from the ground. If the car has a live rear axle, the rear springs are then adjusted so that both rear wheels are an equal distance from the ground. If the car has independent rear suspension, the rear wheels are lowered to the ground and the front of the car jacked up (centrally) until the two front wheels are off the ground. The rear springs are then adjusted so that the chosen rear suspension pick-up point centres are at equal distances from the ground.

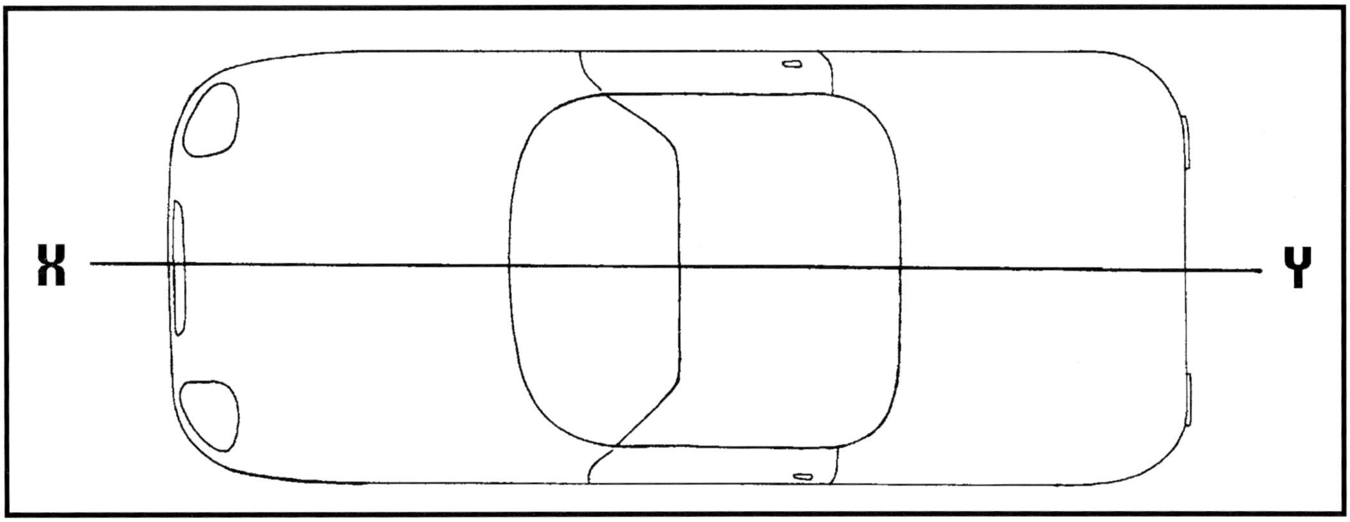

Centreline of car (X-Y).

TYRES

The circumference of tyres on a driven axle fitted with a limited slip differential needs to be identical side to side of the car. There are usually problems if they are not.

What this means is that, if the right hand rear tyre is, say, 1 inch/25.4mm larger in circumference than the tyre on the left hand side of the rear axle, the car will tend to turn to the left as it comes out of a right hand turn under power. The same car will tend to power oversteer when exiting a left hand turn under power. This is because the larger circumference tyre has more drive. This effect only applies, of course, when the rear axle is locked and the engine is quite powerful (torquey). Off-power the situation is not the same.

Depending on how much difference there is, the affect of having two different circumference-sized tyres can also be felt in straight line acceleration. If the tyre on the right is larger than the tyre on the left, the car will tend to turn to the left under full power acceleration; if the tyre on the left is larger, the car will tend to turn to the right under full power acceleration.

If your car has a limited slip differential, make sure that the two tyres which go on the driven axle are the same circumference (to within 0.25in/6.35mm). Cars with tyres of different circumferences are referred to as having "stagger."

Initially, inflate the tyres to the pressure recommended by the car manufacturer, or by the tyre manufacturer if the car is a kit car, but be prepared to decrease or increase the tyre pressures by as much as 5 to 10psi per tyre (if the tyres are under-inflated, expect to hear a lot of tyre noise during hard cornering). The range of tyre pressures for sports cars varies considerably because of the weight of the cars and the size of the tyres frequently used. Some sports cars have a lot of 'rubber' on them and, while this will often reduce the maximum top speed compared to what could be acheived if narrower wheels and tyres were fitted, the cornering ability of the particular car will be excellent. Cars with too much 'rubber' on them frequently need much less psi in the tyres than you might imagine. Experimentation is the way to find out what your particular car responds best to. The range of tyre pressure to experiment with starts at 15psi and generally goes up to 30psi. 15psi, for example, probably sounds quite low and hardly possible, but it actually is fine for certain types of tyre and weights of car.

Check to see how the car goes and handles with a range of tyre pressures. If tyre pressures are too low the car will tend to move around too much, accompanied by a lot of tyre noise. If the tyres are over-inflated the car will not grip as well as it does with lower pressure because the tread surfaces no longer have full contact with the road or track surface.

Run the highest tyre pressures possible conducive to good handling characteristics. On a long term basis, under-inflated tyres tend to wear the edges of the tyre tread more and over-inflated tyres tend to wear the middle of the tyre tread.

If two different tyre diameters are used on the same axle side to side of a car (front or rear), the suspension geometry will usually be slightly out side to side if the car has been wheel weighted.

Tyre circumference is checked with tyres inflated to the recommended pressure: a tape measure is used to measure the tyres' circumference in the centre of the tread.

BRAKES

With excessive toe-out, under extremely hard braking the car may wander slightly or, worse, not feel very controllable. These symtoms may be attributable to excessive static toe-out and/or too much compliance/movement in the bushes/various joints of the suspension (when the car is braked heavily the steering system/suspension joints are heavily loaded, allowing the wheels to toe-out further). When the brakes are applied, the front wheels of any car move towards toe-out.

It's quite possible to set the suspension with an amount of toe-out that is ideal for maximum cornering purposes, but not ideal for maximum braking purposes. If eliminating excessive compliance in steering/suspension joints does not remove the braking instability problem, then you'll know what the maximum amount of safe braking is and must drive within the confines of that limit. Few people, especially racers, would want to sacrifice cornering ability for a very slight gain in braking efficiency, so consider 0.140in/3.5mm of toe-out as the maximum for any car.

It may only be when the car is being used to the full that it becomes quite noticeably unstable - and quite dangerously so. **Warning!** - The performance limits for all adjustments you make have to be established before the car can be used to its maximum potential: this is why testing is **essential**.

Warning! - Testing of this nature simply cannot be done on the public highway: an off road venue is pretty much essential to avoid personal injury and injury to others. A good road surface and wide open spaces are required so that if things go wrong there is plenty of room to manoeuvre out of any situation.

Braking tests are vital so that the driver knows exactly how good the brakes are. This means knowing how much room is required to pull the car up from the speeds likely to be used: such judgement comes from experience. For example, even though race tracks often have signs giving the distance to the next corner, the driver will still have to judge how much braking distance the car needs to reach the speed required to negotiate the corner successfully. All cars are different, meaning that some cars corner better than others and slow quicker. It all comes back to the fact that you must 'know' the car you are driving, and the limits to which it can be taken to get the most out of it.

There is nothing quite as frightening as approaching a corner in a car faster than you have ever approached it before and, suddenly, getting the feeling that the car is not 'settled' as well as it normally is in that particular corner (too late to sprout wings!). Better to find by testing at an earlier time what the capability of the car is and in conditions where no damage is going to be done to yourself or, more importantly, the car! (that's a joke, right?).

When testing brakes, a brake bias valve or proportioning valve can be very useful. If the car is at full speed on a dry surface and the brakes are applied fully, the rear tyres may well have too much braking effect (wheels lock up). With a bias valve fitted, rear braking efficiency can be reduced until the rear brakes are working to the maximum desirable (just at the point of locking up) but not more than that. This is even more important, of course, when the road surface is wet. Once again, the brake bias valve can be adjusted to reduce the amount of braking effort being fed into the rear brakes (to prevent the wheels locking up). Having a brake bias valve within easy reach is the ideal situation so that the brake bias can be adjusted within a second or two.

If the car is tested at full speed, the maximum amount of braking efficiency will be found. While distance signs on the side of the track can be of major benefit, you still need to know the minimum distance that can be left before the brakes have to be applied. Using the signs as reminders is a good idea, once you know how good the brakes are.

Warning! - during all testing procedures you need to take all necessary precautions to protect yourself and bystanders; you also need to be confident that you can handle the car safely if it loses adhesion. In the first instance, markers should be spaced out along the side of the track, one every 100 yards (you can use metres if you prefer) starting at 500 yards (or metres) from a zero point (allow for run-off). Approach the 500 yard marker at full speed and apply the brakes, bringing the car to a dead stop as quickly as possible. Note the distance taken to stop the car. Now consider how well it stopped. Did it pull up straight or did it slither around a bit? Did the front or rear wheels lock up at any stage? Did it pull to one side? Did you feel comfortable with the way that it pulled up? Did it give you a feeling of confidence?

This is also where having some assistance comes in handy because other people (**Warning!** - at a minimum distance of 20 yards/metres away from the side of the track at all times) will be able to observe what actually did happen and perhaps give you a more accurate picture of events. For instance, if the rear brakes locked up they will be able to tell you exactly where they locked up and for how long.

It is also amazing how much difference some practice makes in improving the time and distance taken to stop the car from full speed to a dead stop. In many instances the amount of foot pressure applied to the brake pedal needs to be reduced once speed starts to fall to prevent the wheels locking up. This is where driver skill comes into the equation. At full speed, maximum foot pressure (hydraulic line pressure) will almost always need to be applied but, as speed reduces, pedal pressure will need to be reduced to prevent the wheels locking up. The driver needs to be able to 'feel' the braking efficiency. The object of the exercise is to keep all the wheels at the point of being about to lock but not actually doing so.

Locked wheels are not giving maximum braking efficiency, or stopping ability to the car at all. The odd wisp of smoke coming off a tyre is not too much to worry about, provided the wheel is still turning; but when the tyres have stopped turning and there is plenty of smoke, the situation is out of hand and the car will need a longer distance in which to stop. In this situation release the brake pedal pressure immediately for an instant, and then re-apply pedal pressure but not quite as much. The foregoing applies to a maximum braking test with the car being taken from full speed to a dead stop. In most real world instances of brake use the car does not need to be brought to a halt, but rather slowed to a certain speed. Overall brake bias settings for maximum braking efficiency from maximum speed will usually prove fine for general use.

Under heavy braking the car must pull up square without any slithering

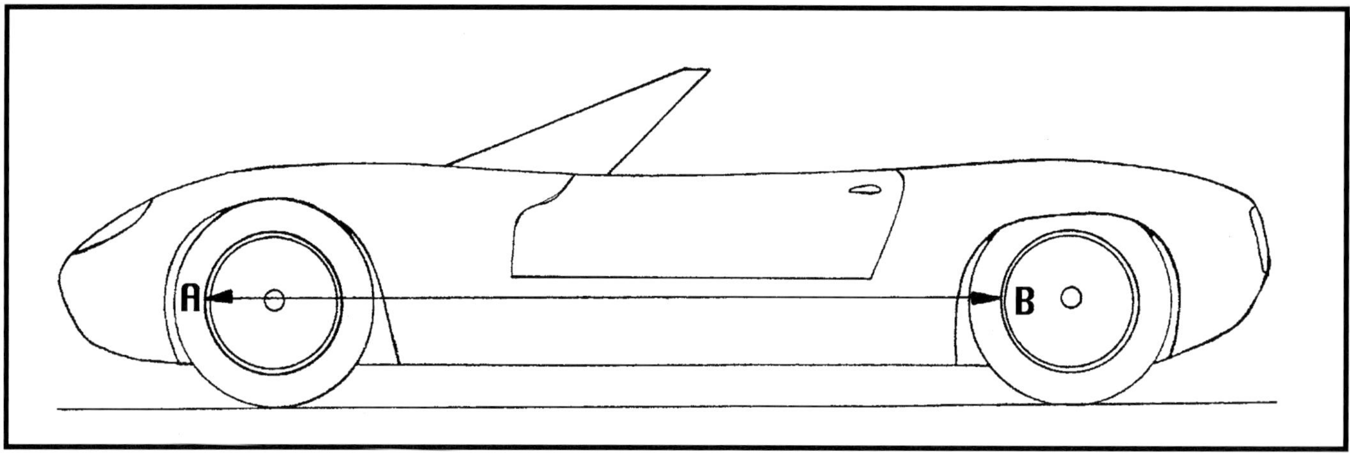

Measure from the front of the front rim (A) to the front of the rear rim (B).

around or rear wheel lock-up. Rear wheel lock-up is often felt as the back of the car moving off line. When this happens, a brake bias valve must be fitted or, if already fitted, adjusted until the rear of the car becomes stable when the brakes are applied. The car must not pull to the right or left (if this happens one of the front brakes is not working correctly). The car must pull up without a wheel, or wheels, locking up. This may involve reducing pedal pressure (reducing hydraulic line pressure) as the car slows to prevent all four wheels locking up. What you definitely don't want is a situation where you have to reduce pedal pressure to prevent the rear wheels locking up - this would mean that hydraulic pressure to the front brakes would be reduced, even though they were not about to lock up anyway. The car will take longer to stop like this. The solution to this problem is to reduce the pressure going to the rear wheels using a brake bias valve, and to keep all four wheels on the point of locking up.

STEERING PULLS TO ONE SIDE

If the car pulls to one side when being driven in a straight line, check to see if the wheelbase (that's the distance wheel centre to wheel centre, front to rear) is the same on both sides of the car. It only takes a 0.125-0.25in/3-6mm difference in wheelbase to cause it to pull to one side. Wheelbase dimensions **must** be identical on both sides of the car.

To check the wheelbase, the steering wheel is placed in the known straight ahead position and a tape measure used to measure rim to rim, back to front of the car on both sides. Use the front of the rim on the front wheel and the front of the rim on the back wheel as datum points. Check that the rim diameters are the same on all four wheels, otherwise the measurements will be different for this reason and not a wheelbase difference.

If the wheelbase is shorter on the right side of the car, the car will tend to turn to the right, and vice versa.

Another thing that will cause the steering to pull to one side is having a tyre on the front of a car (and/or the rear of an independent suspension car) that is not equal in circumference side to side of the tread width. While not being a common problem, it can be difficult to track down. With the tyre off the ground and correctly inflated, measure the circumference in the centre of the tread and then near the edges of the tread on both sides. If the tyre is tapered side to side, the car will pull to one side. The faulty tyre will have to be replaced.

CORNERING PROBLEMS

There are few things worse than driving a car fast and finding that it understeers severely when steering lock is applied on entering a corner. The car feels like it wants to go straight ahead and steers wide of the intended cornering line. **Warning!** - In the extreme this characteristic can be dangerous. The simple fact is that the car does not go where you are pointing it and this can be very annoying, especially when you can't figure out what is really causing the car to do what it's doing. There are a few possibilities here ...

Having a very heavy engine in the front can affect the handling of a sportscar quite dramatically. This is why on kit cars, for instance, which almost always have a tubular chassis, the engine should always be fitted into the car as close to the bulkhead (firewall) as possible. It's always worth

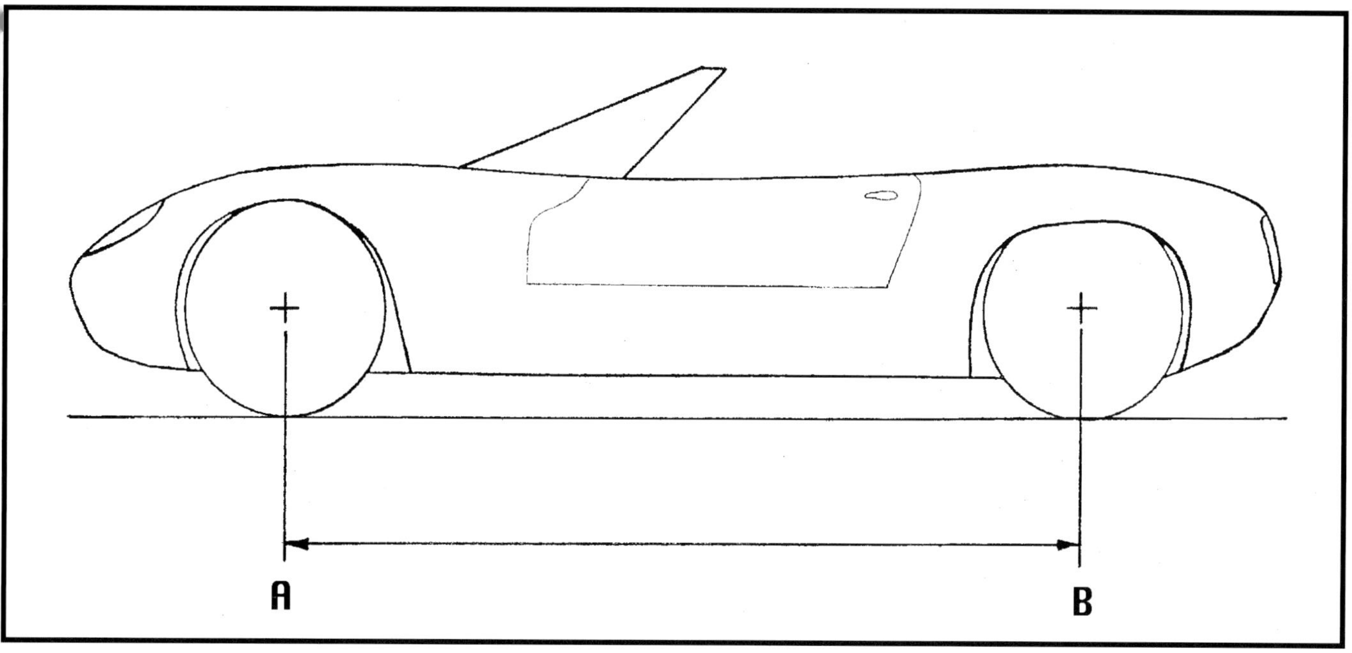

Wheelbase is the distance between "A" and "B."

taking the trouble to get the engine as far back in the chassis as possible. There are plenty of things that can be done to accomplish this: the bulkhead could be slightly reshaped, for instance. In many instances the clutch bellhousing is what gets in the way of being able to set the engine back as far as possible, but sometimes the bellhousing can be cut and welded so that the whole gearbox, bellhousing and engine unit can go back a further 2-3in/50-75mm, or so, in the chassis.

To find out whether the bellhousing can be modified, check to see how far away the clutch pressure plate is from the bellhousing. It is surprising how much clearance there can be and how much a bellhousing can be altered in the appropriate area. An aluminium bellhousing can be Tig welded and a cast iron bellhousing can have mild steel sheet metal braised into position to keep dirt and grime out of the clutch. On the basis of strength, very often the bellhousing does not always need to have strengthening plates welded in where material has been removed, and it may be possible to leave the bellhousing open.

Moving an engine and gearbox which is installed in the front of a car backwards as far as possible improves the weight distribution dramatically. The further back the engine goes the better. On some kit cars, for instance, it's possible to move the engine and gearbox back in the chassis by 3 to 4 inches/75 - 100mm, or even more. There are, of course, usually limits as to how far an engine can be moved back in a chassis.

If your car has, say, 0.125in/3.2mm toe-in and no Ackerman angle built into the steering system, the two front wheels will essentially be 'fighting' each other when steering lock is applied. The front wheel on the inside of the turn is not angled into the turn as much as it should be for best possible turn-in action.

If your car has toe-in and Ackerman steering, it does not automatically mean that it will not understeer. This is because geometry changes caused by Ackerman steering are progressive as more lock is applied to the wheels. This is no good for a car travelling at high speed which is only going to have about 10 degrees of lock applied to the front wheels, and then only for an instant. The geometric action of Ackerman steering will not be enough to do any good, nor will it come into action soon enough. If the steering ends up being turned through 20 degrees or so, the geometric action may well be enough, but it will be too late to be of any use. This is the reason why some cars are seen with huge amounts of static negative camber (5 degrees, or so). The negative camber for optimum tyre support is there, irrespective of how little the steering wheel is turned.

Regardless of the type of steering your car has, setting up the car with toe-out and testing it to see if there is an improvement in cornering ability is essential.

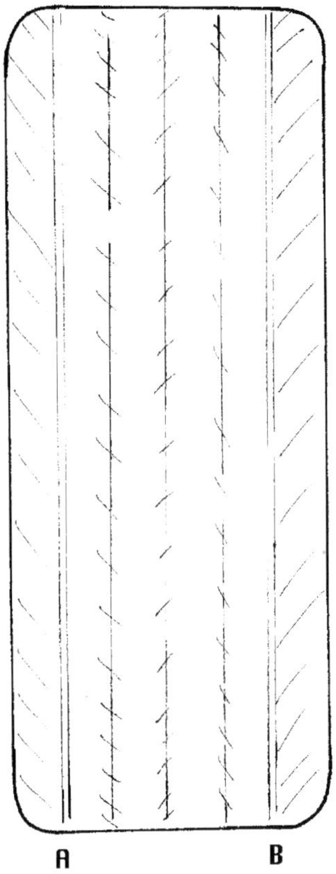

This tyre has a different circumference side to side of the tread.

There is no getting away from it: having toe-out (zero toe, 0.060in/1.5mm toe-out, or 0.125in/3.2mm toe-out) built into the steering geometry almost always leads to better cornering as opposed to having any amount of toe-in. This is because the toe-out is there constantly and, irrespective of how little the steering wheel is actually turned, the wheel on the inside of the turn will *always* have more effective lock on it than the wheel on the outside of the turn.

Use toe out as a tuning tool and run the least amount of toe out that you can get away with while gaining an improvement in handling. Avoid excessive amounts of toe out as more is not necessarily better! Aim for just enough.

If your car has true Ackerman steering and, say, 0.125in/3.2mm toe-out (the general recommended maximum), when there is a serious amount of steering lock on the front wheels (25 degrees or more), the front wheel on the inside of the turn will often have too much lock on it. This will lead to the wheel on the inside of the turn 'dragging' and will cause speed to be scrubbed off rapidly. However, this factor can basically be ignored because, in almost all instances, large amounts of lock (25 degrees, for example) will never be used in high speed situations. It is amazing how little lock is actually applied in most situations. Frequently as little as between 5 - 15 degrees is all that is ever used.

This factor of a small amount of steering lock needing to be used is the reason why on many circuit racing cars large amounts of negative camber are built into the steering geometry so that, irrespective of the amount of lock actually used, the front wheels have the required amount of negative camber on them to give the front tyre on the outside of the turn sufficient support under extreme cornering conditions. The other factor here is that very often the castor cannot be altered all that much (race rules) but generally the negative camber is there in such amounts to ensure that when it really matters (in high speed cornering situations) the front wheel tyre attitude is dead right (that's the lefthand front tyre of a car turning right and the righthand front tyre of a car turning left). This results in the lowest possible lap times. Braking efficiency is compromised slightly because of the large amount of negative camber but it's the lesser of the two evils.

Warning! - If your car has toe-in and you want to try toe-out, try setting the car up with 0.125in/3.2mm toe-out and then check the braking performance from progressively higher speeds - sometimes a car will prove unstable under heavy braking with toe-out, this is dangerous and unacceptable.

Tyres obviously have a fundamental role in cornering performance. Tyres that, while having plenty of tread, have gone 'hard' are no good at all; rubber deteriorates over time, especially in the sun. Take your racing rubber off the car and store it in black plastic rubbish (trash) bags. Deflate the tyres but do not rest them tread down on the ground as this can lead to permanent distortion of the tread if the tyres are left in one place too long. If the tyres are going to be left on the car but the car not used, jack up the car so the wheels are clear of the ground, deflate the tyres and cover the tyres with black plastic bags.

Tyre technology is improving all the time and, while there are many well-known tyres on the market that have been around for some time, tyres are constantly changing. Always buy the best new tyres you can afford. Soft compound tyres grip better than hard compound tyres, but don't last as long.

Large diameter wheels (15-16in as opposed to 13in) and low profile tyres (45, 50 or 55 series) offer the best handling characteristics - provided the suspension geometry is keeping the tread supported correctly and on the road or track surface. Tyres like this offer less compliance compared to small diameter high profile tyres (13in by 70 series) so the geometry just has to be right to get the best grip out of them.

Note that it is quite possible to fit very expensive large diameter, low

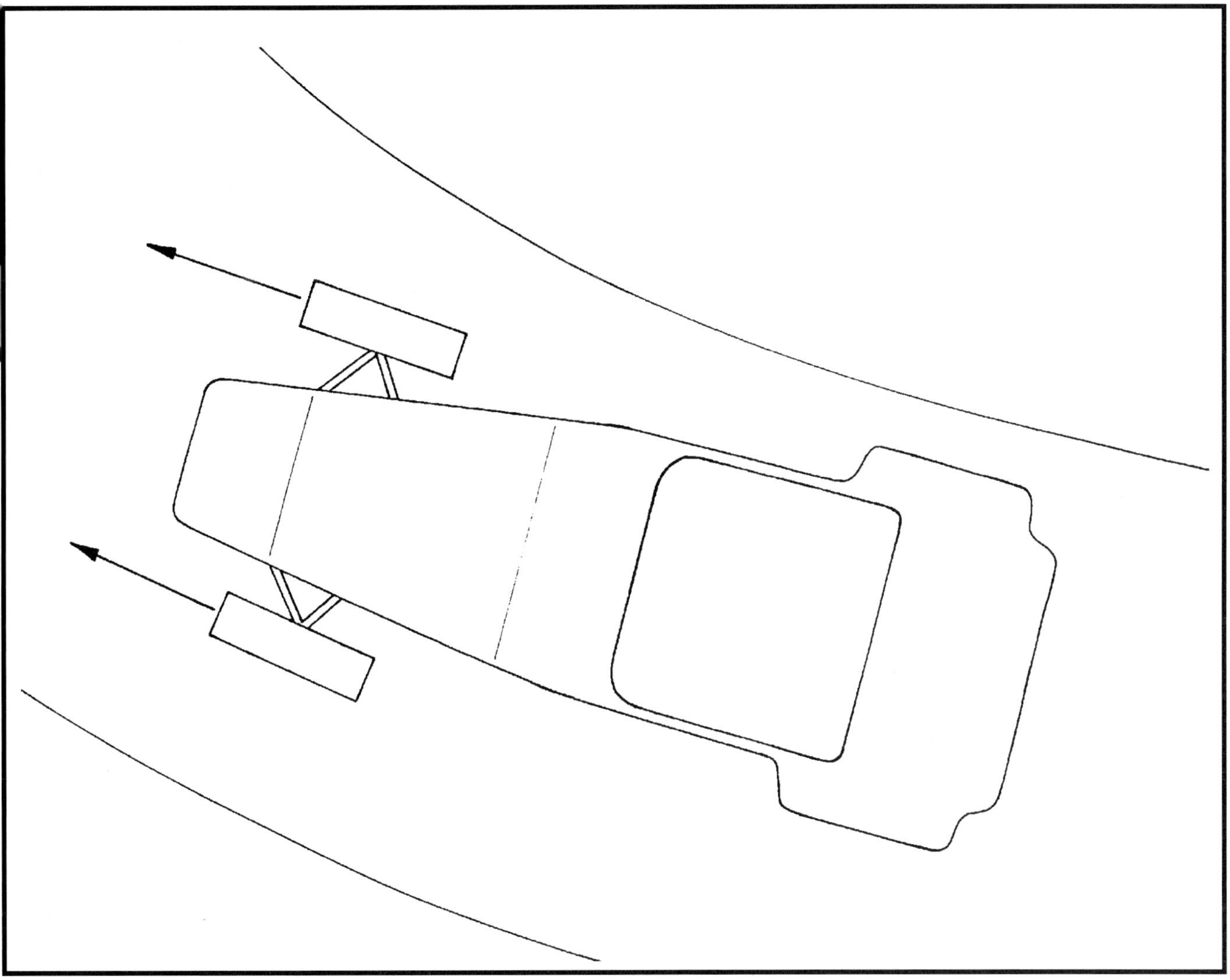

Car with front wheel toe-in turning right. The right hand front wheel is not turning in enough to do any good. Arrows at the front of the wheels show that the wheels are on convergent lines.

profile tyres on to a car which doesn't have particularly good suspension geometry, and end up with a car that handles worse than in original condition. The reason is that the tyres just don't have any 'give' in them, whereas the previously fitted large profile tyres did. It's not really the tyres that are at fault.

Many low profile radial tyres now have rigid sidewalls (Michelin Pilot SX GTs, for example) and this type of tyre grips exceedingly well provided the suspension geometry is set to suit it. The tyre treads must be in full contact with the road or track surface during hard cornering. Avoid lots of negative camber during hard cornering (that's 2 degrees or more) and more than 2 degrees of suspension geometry, body roll induced positive camber during hard cornering, for that matter, on the front wheel on the outside of the turn (a visual estimate can be made by an observer who understands what is being looked for).

With the car's suspension set up statically, the ideal criteria may well have been applied and met; however, once the car is in motion other factors come into play: the main one is body roll. Body roll causes suspension/steering geometry changes and, generally, the more body roll there is the greater the change in the attitude of the wheels (usually in the wrong

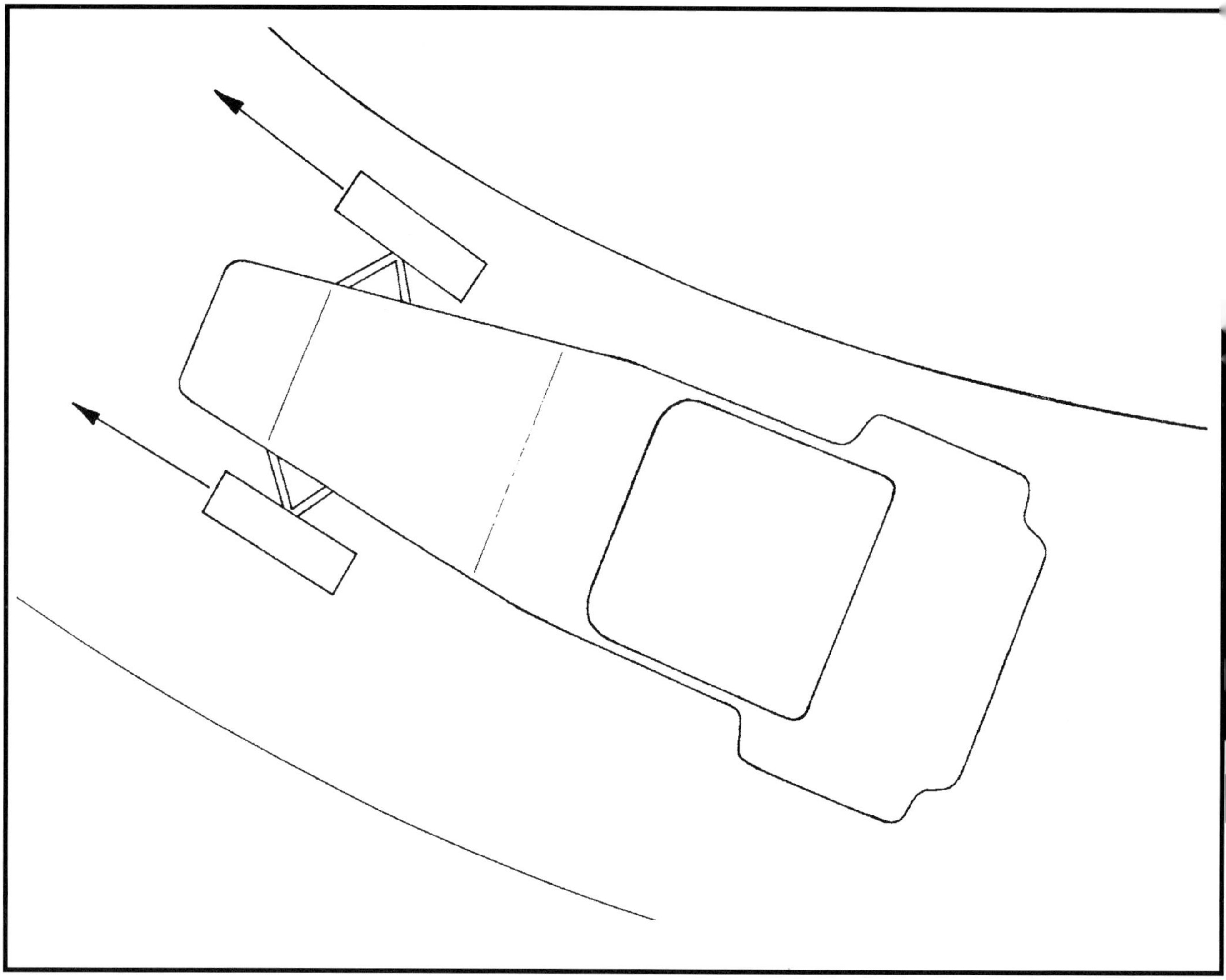

Car with front toe-out turning right. Right hand front wheel is turning in more than the left hand front wheel. Wheels are not 'fighting' each other. Arrows at the front of the wheels show that wheels are on divergent lines.

direction). Sportscars do not normally exhibit too much body roll because of their low centre of gravity (major weight concentrated very low down in the structure of the car). An inherently low amount of body roll can, however, mean that a car can have mediocre suspension geometry and still handle well. There are several kit cars, for example, that fall into this category. They are not unsafe, but do not handle as well as they could if a bit more thought had gone into geometry at the design stage.

When the tyre tread is not fully in contact with the road surface during cornering, the tyres do not grip as well as they do if in maximum contact.

Some sportscars are set up by the factory with a lot of static negative camber (4 or 5 degrees), when the front wheels are in the straight ahead position, and this can lead to severe understeer during cornering. Cars like this frequently do not handle well in a turn, the very thing the negative camber is supposed to help. The problem is that, in the straight ahead position, the tyres are not really in full contact with the road. The edges of the tyres nearest the centre line of the car have more of the tread in contact with the road or track surface than the outer edges. Most cars do not actually need much steering lock to negotiate corners, which is why racing saloon

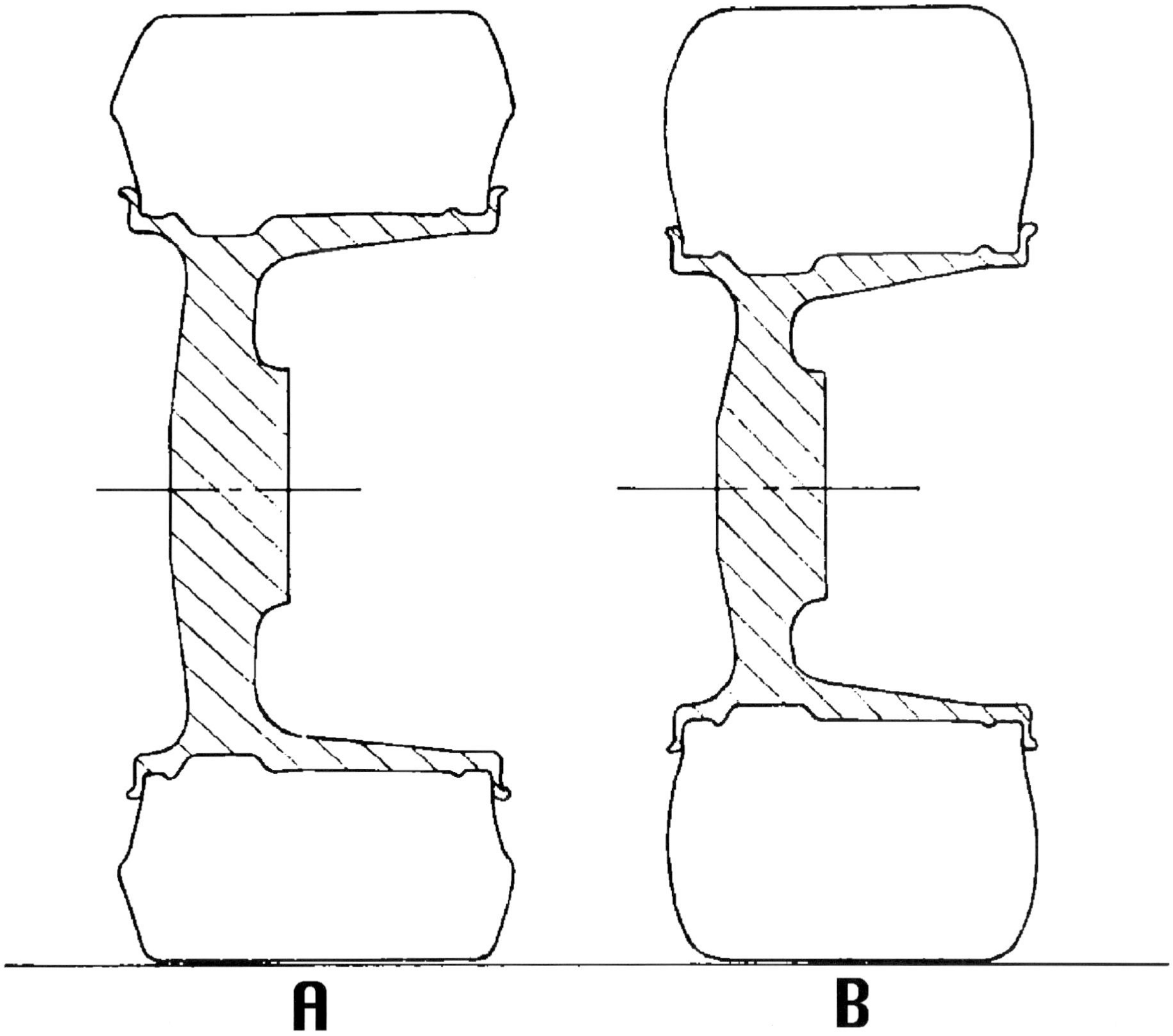

Tyre "A" is a rigid-sidewalled, low profile 15 inch item. Tyre "B" is a high profile 13 inch item. The circumference of both tyres is the same.

cars and single-seater racing cars, for example, often have a lot of static negative camber. Invariably in these cases the cars have the best racing tyres and the front tyres are poised for immediate action by having optimum wheel attitude built into them. When cars are set up with this sort of geometry only one wheel will be 'right' in the corner. That is, if a car is turning right, the left hand front wheel will have optimum attitude and if that same car is turning left the right hand front wheel will have optimum attitude. In each situation the opposing wheel is only partially in contact with the track surface.

Just because many racing saloon cars and single-seater racing cars are seen to have a lot of static negative camber, it does not mean that this is right for a sportscar fitted with radial tyres and travelling, by comparison, at medium speeds. When a car like this turns a right hand corner, for example, the left hand front tyre gains negative camber via the positive castor and kingpin inclination (kpi) built into the front suspension and loses negative camber due to body roll.

The solution to this situation involves making sure that, when the car is negotiating any turn at full speed, the wheel on the outside of the turn (that's the right hand front wheel on a car turning left and vice versa) has no more than 2 degrees of negative camber (and no more than 2 degrees of positive camber, should the suspension allow the front wheel to go that far). This, of course, means that all factors have been taken into account, such as body roll, castor and kingpin inclination. The way to check whether or not the front wheels have too much negative camber on them for high speed cornering, is to look at the tread of the tyres. If the inside portion of the tyre tread is showing signs of major 'scuffing' and excessive wear, compared to the rest of the tyre's tread, then the chances are that the suspension geometry is causing the front wheels to have too much negative camber on them in this situation. Reset the suspension with less static negative camber, or reduce the castor, or both. There won't usually be any loss of tyre adhesion by reducing the dynamic negative camber, in fact grip will often improve and the tyres will generally wear more evenly.

After all adjustments have been made to the suspension, the question is: in practice, does the suspension/ steering set-up give the wheels optimum attitude? This can be checked visually with the car in action and, once you know what you are looking for, it is quite easy to spot something that is not right. For instance, if the car is turning right at high speed, it only takes an observer to tell you that the left hand front wheel is leaning a lot at the top and the body is leaning over a lot too for you to know that your car has a significant amount of body roll, and the left hand front wheel has a lot of positive camber on it in this cornering situation. Once you've observed the car's dynamic behaviour, it's easy to rectify problems with further adjustments. Sensible adjustments (no more than one at a time) - and thorough testing of each adjustment - is what is required to ascertain how much of an improvement has been made.

CONCLUSION

There are plenty of things to check to make sure that the car is basically free from obvious suspension/steering setting defects. In far too many instances the problems that a standard or badly modified car exhibits will ultimately be quite simple to eliminate. All car suspension systems are slightly different by design and in the size of the various components, but all cars respond to the same factors to varying degrees; things like castor, negative camber, zero toe, toe-out, for example. The attitude of the wheels in various dynamic situations, and the weights acting on the wheels, is what good handling is all about.

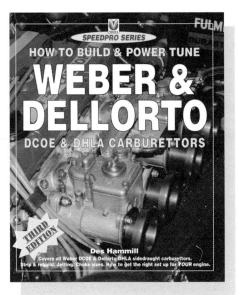

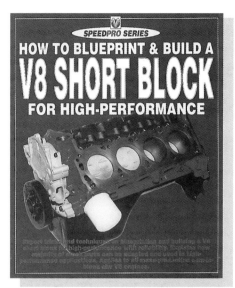

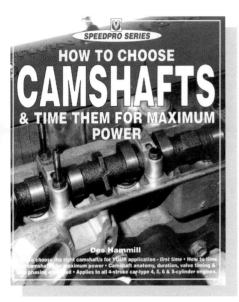

ALSO FROM VELOCE PUBLISHING -

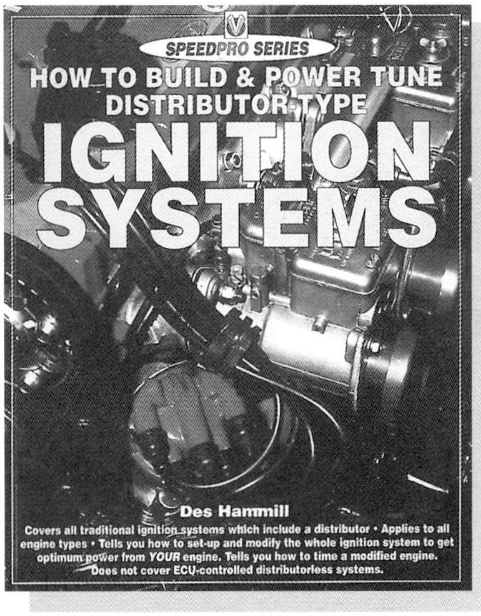

HOW TO BUILD & POWER TUNE DISTRIBUTOR TYPE IGNITION SYSTEMS

by Des Hammill

ISBN 1 903706 91 2
Price £13.99*

A book in the ***SpeedPro*** series. Expert practical advice from an experienced race engine builder on how to build an ignition system that delivers maximum power reliably. A lot of rubbish is talked about ignition systems and there's a bewildering choice of expensive aftermarket parts which all claim to deliver more power. Des Hammill cuts through the myth and hyperbole and tells readers what *really* works, so that they can build an excellent system without wasting money on parts and systems that simply don't deliver.

Ignition timing and advance curves for modified engines is another minefield for the inexperienced, but Des uses his expert knowledge to tell readers how to optimise the ignition timing of *any* high performance engine.

The book applies to all four-stroke gasoline/petrol engines with distributor-type ignition systems, including those using electronic ignition modules: it does not cover engines controlled by ECUs (electronic control units).

CONTENTS

Why modified engines need more idle speed advance • Static idle speed advance setting • Estimating total advance settings • Vacuum advance • Ignition timing marks • Distributor basics • Altering rate of advance • Setting total advance • Quality of spark •

SPECIFICATION

Softback • 250 x 207mm (portrait) • 64 pages • Over 70 black & white photographs and line illustrations.

RETAIL SALES

Veloce books are stocked by or can be ordered from bookshops and specialist mail order companies. Alternatively, Veloce can supply direct (credit cards accepted).

* *Price subject to change.*

Veloce Publishing Ltd, 33 Trinity Street, Dorchester, Dorset DT1 1TT, England. Tel: 01305 260068/ Fax: 01305 268864/E-mail: veloce@veloce.co.uk

ALSO FROM VELOCE PUBLISHING -

HOW TO BUILD, MODIFY & POWER TUNE CYLINDER HEADS

- Updated & Revised Edition
by Peter Burgess & David Golan

ISBN 1 903706 76 9
Price £16.99*

A book in the ***SpeedPro*** series.
• The complete practical guide to successfully modifying cylinder heads for maximum power, economy and reliability.
• Understandable language and clear illustrations.
• Avoids wasting money on modifications that don't work.
• Applies to almost every car/ motorcycle (does not apply to 2-stroke engines).
• Applies to road and track applications.
• Peter Burgess is a professional race engine builder. David Gollan B ENG HONS is a professional engineer.

CONTENTS
Horsepower and torque • Equipment and tools • Airflow • Building a flowbench • Porting • Valves, valve seats and inserts, valve guides, valve springs • Unleaded fuel conversion • Fuel economy • Includes an overview of camshafts, exhaust systems, ignition, cylinder blocks • Case studies of a selection of popular cylinder heads • Index.

SPECIFICATION
Paperback. 250 x 207mm (portrait). 112 pages. Over 150 black and white photographs/line illustrations.

RETAIL SALES
Veloce books are stocked by or can be ordered from bookshops and specialist mail order companies. Alternatively, Veloce can supply direct (credit cards accepted).

* *Price subject to change.*

Veloce Publishing Ltd, 33 Trinity Street, Dorchester, Dorset DT1 1TT, England. Tel: 01305 260068/ Fax: 01305 268864/E-mail: veloce@veloce.co.uk

Visit Veloce on the Web - www.veloce.co.uk

ALSO FROM VELOCE PUBLISHING -

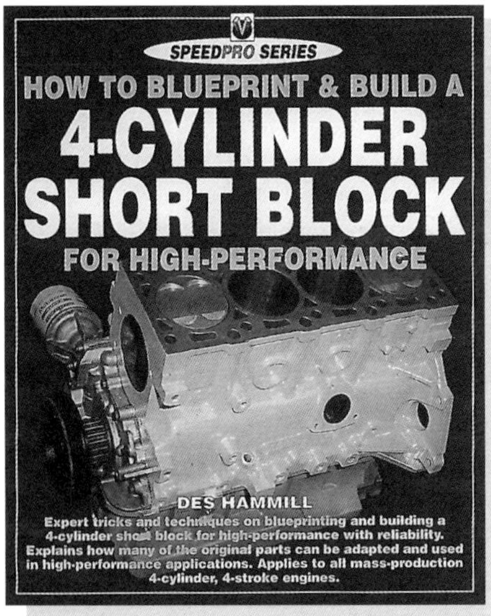

HOW TO BLUEPRINT & BUILD A 4-CYLINDER SHORT BLOCK FOR HIGH PERFORMANCE

by Des Hammill

ISBN 1 903706 92 0
Price £16.99*

A book in the ***SpeedPro*** series.
- Applies to all 4-cylinder car engines (except diesel & two-stroke).
- Essential reading for millions of car owners looking for more power.
- Expert advice in non-technical English accompanied by clear photos & line illustrations.
- Saves money by eliminating techniques that don't work and by maximising the use of standard components.
- Written by a professional competition engine builder.

CONTENTS

A complete practical guide on how to blueprint (optimize all aspects of specification) any 4-cylinder, four-stroke engine's short block to obtain maximum performance and reliability without wasting money on over-specced parts. Includes choosing components, crankshaft & conrod bearings, cylinder block, connecting rods, pistons, piston to valve clearances, camshaft, engine balancing, timing gear, lubrication system, professional check-build procedures and much more. Index.

SPECIFICATION

Paperback. 250 X 207mm (portrait). 112 pages. Around 200 black & white photographs/ illustrations.

RETAIL SALES

Veloce books are stocked by or can be ordered from bookshops and specialist mail order companies. Alternatively, Veloce can supply direct (credit cards accepted).

* *Price subject to change.*

Veloce Publishing Ltd, 33 Trinity Street, Dorchester, Dorset DT1 1TT, England. Tel: 01305 260068/ Fax: 01305 268864/E-mail: veloce@veloce.co.uk

ALSO FROM VELOCE PUBLISHING -

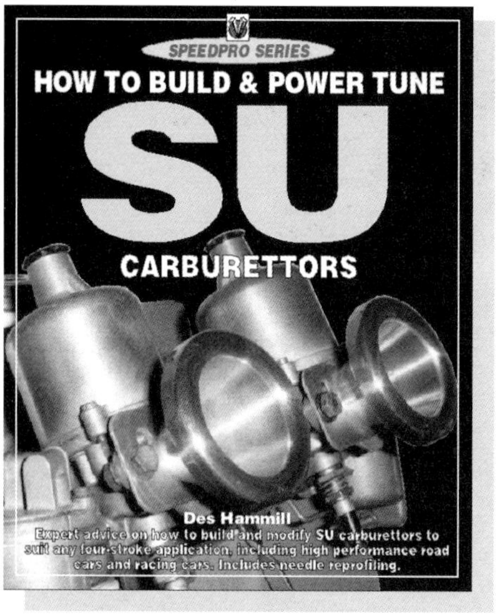

HOW TO BUILD & POWER TUNE SU CARBURETTORS

by Des Hammill

ISBN 1 903706 98 X
Price £13.99*

A book in the ***SpeedPro*** series.
• The complete practical guide to modifying SUs for high performance applications.
• Step-by-step illustrated procedures.
• Millions of cars are equipped with SU carburettors.
• Includes needle profiling.
• Des Hammill is an engineer and professional race engine builder.

CONTENTS
Introduction • Preparation • Inlet manifolds • What size carburettor(s)? • Needles • Altering needles • Choosing starting point needles • Carburettor tuning sequence • Rejetting (engines equipped with SUs as standard
• Rejetting (other engines)
• Modifications for racing engines
• Appendix: How an SU works
• Index

SPECIFICATION
Paperback. 250 x 207mm (portrait). 64 pages. Over 70 black and white photographs/line illustrations.

RETAIL SALES
Veloce books are stocked by or can be ordered from bookshops and specialist mail order companies. Alternatively, Veloce can supply direct (credit cards accepted).

* *Price subject to change.*

Veloce Publishing Ltd, 33 Trinity Street, Dorchester, Dorset DT1 1TT, England. Tel: 01305 260068/ Fax: 01305 268864/E-mail: veloce@veloce.co.uk

Index

NOTES